For Christ's Sake

pressing the refresh button on the

life of Jesus

Glenville Whittaker

ISBN: 1496033043
ISBN-13: 9781496033048

Cover design and illustration by Kay Devey
Edited by Yolande de Vogel
www.forchristssakebook.com
www.glenvillewhittaker.com

"Not all true things are to be said to all men"
– *Clement of Alexandria*

Contents

Introduction

These past fifty years have been exciting ones in the field of Biblical research. More discoveries have been made than in the entire previous two millennia. It had been said of one of the experts, the venerable Professor Vermes, that no one since the first century knew more about Jesus Christ, and the claim is made even more astounding when we consider that others, such as the American professor, E.P. Sanders, can compete with him for such a title.

Yet with so much academic expertise being brought to bear on the subject, it is disheartening to see that a fundamental line of inquiry into the meaning of Jesus has been paid so little attention; a line of inquiry that might reveal the real truth about what he actually did that convinced his disciples, long before his crucifixion and 'resurrection', that he was indeed the 'Son of God'.

During the course of this investigation, we might well discover that Jesus of Nazareth – posthumously called Jesus Christ – wasn't the man we thought he was. Not necessarily someone sent by God to try to

steer humanity into better ways, and then, hardly had
he started, found himself arrested and executed in an
ignominious manner which cast doubt on his divine credentials, until a new element came into play: the theory
that the death had been part of the plan all along. Not
someone who died for sinners, so that they might be
saved – the very centerpiece of modern Christian belief.
And not necessarily a kindly man who walked on water
and healed incurables with a touch of his hand and a
sign of the cross.

We might even discover that he did not fit the modern depiction of the 'historical Jesus', freed from the
religious imagery that has grown up around him over
these past two millennia; a simple preacher trying to
make his Jewish countrymen turn back to the Jehovah
they had abandoned. And we might well ask ourselves,
if all this is stripped away, what could possibly remain to
justify his seminal role in human history?

It is time to look again at this colossal icon of humanity, and see what can be recovered from the conflagra-
tion of recent decades, decades where new scholarship
was supposed to have revealed the real truth about him,
but has left those who want to know as divided, as misin-
formed, as ever.

The man was there. The man did something. The
man taught something. Yet it is a lesson that has been
long lost. This book looks at Jesus again, in a new light,

to deduce what he was really all about, why he made such a profound impression on his contemporaries, and we make a fundamental discovery that has been hidden for nearly twenty centuries.

If there is some truth in this line of thinking, the implications are far-reaching. The Christian churches in particular will be called upon to look deeply into what they stand for, and make profound adjustments which may be uncomfortable but which might well enable them to prosper and thrive for a further two millennia, or at least until a new understanding of the nature of man's relationship with the divine renders them surplus to requirements.

Before we start this journey of discovery, we will be encouraged to suspend any belief in miracles, and to acknowledge the possibility that no miracles, as we understand the term, were performed by Jesus. He did not walk on water, he did not rise from the dead, and his mother was not a virgin. We acknowledge the uncomfortable truth that founding a new religion was not on his agenda, and we have also to take on board the unpalatable thought that world peace and the abolition of poverty also did not feature highly on his to-do list.

Biblical research is like a gigantic ocean-going vessel. It takes a great deal to change its course. This book surveys the renaissance it has undergone over the past half-century, but observes with consternation its reluctance to let go of deeply held convictions and look at the subject anew. The transition from the accepted view of Jesus as a serene holy figure gliding calmly and inexorably, like a Disney river-boat ride, towards his preordained destiny, to an altogether more real and down-to-earth historical character is welcome. But the mystery of the man, and what he saw as his life's purpose, has not been uncovered.

This is what this book attempts to address. We examine the clues that indicate that Jesus was primarily not about fine words and a profound teaching that linked the human being to a divine father, but was able to lead his followers into an actual inner experience of this source, this inner heaven, and conclude that it was this special ability that made him so unique. Something so far undetected was taking place, something of incandescent importance, which the gospels cover in a light mist that has remained impenetrable over the centuries.

Our efforts might represent a little puffing tug-boat trying to nudge the giant tanker onto a different course: a seemingly hopeless task. But it is important that the adjustment be made before Christianity dies completely as a living remembrance of the iconic figure at its heart. We will walk down a path we thought we knew well, but this time, like amateur detectives, see if we can spot any valuable little clues the great minds might have overlooked.

It is a fascinating journey, and it needs to begin with a survey of these golden years of Biblical discovery, to see how they are finally coming, like a film without a conclusion, to a frustrating end, and what we can do to put this unwieldy vehicle back on the track.

Chapter One

Looking Anew

For nearly two thousand years Jesus has been worshipped as a living God, as part of a Trinity, of three aspects of divinity, with hardly a question asked about the underlying foundations of Christianity. Once the dust had settled on the embryonic stages of the first four hundred years or so after he lived, the religion remained unchanged, and was so well-established that even to challenge its basic premises was classed a gross heresy, punishable by excommunication or death. The reformation in the sixteenth century was a rebellion not against Christian fundamentals but against the wealth and corruption of the Catholic church, given that Jesus seemed in some of his sayings – but not others – to recommend poverty and simplicity. In short, the Catholic church had an unassailable monopoly on the Christian faith, and only lost the northern half of Europe to Protestantism because of its own venality and corruption. If Luther had not nailed his 95 objections to the door of his church in Wittenberg in 1517, triggering the protestant revolution, someone else would have soon done something similar in Scandinavia, Hungary, Poland or Britain. It was a revolution waiting to happen. What he objected to, in particular, was the sale of indulgences, which allowed you to be forgiven for a sin in advance of committing it – for an appropriate fee. As the church's shameless ditty of the time went: "As soon as the coin in the coffer rings, the soul into heaven springs", your payment, in effect, wiping out your sin.

But nobody was challenging the essence of Christianity. You merely chose – or had chosen for you – whether to go with the gold-plated and incense-perfumed opulence of Catholicism or the ascetic, stark, wooden-altared simplicity of the protesters. There was also, of course, the substantial doctrinal issue of whether, in the mass, you were actually eating the body and drinking the blood of Christ or only symbolically eating the body and drinking the blood. On these differences, far more Christians were tortured and killed than by the emperors in pre-Christian Rome.

But gradually, even the basic building blocks of the faith, sacrosanct and permanent, began to feel the uncomfortable chipping of awkward questions and points of debate as, over the past couple of hundred years or so, scholars, theologians and historians have tried to look at the life of Jesus in a more dispassionate way. Previously there was no reason to examine those early beginnings. Everything you needed to know was already written down in the gospels. But the age of enlightenment, of scientific and rational enquiry, towards the end of the eighteenth century, saw the celebration of a new religion: reason, the very nemesis of faith-based unquestioning belief. It was no longer acceptable that an answer should be "Because God said so", or "Because Jesus said so", or "Because the Bible said so", or even, "Because the church said so". In the world of science, of rationality, it would never do to accept something as unchallengeable on such grounds. The issue had to be probed, turned over, examined, looked into, to see if there was verifiable evidence behind whatever was being postulated.

Two major nineteenth century turning points opened the floodgates of inquiry. Firstly, in 1859, Darwin's *On The Origin of Species* came along to say that the world was not 4,004 years old at the time of Christ's birth after all, but several billion. Far worse than this, as the number of years since the world began is not in itself of any importance, the theory of evolution led to the inexorable conclusion that Adam and Eve had simply not existed. This was heady stuff, making the more traditional Victorians reach for the smelling salts and steady themselves against an ornate dining room chair. If this rock-solid and believed-for-eons account of the creation was not true, then how could any part of the Bible remain sacrosanct, authorized by God himself? In particular, if there were no original sinners, how could there be that mainstay of Christian faith, original sin? In an earlier age, we can be absolutely sure that Darwin would have been consigned to an even worse fate than Galileo, who was only imprisoned and forced to renounce his conclusions, for to question the plain fact that the sun, like all other heavenly bodies, circumnavigates the earth was small fry compared to the denial of the events described in the first three chapters of *Genesis*.

Darwin's premise, unlike Galileo's, meant that religion itself was being called to account, for it had made a rod for its own back by declaring the Bible to be the 'Word of God', when it was no more than a collection of diverse writings assembled as a 'book' by people who appeared in some cases to have self-interested reasons for their choices, a book which was declared as inviolably sacred as the *Koran* in Islam or the *Guru Granth Sahib* in the more recent Sikh faith, which is indeed worshipped as the supreme deity itself. It meant that if one part of this divinely ordained narrative fell, then no part was safe.

The second tsunami that hit Victorian religious rectitude was the *Life of Jesus* published by the German theologian David Strauss in the 1840's, which stated that Jesus' miraculous acts simply did not happen, but were myths that had grown to embellish the claim that he was, in fact, 'God'. Written before Darwin's book, it was not published in England until translated by the author of *Middlemarch*, the woman known as George Eliot, in 1860, just one year after Darwin's. It was a task which led to her experiencing, as many people handling what could be described as a poisoned chalice were to do over the next hundred and fifty years, a major crisis of personal faith.

More recently, newly discovered texts and forensic scholarship have portrayed Jesus and the subsequent beginnings of the Christian religion in a very different light from that previously handed down to us. In particular, the search for the 'historical truth' about Jesus and his works on the one hand, which started in Germany in the late nineteenth century, and the discovery of the Gnostic gospels in 1945 on the other, have swung Christian scholarship in completely new directions, presenting him not as a living God, a Messiah, floating through his pre-ordained brief stay on Earth, but as a much more interesting and real person, and most importantly, yielding fresh insights into what kind of man he was and what he was actually doing during the couple or so years of his work, or 'ministry'.

The result is that, over the past forty years or so, the scholars have had a field day. New heroes and heroines, giants in the world of Christian theology, have emerged as masters and mistresses of this new terrain. One of them, the redoubtable Elaine Pagels, the interpreter of the Gnostic gospels, was even named as one of the most influential spiritual personalities on the planet, ahead of established religious leaders such as the Pope and the Archbishop of Canterbury, although not, significantly, of the Dalai Llama, who has garnered great personal respect for his meaningful comments based, one feels, on deep inner wisdom rather than official teaching. We then have the doyen of first century authorities, the late British, although Hungarian-born, Jewish writer, Geza Vermes, piling in with inscrutably detailed scholarship on every nuance of the New Testament texts and early Christian development.

The great British writer Karen Armstrong has opened up whole panoramas of reliable, probing investigations into the nature of divinity, God and religion. Professor Michael Goulder, before his recent death, shone a new and penetrating light onto those first decades after Christ died, while Professor Maurice Casey has used his great expertise in the languages of the time to arrive at a historically 'independent' interpretation of the New Testament. Most recently, we have seen a revisiting, without real evidence, of the theory that Jesus was no more than a nationalist revolutionary, a man of the sword, who after his death was transformed by his followers into a man of peace to avoid antagonizing the Romans after the destruction of the temple in Jerusalem in 70 C.E. And meanwhile, a group of mainly American-based inquiring historical theologians are ferreting ever more minutely into every aspect of the 'historical Jesus', carrying with them a small side-group who still question whether Jesus actually existed, or was a figment of the gospel writers' imaginations, designed to embellish their attempts to revive a moribund Jewish spiritual landscape.

It is accepted that if the evidence for Jesus as a real person had to rely on the New Testament gospels alone, there would be some grounds for this line of thought: it has been said that their clear biases and the many inconsistencies between their various accounts would not hold up in any court of law or scholarship. However, few and slender though they be, and in themselves sometimes of questionable authenticity, there are sufficient references to this first century Jewish trouble-maker and his eventual execution from non-Christian commentators and historians of the time to give the Nazarene the benefit of any doubt. This question of Jesus' existence has therefore become a minor debate on the fringe of most serious research, where the great players of this golden age of Biblical scholarship are busy plying their trade as we speak. The books by these new authorities are now essential reading, as important in their own way as the scriptures they interpret.

The controversies which have developed over the past half-century have revealed a vast amount of new information on early Christianity. We now think we know that an enormous conflict broke out in the decades after Jesus' crucifixion between Peter and Paul over whether it was right to spread the good news about Jesus in the non-Jewish world. We think we know that from the outset there was confusion as to whether Jesus really appeared in person after his death, was seen in 'bereavement visions' by his disciples, or whether the whole resurrection story was invented by Paul in support

of his new 'church'. We think we know that Mary
Magdalene was a particular favorite of Jesus, and that,
after his death, Peter vented his long-simmering frustration about this closeness in a disgracefully sexist manner, knowing full well that he would never have dared
to do so while Jesus was still alive. We think we know
that Jesus was not regarded as 'God', or the Messiah,
'Christ', until long after he died, but was viewed in his
life as a teacher and 'healer' who might have had a special connection with God, but did not share his identity.
We think we know that Jesus *might* have been, but probably wasn't, a charismatic traveling preacher who dealt
in magic spells and was an accomplished hypnotist. We
do *not* think there is any credence in the admirably
researched book by John Allegro purporting to demonstrate that Jesus was not man but a mushroom, and
the early Christian religion a cult based on psychedelic
hallucinations.

But we think we know that there was quite an edgy
rivalry between John the Baptist and Jesus, and their
respective followers, in which John might have come
out on top were it not for his untimely death. We also
think we know – and, let's be frank, there is no dispute
about this – that a serious skirmish developed in the
fourth century between the Catholic church's adoption
of a theory never expounded by Jesus, that all human
beings carry the guilt of the original sin of Adam and
Eve, and even new-born babies are refused entry into
heaven unless baptized, and those led by the admirable

British scholar Pelagius who thought this was a nonsense too far. And perhaps most of all we think we know that an almighty war of ideas and words was fought in the first three centuries after Jesus' execution between those who believed he wanted his followers to seek and find God within themselves through an inner process called *gnosis*, and those who were pushing for a fixed and monolithic religion, where what was needed was a declaration of belief that Christ was the Lord and adherence to a growing code of doctrines and ritualistic practices.

It would be hard to come across any book or any period in history that has been scrutinized as intently as the New Testament and the early years of Christianity. So why should another little volume be needed? Quite simply, it is because something more can be said, a new perspective taken, revealing essential truths and positions not previously given weight or consideration. It is based on a sense that in spite of the erudition, the scholarship, the debate, the forensic enquiry of the past few decades, something is still missing: a key part of the Jesus story has not yet been told. The exciting surge in Christian scholarship over the past half-century, which promised so much, has become stuck in the mire. Something is needed to provide it with a new push, a new impetus that will unstick those wheels and send the vehicle merrily on its way, and if that push has to come not from within the walls of the citadel of scholarship but from the fields beyond, so be it.

The central theme of this book is that Jesus had no supernatural powers or abilities, that the notion of miracles has to be removed unequivocally from the equation, but that once this is done enough evidence will remain to demonstrate that he possessed an entirely different talent: the ability to transport people who met his strict qualifications into an inner, and apparently real, experience where they were convinced they had been in the Kingdom of Heaven. This ability was the beginning and the end, the alpha and the omega, of his work. This is what he felt he was charged to do and what accounts for the undying love of his disciples.

It follows that he had no intention of founding a new religion to replace an old, nor intended to allow himself to be crucified in order to have people's 'sins' forgiven. It follows that his miraculous healings did not happen, but were allegories for the inner revealing he was able to perform. It follows also that the mainstay of subsequent belief in him – his resurrection – did not actually take place, but was also a metaphor for receiving the gift of 'new life' he was able to bestow.

It is true that the 'initiation theory' has already surfaced as a result of references to such a process in the Gnostic gospels, and has also been mooted in the much-disputed scholarship of a controversial American professor. But most of academia reject the notion, and amongst those who accept it the furthest the idea has been taken is the proposition that Jesus may have had hypnotic powers, possibly combining with incantations and magical procedures, which enabled him to hypnotize his followers so that they had a conviction they had been transported to an inner 'kingdom'.

This book will examine the evidence for these theories, taking a new look at Jesus and the controversies surrounding him to establish their truth or otherwise. In this journey of discovery we will ask to what extent are there any clues to be found in the original four gospels and the other New Testament books, and whether any light can be thrown from the relatively recently discovered writings of the so-called Gnostics and the mysterious contemporaneous sect, the Essenes. Can we find comparisons in other spiritual traditions that support these ideas? And if this new thinking is to gradually replace the old, does it leave any room for Christianity at all in today's societies?

Beside the detailed works of real scholarship, mainly aimed at fellow academics, there has been a spate of recent popular books on the subject which have proved pleasing and insightful, but at the same time only underline what little we know about the man at the heart of it all, as opposed to the avalanche of either speculation and theory or extraneous information. How fortunate, for example, for that spellbinding historian, Diarmaid MacCulloch, that the assignment for his wide-ranging television series and subsequent book was the history of Christianity and not the history of Christ. This immensely informative and readable study extends to over a thousand pages, of which less than twenty are about the life of Christ himself, and of these most are about his birth and death: his actual deeds and teachings are covered in less than double digit figures, while the essence of the story, the miracles and healings by which Jesus said he could be known and recognized, take up just one sentence. You could say, but of course, two thousand years of Christian history do not allow very much time for such a short period to deserve more than a cursory look, but likewise one could argue that this 'short period' is the most important of all the periods, long or short, that were to follow in the long history of this religion. But MacCulloch's work at least demonstrates what an enormous gap exists between what Jesus taught and what later came to be expounded as his teachings.

On the other hand, the immensely popular 'historical' life of Jesus by A.N. Wilson sticks to its subject, but so meager is the raw information with which the author has to work that only a fraction refers to clear facts, the other nine-tenths of the iceberg being devoted to what we could call informed speculation. Seldom has so much been made of so little, such a confection of ideas whipped up from a new interpretation of a word, phrase or allusion. Why, for example, was Jesus, a mere guest, asked to perform the wine miracle at a wedding? Quite simple, declares Wilson; it was because he himself was the bridegroom of course, and had therefore some responsibility to ensure that the drinks didn't dry up. Why was the tomb empty come Sunday morning? Isn't it obvious? His family had retrieved the corpse to carry it back to Nazareth for burial. And what are we to make of Paul's dubious claim that he had come across the living Jesus? Leaping in where angels fear to tread, or at least where no scholar had previously ventured, Wilson boldly asserts that of course, Paul must have been the chief priest's assistant at the arrest of Jesus, Malchus – the one who had his ear severed by the apostle Peter – and consequently was present at the trial and crucifixion; hence his sense of guilt and determination to make the death on the cross the starting point for his new religion. Such flights of fancy do not make the book any less enjoyable, and in many respects Wilson's informed speculations might have some truth about them. But at this stage, we just do not know. The fact that he can pop them in without raising eyebrows shows just how little hard evidence we have about the actual life of Jesus.

Both of these recent popular writers agree, however, that the man Jesus was a contradiction: on the one hand forthright, challenging, prone to anger, and not someone we would like to encounter while struggling to get on a bus at a crowded bus stop in the rush hour; on the other a gentle messenger of peace who put children at the heart of his teachings for their innocence and lack of guile, and would probably be still waiting for a bus at midnight, having let everyone else board before him. They would also agree that precious little can be known of 'the historical Jesus', to such an extent that many of the words he is reported to have spoken can be demonstrated, in all probability, to have been later additions by people wanting to color his teachings in a particular way, making their story appeal more to the Jews, who did not like the idea of a new leader getting himself arrested and crucified before he had progressed very far with ushering in his new 'kingdom', or to the non-Jews, the gentiles, who worried about having to be circumcised and follow other Jewish traditions if they joined this otherwise attractive Jewish sect.

This leaves even less original material relating to Jesus' life and teachings, to the extent that MacCulloch, Wilson and the other recent writers on Christ agree with that doyenne of religious pundits, Karen Armstrong, when she says the life of Jesus is 'an enigma'.

This little book is going to flit over the landscape of Jesus' life like a busy helicopter, soaring high here, swooping low there, looking at what might really have been happening beneath the haze and the mist obscuring the scene. Sometimes we'll have to visit the near future, the few decades, maybe a century or two, after that little flurry of activity beside the Sea of Galilee around the year thirty, and occasionally take a quick trip to another landscape altogether in the search for clues that might help us understand what was really going on. Because in spite of the tremendous amount of scholarship on the subject, as we look down from our cockpit in the sky, one thing is for sure: we are still a long way from any real insight about that little sandaled man resting by those fishing boats surrounded by his loyal and, for a time, joyous band of followers.

I like Jesus. I would love to have met him, passed time with him, played a game of checkers, sat on the shore lightly discussing his views on the divine and the current political situation while eating some grilled fish washed down by a shared gourd of wine. But I sense that I may not have found him an easy man to be friends with, and when he came to his terrible end, while shouting at the soldiers to leave him alone, and risking my own freedom or life in doing so, some little voice within me might have been saying: "You brought it on yourself, you fool. There was no need. Why did you do it?"

So, let's go back, both to the original sources and to the 'new discoveries' of the past century or two, and see if the former can yield any new leads previously missed, and, for the latter, whether it was worth the effort of their being discovered and dwelt upon like so many tea leaves at the bottom of the proverbial teacup.

Chapter Two

The Virgin Birth

When we examine the array of books on the subject of Jesus and Christianity, one fact stands out clearly: they have in the main been about the period *after* Jesus' life. Until the recent avalanche of research and discovery, not too many scholars and theologians actually looked closely at that short period of his own time and teachings on earth. One reason for this is evident from what we have just observed: there is a wealth of fascinating information, material, controversy and sheer good old history covering the decades and centuries following the crucifixion. What is not to like? It is as if a newly discovered archaeological site were glittering with treasures, artifacts and manuscripts, just waiting for the excavator's trowel and the historian's analysis. Never mind that the man who laid down the foundations of this site is remembered only by a faded little plaque in a relatively unnoticed corner. Certainly, give the man his due, is the unspoken message, but the influence of Christianity and the various world-wide religions that have grown under that umbrella has become far more than the story of its

17

For Christ's Sake

originator – we will not say founder, for Jesus would not have wanted to be known as the founder of a religion. A comparison could be made with the world-famous soft drink. John Pemberton was the crazed but inspirational scientist who invented *Coca-Cola*, yet his invention was taken up, some would say stolen, almost from under his nose by Asa Candler who, with the publicist Frank Robinson, made it the global brand it is today. Jesus created the product, but others created the brand.

The other reason is simply the comparative dearth of interesting or relevant new material about the life of Jesus himself. No wonder that Karen Armstrong calls it an enigma. No wonder that so solid a historian as Dairmaid MacCullogh does little more than set down a marker saying this is where it started, without undertaking further examination. An array of historians have joined them in bemoaning the unappealing but inescapable fact that so little is actually known about the Galilean who kicked it all off.

But a second interesting feature about research into the beginnings of Christianity is how much attention is paid to the history of the Jewish faith in the centuries *before* Jesus. This is based on a common misapprehension: a conviction, strongly held but not strongly tested, that the history of Semitism is relevant because Jesus' purpose was to put Judaism back on the right track after it had fallen into some disrepair after the heady days of Abraham, Moses, David, Isaiah and the prophets. This thesis is not

18

borne out by the facts of how Jesus explained his mission and his work. He acknowledges the past, and refers occasionally to the great figures of Jewish history, but makes it quite clear that he is not here to revive the faith or to repair its workings. His attitude is reminiscent of Monty Python's repetitive joke: "And now for something completely different". He is coming to offer a fresh start. New wine will simply not go into old bottles, or rather wineskins, as he says to make this very point; they will stretch, break and simply prove incapable of holding it.

Jesus had seen nothing wrong with Judaism, while pointing his finger strongly at its leaders, the Pharisees, whom he called hypocrites for their pride, their immersion in dogma and an outer show of correctness. But his main work, and the main thrust of his teachings, was nothing to do with the history of Judaism; it was about an altogether new way of knowing the divine.

There are many simple and easily explained anomalies about the dating and circumstances of Jesus' birth. One of the most quirky facts of the search for the 'real Jesus' is, of course, that he was born four years before Christ, in 4 B.C., or, as it is now politically correct to say, in an attempt to confuse millions of schoolchildren, B.C.E. – before the 'common era'. This was simply deduced by looking at the date of the death of that decidedly evil king Herod – the one of whom it is said that he ordered all male babies in

Bethlehem to be killed – since two gospels state Jesus was born during his reign. He died in 4 B.C.E. so Jesus could not have been born later than this date. We know that he was executed around 30 C.E. – Geza Vermes, the most fastidious of Biblical scholars, claims the actual date was Friday, April 7 of that year – which means he was around the age of thirty-four when he met his untimely end. The figures don't exactly add up, and there is room for confusion when trying to establish how long Jesus' 'ministry' lasted: one year according to Matthew, Mark and Luke, who have him visit Jerusalem only on that one last fateful occasion; three years according to John, who has him visit Jerusalem several times. Vermes proposes that it might have been no more than six months, basing this opinion on the fact of there being two other annual occasions beside the Passover when Jews would be required to visit the Jerusalem temple, and as these are *not* mentioned in the gospels it can be assumed Jesus' period of activity covered only the six months which included the Passover: from Autumn 29 C.E. to Spring 30 C.E. It seems far too short a period for Jesus to carry out the full list of engagements and activities attributed to him and this theory is probably wrong, especially in view of Luke's comment that "his parents went to Jerusalem every year at the feast of the Passover," indicating they only needed to visit the capital once annually. We should also observe the build-up of an intense and profound devotion to Jesus during his period of teaching, often based on real familiarity and mutual love, which does not seem to match a relatively brief time-scale for his work: this consideration should be given at least as much value as searching for clues about visits to Jerusalem and numbers of Passovers. The length of Jesus' ministry is not of vital importance, and by and large we can leave the experts to continue their deliberations both into this question and that of Jesus' age, while recognizing that one of his challengers said to him, "You are not yet fifty", which could indicate he was older than generally assumed.

Most theologians now also accept that the story of the birth in a manger in Bethlehem, even when stripped of its miraculous content, is probably fictitious. There was no census at the time of Jesus' birth, although it appears there *was* one ten years later; it is generally assumed the two gospel writers who cover the nativity legend conflated the facts and circumstances to suit their story. Even if there had been a census, calling on all citizens to travel to their 'own town', it would probably not have required a resident of Nazareth in the Galilee area to travel to the equally insignificant town of Bethlehem at the other end of the country.

Cue the importance of this little village as the home town of that most illustrious of Jewish kings, David, and the importance of having Jesus as a potential new Jewish Messiah come from there also. It is unfortunate that in the extensive genealogy provided by Matthew to prove Jesus was actually descended from King David, the last person in the line was the cuckolded Joseph, whom Matthew had just made clear was not actually Jesus' father. The picture is further clouded by the recent discovery of the remains of another small town called Bethlehem, this time just a few miles away from Nazareth. Mary may possibly have gone there to have her baby at the home of a friend or relative who lived there, and the later gospel writers were happy to build on this fortuitous coincidence.

The nativity *might* have happened, but it is generally considered likely that the story of the birth, with its strong connection to David, is a later addition, to make Jesus more acceptable to Jewish society in the years after the crucifixion. The same thinking is what possibly lies behind the story of the killing of newborn boys, with its parallel to the Old Testament account of Moses, where, allegedly, first-born boys really were slaughtered, not by Herod but by the vindictive Old Testament 'God', considered by some of the Gnostic gospels as an imposter whom Jesus came to replace with the real thing, the 'God of Love'. In the case of what happened in Egypt, however, the Jews would have very much welcomed the slaughter as it led to their escape from slavery; their first-born were, unlike the Egyptian children, 'passed over', an event celebrated annually to this day, and at the time of year when Jesus met his fate. As for the precise date of Jesus' birth, we are in the dark, Geza Vermes pointing out drily that the odds of him having been born on December 25 are one in three hundred and sixty-five.

Lastly, the idea of animals in attendance didn't come along for many centuries, but we can surely be grateful for the charm this innovation has added to countless nativity plays during Christmas celebrations.

Is any of this relevant? Is the precise year of his birth important? Does it matter that he was possibly not born in Bethlehem, or that his parents might not have hidden in Egypt to avoid the wrath of Herod? Not in the least.

* * *

Likewise, it would be hard to find any rational person today, outside of Catholic circles, who honestly believes Mary was a virgin, and the birth of her son was the result of an 'immaculate conception'. It is now accepted that the word for a young woman or girl used in the eight hundred year-old prediction by the prophet Isaiah of the future birth of a great leader, the Hebrew *alma*, was translated when quoted by Matthew into the Greek word *parthenos*, meaning *virgin*, either accidentally or deliberately, to make it appear that Jesus really was fathered by God.

The later church, wound up in the question of Jesus' own divinity, decided that Mary must have been a virgin throughout her life. The thought of the Holy Mother, the bride of God himself, having sex was simply...well, unthinkable. It is a position difficult to square with the clear assertion in the gospels that Jesus had brothers and sisters – four of the former and at least two of the latter.

A hundred and fifty years after Jesus died, an Egyptian philosopher named Celsus launched a vicious attack on the Christian faith, which was gradually making in-roads on the allegiance to his beloved Plato. His libelous rant included the proposition that Mary had been something of a loose woman, and, while betrothed to Joseph, had an affair with a Roman centurion called Pantera. There was a flurry of excitement some years ago when the grave of a Roman soldier of that name was discovered in Germany, prompting speculation that Jesus' real father was a soldier on a tour of duty who got his girl pregnant, before later being reassigned to fight in Germany. I don't like this slur on Mary's character. She may not have been divinely impregnated, nor worthy of being raised by the church to a figure of almost equal importance to her son, but she was the busy mother of a respectable and presumably hard-working family who stood by her wayward son when, on the cross, most others abandoned him.

We could speculate that, if Jesus had a Roman soldier as a father, his genes might have given him an appearance and demeanor that could have caused comment by the gospel writers, or, if Jesus *were* half centurion, or half Roman, somebody might also have mentioned this fact to Pontius Pilate, who might have treated him more respectfully, and not handed him over to the mob. Presumably, as with American soldiers in Vietnam, or those stationed in England during the Second World War, a large number of relationships with local girls might have taken place with a mixed-race stratum of offspring, so the theory, although firmly rejected, is not beyond the realms of possibility.

The critic Celsus himself, while speculating on the centurion theory, also states that Jesus was physically ugly, on no deeper grounds than that someone who had led such a wretched life and ended up so ignominiously must have lacked any semblance of beauty or nobility. Real clues about his appearance are non-existent, although the biographer Paul Johnson makes much of frequent references to Jesus 'looking at' his disciples, or others he was addressing, to surmise that he must have had a 'penetrating gaze', which does not necessarily follow. If eyes are the windows to the soul, we can expect Jesus' to be, yes, challenging, deep, but also loving and almost entrancing – good eyes if you happen to be, as several scholars have claimed Jesus was, a charismatic hypnotist. Or, alternatively, a channel to a profound inner self-awareness.

Although we have no evidence at all of Jesus' physical appearance, each of us probably cannot escape a personal mind's eye picture of what the man looked like: almost certainly bearded, slightly gaunt, with a powerful aura of personal strength and integrity. But not a clue about his actual appearance is found in the gospels. If we wanted to pursue the issue, we can acknowledge that adult human beings of that period were around half a foot shorter than those of today, and Jesus most probably had the normal features associated with that part of the world, given that there is no racial or genetic distinction between Jewish people and those of surrounding areas: black hair, possibly greying as he entered early middle age, dark eyes and an Eastern Mediterranean complexion. Whatever his appearance, there are sufficient references to the graciousness of his speech, the expressiveness of his face, and what one expert has called the tenderness detectable in his personality to conclude he was probably an attractive human being.

The first artistic depiction of Jesus, from Greco-Roman times, showed him as resembling the sun-god Apollo: a handsome youth with curly hair, carrying a wand with which he performed his miracles. Later he became a more serious figure, with a solemn expression and a bearded face, more in line, it is believed, with classical sculptures of Jupiter, king of the gods. Later still, as the passion of Christ began to play a central role in the religion's iconography and suffering was put at the heart of the new faith, the anguished harrowed aspect of the Turin shroud gained predominance. In recent centuries, northern European societies have portrayed him as kindly and wise, even blonde and blue-eyed, while in Africa we have black Christs, and in the Far East he bears oriental features. In short, each society portrays him in a way they would like him to appear. As for his dress, we think of him wearing a robe of sorts, although it might not have been the elegant, flowing toga of our ideal visions: the bleeding woman touched 'the fringe of his cloak', and the word 'fringe' has been suggested to mean tassels of the kind that decorated the hems of the rabbis' garb, though Jesus, not being a rabbi in the traditional sense, would probably not be found wearing the extravagant robes adorned with tassels and bells worn by the rabbinical class. It is known that men of the time probably wore a loincloth and then two items of clothing, a kind of shift or undergarment, covered by a cloak or gown. We also know from John's famous saying about fastening the straps on his sandals that this would have been his normal footwear, although, let us remember, John had not actually seen Jesus before making this remark.

The essential fact is that neither Jesus' appearance, nor his parentage, nor the circumstances of his birth have any relevance to the man and his teachings, and can safely be relegated to the category of 'peripheral information'. But the whole nativity narrative is beautiful, is it not, and as journalists the world over know full well, why should the truth get in the way of a good story?

* * *

The point of the 'virgin' myth is to demonstrate that Jesus was indeed the 'Son of God' not only in a metaphorical, spiritual or abstract way but physically as well. If there had been such things as birth certificates at the time, Jesus' would have been a very unusual one indeed.

Why should the story of the nativity of Jesus, with its miraculous elements, have been included in the Bible, if it were not true? We can be grateful for certain non-miraculous facts, which had no need to be invented: Mary (actually called Miriam), a teenager, and her betrothed Joseph having a son whom they named Jesus (Yeshuah) before the death of King Herod in 4 B.C.E. But the place of birth, together with the miraculous occurrences, are inserted to give added resonance to the theme which the gospels wished to propound: that a Messiah – a Jewish savior – was born with powerful supernatural signs of his authenticity in the very city of the great Jewish leader, David. Geza Vermes concludes that the two gospels which relate the story, Matthew and Luke, added their versions of the nativity to an already written account of the actual life of the adult Jesus to provide an infancy addendum, creating a prologue to the real story of Jesus which is comparable to the equally dubious accounts, at the end of his adult life, of after-death reappearances. Together they formed two miraculous bookends to what would otherwise be a straightforward account of the life and death of a most impressive historical figure. Both bookends populate their stories with miracles, apparitions and angels that are for the most part absent from the main, and vastly more believable, biography. As Vermes says, it is stretching credulity that the colorful and amazing sequence of events at the beginning of his life is not referred to once during the rest of the gospels, and is ignored altogether by the two remaining evangelists, Mark and John. This does not necessarily constitute irrefutable proof of the later addition theory, but it does push the envelope a long way forward.

There is, of course, a further reason why we can be sure that whatever else Mary might have been at the time of Jesus' birth, she was certainly not a virgin. This reason is simply that, in the absence of *in vitro* fertilization in the first century B.C.E., a miracle would have had to take place, and one essential fact amongst all the disputed ones stands undeniably true: no miracles, as we understand the word, took place during the lifetime of Jesus. As with references in the gospels to walking on water, raising the dead, coming back to life after execution, defying gravity to rise into the clouds, making the blind see and the lame walk, or simply feeding huge numbers on small amounts of victuals, we may rest assured that those miracles surrounding his birth simply did not take place. This is the perennial dilemma of Christian scholarship. Real historians need to approach their subject in as unbiased a way as they can, but Christian historians are shackled from the start by their fundamental belief that miracles either took place, or might have taken place, and are unable to discard this premise while remaining true to their faith.

Any serious study of Jesus has to take this refutation of miraculous acts as an elementary statement of truth, and we will look presently at why they figure so prominently in the scriptures. What the equation leaves us with once these erroneous flights of fancy are removed might give us a clearer view of the man himself, and what he was up to.

For now at least, we can safely ascertain that no virgin birth took place, and nor for that matter did any prior communication to Jesus' mother by an angel, of the Lord or otherwise, for we can state with equal certainty that angels as they are generally understood have not appeared to prophesy upcoming events. As with any mother-to-be living before the scientific advances of our own time, until the birth actually took place, Mary would have no indication of the gender of the child she was bearing.

It would be far more likely, since it would not have been a miraculous act, that a paranoid king demanded the killing of male newborn children. There is no record of Herod ordering such a deed, although that does not prove it did not happen. Such a ruling would register so small on the seismological scale of political decisions at the time that we would not expect a record of it to exist. No, the reason we can say with certainty that the culling of the boys did not happen is that it would have come about as a result of wise men from the east – considered to be three but no number is given in the Bible – reading from their astrological charts that a new king was born, and being guided to him by the wondrous star hovering over the manger. In short: another miracle.

And miracles did not happen.

Chapter Three

The Early Times

Discounting the story of his birth, which is about things happening to him rather than him making things happen, the first mention of Jesus is his being found as a twelve-year-old in the temple, "sitting amongst the teachers and asking them questions, making people amazed by his understanding and his answers". This is probably a true story, for it serves no other purpose than information. If it, like the birth tale, had been a fantasy, we might have expected some miraculous ingredient or powerful event to be recounted, as testimony to the child's role as 'Son of God'. The story is reminiscent of the film, *Home Alone*, for we are told that when Jesus stayed behind in Jerusalem, "his parents did not know it, but supposing him to be in the group they went a day's journey" before they realized he was missing, "searched among their relatives and acquaintances," and then returned to the city where they searched for a further three days before discovering him in the temple.

How did Luke, the evangelist who set it down in writing, know about it? The story would have been witnessed by none of the disciples with the possible exception of James, Jesus' brother, though it is unlikely his parents took him back to Jerusalem for their search, leaving him instead in the care of friends or relatives. If not James, perhaps Mary, Jesus' mother herself, if she spent time at the Jerusalem base of the disciples during the years after her son's death, recounted the tale, and the tender manner in which the story ends – "his mother treasured up all these things in her heart" – indicates the probability that she was the story's source.

This temple incident indicates that Jesus as a boy was not yet a teacher. He had 'understanding' which would lead him over the next fifteen or so years to develop into the person he was to become, but was not thus far 'the one'. The precocious boy did not yet have 'the authority', as it was later called, or he would not be asking questions. He was undoubtedly beginning his journey, his transformation, because when it was his turn to respond to the teachers' questions to him, they were astonished by his answers.

Where would the boy have stayed during those five days alone? Sleeping rough in the temple courtyard, feeling aggrieved at the money-changing activity he saw going on around him, while during the days realizing how far removed from true understanding of the divine the temple priests really were? Or maybe being taken in by a kindly Essene family living in the nearby Essene quarter, and learning from them something of that sect's more gentle teaching of an inner communion with a loving god.

If we could go back in time and meet a famous personality of our choice, we could do far worse than visit the boy Jesus in the temple, passing his time while waiting for his mother to catch the next plane from Paris.

* * *

Much speculation has developed to explain the missing period in Jesus' life, the time between the age of twelve – the temple incident – and his appearing to be baptized by John and beginning his teachings. The fact is of course that nothing tangible is known, and further, that no-one from his later following was with him during this period of development, or stories about it would be expected to have crept into the verbal history that had been swirling around for the four or six decades after his death before the gospels were written.

There is a clue, however, that tells us something. This is the wonderment at 'the gracious words that were coming from his mouth' expressed by people from his own locality who remembered him. They are reported to have asked: "Isn't this Jesus the carpenter's son from Nazareth?" If he had been absent from home for an excessively long period, say from soon after the temple incident, they might not have remembered him in such terms; the distance in time would have been too great. The difference in his appearance from an early or even late teenager to a bearded man in his late twenties or early thirties would have been too much for him to be so readily identified. But a few years absence only would have meant that, on his return, he was still recognizable.

The inference is that at some point in his adult-hood, maybe already in his twenties, he had left the family home to go off and, not to put too fine a point on it, learn his trade, not the trade of a joiner but that of a formidable teacher of truth. We might also assume that he did not abandon his family. Throughout his ministry, as his period of teachings is generally called, they are in the background, often being insulted by him, visiting him, attending the wedding with him and worrying about his sanity. These clear clues indicate that, black sheep though he might have been, he was still closely linked to his mother, brothers and sisters; he did not sever his family ties. The incident where he refused his family admission to his meeting on the grounds that his followers were his real family no doubt took place, but in the context it sounds as if he was simply using them as a rhetorical example. His disciples were his family in a spiritual sense, which was not to deny his physical family the respect and love due to them. He would probably have been found sharing a meal with them later in the day. If they were not close, why was his mother there at his crucifixion, why did he ask his 'beloved disciple' to take care of her, and why did his brother James become the leader of the Jerusalem Christians after his death?

Where did he go during his 'missing years'? The major theories have been lined up: possibly India, with its strong tradition of spiritual understanding; maybe Egypt, which again harbored ancient and somewhat occult teachings – a favored option for those who now consider Jesus was some kind of magician. Paul Johnson in his biography surmises that he worked in a number of occupations, giving him the knowledge of trades, farming, fishing and agriculture that he was to use so extensively in his teachings and parables. A strong case can be made for the possibility that he stayed in Israel, in the secret walled compound of the Essenes, the mysterious sect whose writings, the Dead Sea Scrolls, were discovered in the twentieth century.

We can speculate without reaching a conclusion, but new ingredients can be added to the speculation. In cultures where some kind of revelatory activity from people deemed to have an inner connection with the divine appears to have been present – and India is one of these – the skill, the understanding, the 'gift', is passed from a teacher to a student, who might then became a master himself. Possibly, during his missing years, Jesus encountered and attached himself to such a teacher, and either had the torch of 'mastership' passed on to him, or experienced during this time such a connection within himself with the source of life, God or 'the father', that he felt himself ready and able to deliver the message to his own people. This is a controversial theory, for it presumes Jesus might have had a predecessor, with the implication that he was not the only teacher of what his disciples came to call 'the way'.

It takes away the total uniqueness of Jesus and his teachings, and it is telling that Jesus himself never refers to any previous 'master' who passed the torch on to him. There is, however, one candidate for this role of mentor or predecessor who stands out as possessing the strongest credentials – John the Baptist – and we will look at the mysterious relationship between the two more closely in the following chapters.

There is an interesting parallel with the life of Shakespeare, who can be seen to have attended Stratford-upon-Avon grammar school as a boy but then disappears entirely from our view until he emerges as a fully-fledged playwright, the author of *Love's Labor's Lost* and *Romeo and Juliet*, in September 1593, at the ripe old age of twenty-nine. What was Shakespeare doing during these missing years? Acting as a player in a traveling troupe, perhaps learning the craft of the theater? Possibly having a career at sea, explaining his detailed knowledge of seamanship as revealed in *The Tempest* and other plays? Or – a popular line of belief given the number of plays set there – spending years in Italy, thereby explaining his great familiarity with that country? Even more contentious is the theory that the author had been someone else altogether, possibly the playwright Christopher Marlowe, who disappeared mysteriously in May 1593, again at age twenty-nine, four months before the first appearance in print of the name of Shakespeare.

There is no question that the Jesus who appeared as a mature man at John's riverside base was the same one who had astonished the temple elders twenty or more years earlier. Only in fiction, in the recent novel, *The Good Man Jesus and the Scoundrel Christ*, by Philip Pullman, does the notion of a counterfeit savior arise, and that at the end of his life's work, not the beginning. Nevertheless, as with the Bard of Avon, the theories of what Jesus did in his missing years are, to coin a phrase, legion, and evidence to support any of them is similarly lacking.

We do, however, have one great ally in the tools of the historical investigator – common sense. This tells us that apples do not usually fall far from the tree. Somehow it does not ring true that the youth from Nazareth would strike out for what must have seemed like the other side of the world in search of his spiritual education. The Middle East was already a land full of remote closed religious communities of one kind or another as well as a rich and long tradition in monotheistic experience, together with a strong line of prophets, 'messengers of God'. In support of the recently popular theory that Jesus was some kind of magician, with a repertoire of spells and cures, it was also a land where such people were as populous as snake oil salesmen in the Wild West. We could surmise that it is at least as probable as any other theory that he spent the missing years somewhere near his homeland.

The final theory is, perhaps, the most obvious of all: that he did not go anywhere, but stayed dutifully at home helping with family affairs, working in the carpentry or stonemasonry business – the word for both is, in the Greek of the Bible, the same – or in the smallholding it is now believed relatively prosperous artisan families of that time owned on the outskirts of the town.

The fact that nothing is said in the gospels about the 'missing period' does not necessarily mean that Jesus was missing.

Chapter Four

A Tale of Two Baptisms

All is speculation, and, sadly, it is also extremely unlikely that we will discover more about the role of John the Baptist, which is left tantalizingly unexplained by his two appearances in the gospel texts: his early encounter with Jesus by the riverside, and his arrest and execution by Herod – the son of the Herod who reigned at the time of Jesus' birth. But clues abound which arguably reveal more about Jesus than any other gospel episode. Here Jesus encounters somebody who is not a disciple, nor a supplicant for his miraculous cures, nor a sworn enemy, but, for the one and only time, someone in the same business as himself – drawing people in some way more closely into God's ambit.

The Biblical references to John – his baptizing of Jesus in the river Jordan, and his later execution – are relatively brief, but this doesn't stop them being two of the most evocative and colorful stories in the New Testament. Not only did the two men share a vocation, but they were also to share a similar fate. The story of

John's end was in its way as dramatic as that of Jesus, the king, like Pontius Pilate, finding himself having to acquiesce to demands he felt he could not refuse. There is a poignant similarity between the two deaths: unjust, premature, and brutal.

There are other similarities. Their careers – if we can call them such – intertwine; they are sometimes confused for each other. It is now generally believed by scholars that many of John's followers became disciples of Jesus after his death, and long after Jesus' own execution the apostle Paul found groups of John's followers who now fell readily into the Christian fold. The claim by Luke that they were cousins, while generally considered to be an invention, also indicates a strong affinity between the two men.

The story of John's birth, with his father coincidentally being visited by the same angel, Gabriel, who a little later was to visit Jesus' mother, foretelling the birth of a great prophet who will bring salvation "and give light to those who sit in darkness" may well be a fabrication, like the annunciation widely considered a 'later addition', but it demonstrates the equality of the two men and the similarity of their calling. At this stage one is not greater than the other.

John also has his missing years, before appearing either by the river Jordan, or "in the region around the Jordan", baptizing people and preparing them for the coming of God's kingdom. He was well-established and well-known even before his meeting with Jesus. Josephus, the reliable 'neutral' commentator on these times in Israel, gives him considerable attention, certainly more than Jesus himself. He mentions him baptizing and tells how his eloquence affected and moved many people, although he gives no clue of what he actually said or taught, leaving the gospels as the only source for his message and how he conveyed it. He is also mentioned in the *Koran* as a great prophet, although there is no reference to his baptisms or his meeting with Jesus.

But the entire account of John's relationship with Jesus is an uncomfortable one for Christianity, for it clearly asserts that John not only came before Jesus but that Jesus was John's disciple. The idea of Jesus being number two does not sit well with his reputation as the Son of God. The gospels skirt round this by saying that John's superiority is just a pretense the two men go through for the sake of appearances, but it doesn't sound plausible. The episode, as Professor Robert M. Price asserts, is a serious 'embarrassment', "bequeathing a terrible theological headache to subsequent Christians".

From the gospels we learn that John is predicting the imminent arrival of God's kingdom together with a new master who will usher it in, and is telling people to repent and have their sins forgiven so that they will be ready for it: three separate and major themes in one short statement. First of all the prediction about God's kingdom: this is not considered to be the same as Jesus' many references to the Kingdom of Heaven. John is usually understood – and possibly misunderstood – to be referring to a renewed Israel, free of Roman occupation, dignity restored, where God's writ rules. Jesus is not talking about a physical location but another place altogether, which can be entered by a privileged few. This is new ground. The notion of heaven as being a place where God actually lives and which can be entered by mere mortals is alien to Jewish thinking, then and now. But an earthly kingdom was not only plausible; in first century Judea, with its very existence under threat, it was fervently hoped for.

We should also bear in mind that the word 'repent' did not originally carry the interpretation it has acquired of asking for forgiveness, nor of reverting back to belief in the old Hebrew God; it meant, simply, 'turn around', and could be referring to an inner turning towards a God whom Jesus was later to claim was 'within'.

John also claims to remove people's sins by baptizing them in the River Jordan – a completely new kind of ritual previously unmentioned in the scriptures. Jesus on the other hand did not perform water baptisms, and was not much concerned with people's sins: as Professor Sanders, the pre-eminent American New Testament expert, points out, forgiveness of sins "was not one of the major themes of Jesus' own message". It didn't particularly matter that you were a sinner, and he incurred the wrath of the Pharisees for enjoying the company of sinners. Jesus did not condone sin – "Sin no more," he told the woman who had been 'caught in adultery' whom he saved from being stoned – but he had a more serious agenda than John. "The good news about God," says Sanders, referring to the teachings of Jesus, "is a much more powerful message than a standard exhortation to give up wickedness and turn over a new leaf". We can also note that whilst John's teachings relied heavily on a fire and brimstone approach, Jesus, though also having his gnashing of teeth moments, generally emphasized a God of kindness and love.

John claims he is not only baptizing, but is fulfilling prophesy by "preparing the way of the Lord, and making his path straight," a quote from the Old Testament book of the prophet Isaiah. It is assumed this means he had a God-given duty to watch out for the arrival of Jesus, the 'Lord'. But the Old Testament use of the word 'Lord' is only ever in reference to God himself, not a messenger, representative or 'son' of the divine, and 'the way' presumably refers not to the path Jesus was to take, whatever that may be, but to a path by which ordinary people can access the divine. In the same way, it is widely assumed John was expressing the universal desire of Jews to be rid of the oppressive occupiers, the Romans, and the kingdom he spoke of was an independent Jewish state.

It is the theme alighted upon by those who think Jesus must have been a military leader, or at least a social revolutionary. Certainly, it is believed, people had been hoping for the arrival of a new David, a Jewish Messiah, who would drive out the Romans and bring freedom to the Jewish people, for a considerable time. Uprisings occurred both in the decades before and after the events of the New Testament. But this feeling is expressed nowhere by John in any of his utterances, no more than it was to be by Jesus during his ministry. The reliable chronicler Josephus portrays neither man in political, military or revolutionary terms. Neither of them seemed unduly concerned by the political situation they worked in, while Jesus himself came from the Galilee, the one part of the Israeli homeland which existed relatively peacefully alongside the Roman occupiers and, when the great rebellion came in 66 C.E., was spared by the avenging legions.

Nevertheless, it appears that something happened at his riverside station that made John endorse his new recruit as an outstanding pupil, and we will have to discover what that was. For now, we need only acknowledge that there is unusual concurrence amongst the Biblical experts that the theme of John as the heraldic figure announcing Jesus' imminent arrival was subsequently created by Christian chroniclers in support of their message that Jesus was indeed the God-sent Jewish savior whose arrival had been predicted by no less a figure than the great Isaiah himself.

If John did in fact have inside knowledge about Jesus' impending arrival, as implied in the quote about someone coming, "the straps of whose sandals I am not fit to unfasten", once again we come across a part of the recorded life of Jesus that requires us to believe not in a miracle but in miracle's younger sister, the ability to know the future, which neither man possessed. If Jesus were indeed going to blaze a trail of good works and explosively powerful teachings for the short period of his ministry, he presumably had no need of anyone to announce his arrival, and could have just commenced his work as soon as he felt ready to do so. He did not need John's permission, blessing, or indeed, baptism. In none of his many teachings, parables and speeches does he mention his endorsement by John. If, indeed, he did receive such an endorsement, it counted for little with him. So why did he go to John at all? The only reason would be for him to receive some esoteric teachings, training, or instruction, in which he quickly became so proficient that he felt empowered, once John had been forced to retire, to begin his own mission.

We might ask why John's river immersion prepared people for the arrival of Jesus, as there is no obvious connection. When Jesus began his own work, he did not ask people if they had previously been baptized by John: it was irrelevant. Why, in any event, should John's immersion mean one's sins were forgiven? People might believe their sins were being washed away but this is all it would be: a belief. And taking this further, why should

Jesus, already, apparently, completely without sin, need such a baptism, especially from someone apparently inferior to him? The gospel writers clearly saw this flaw in their story, and had Jesus explain it by the weak excuse, "Let it be so for now, for thus it is fitting for us to fulfill all righteousness".

A further difficulty for proponents of the later Christian interpretation of the relationship between John and Jesus is the clear inference that while the gospels have John acknowledging that Jesus was indeed the great master whose arrival he had been predicting, he does not subsequently become Jesus' follower, preferring instead to continue his own teachings with his own disciples. If John saw his life's purpose as predicting the arrival of Jesus, one would expect him to throw in his lot with him once he had identified him as the expected Messiah. But this does not happen.

Regardless of these anomalies, at the time of John's encounter with Jesus there is no doubt that he is a great success. He has a large following, and he is causing such a stir that the official religious 'police', the Sadducees and Pharisees, come down to check him out. He in turn treats them with great disrespect, famously calling them a 'brood of vipers'. Tact is not the Baptist's strong point, and this confrontation might well have led to Herod, upon hearing it, marking the Baptist's card. It is entirely plausible to suggest that at some point, amongst the many young men who flocked to his banner was one who, from the moment of his baptism, stood out as exceptional, somebody afire with the gift of god-centeredness. It shone from his personality; his words, once he had received the 'baptism', were self-evidently coming from a place of profound understanding. John might well have recognized in him someone with enormous potential, and endorsed him not miraculously before Jesus even appears on his radar, but simply from his own observation of this outstanding disciple.

We finally arrive at the essence, the very nub of the story of John – his baptism of Jesus – and examine the confusion that is built into the scenario by the introduction of two different kinds of baptism: the baptism in water, which John is able to do, and the much more effective baptism in spirit or 'Holy Spirit and fire' that he says "one who is mightier than I" is able to perform. Then comes the sequence of events. First, Jesus is baptized by John, a baptism which John believes is unnecessary since Jesus should be baptizing *him*. But then, *after* Jesus 'had left the water' and 'prayed' – a word we need to remove from its present definition to something much more profound – he experienced a different baptism in which 'the heavens were opened to him' and he saw the spirit of God 'descending like a dove and coming to rest on him'. The first three gospels, but not the fourth, report a 'voice from heaven' being heard at this stage in the proceedings, saying, "This is my beloved son, in whom

I am well pleased". It is a beautiful phrase, expressing a sentiment any parent of a son or daughter would recognize. If God could speak, it is the sort of thing we would expect him to say of his son. However, all-powerful as he may be, we can unequivocally accept that God is not able to speak with a disembodied human voice. He is *not* a ventriloquist.

Notwithstanding the words 'spoken' by God, the description of this episode leaves no room for doubt: this is the spiritual baptism that John has predicted "someone mightier than I" would be able to perform. Throughout this book we will come across similar baptisms taking place. The best-known one is the sudden 'conversion' of Paul on his way to Damascus, when besides being "filled with the Holy Spirit", "a light from heaven flashed around him" and he heard the voice of Jesus. It is a coincidence that seems to have eluded many investigators that these accounts are uncannily similar in nature and are evidently examples of the 'baptism in the spirit' which John speaks of *before* Jesus begins his work, and which Jesus himself experiences *after* his water baptism.

In most instances we will refer to, the baptism in spirit, like the baptism in water, comes about through the agency of another person; it doesn't just happen of its own accord. In Paul's case, although the sequence of events is convoluted, someone called Ananias is the one authorized by God to 'lay his hands' on him. For the most part in the New Testament, it is Jesus himself who is the conductor, the 'layer of hands', and after Jesus has gone it appears his disciples continue to perform this spiritual baptism on his behalf. We later learn, for example, that the apostles Peter and John, visiting new 'converts' in Samaria, "laid their hands on them, and they received the Holy Spirit". It is obviously a skill that not just anyone can employ, for after seeing Peter performing his baptism in the spirit, someone called Simon offers to buy the secret: "Give me this power also, so that anyone on whom I lay my hands may receive the Holy Spirit". Peter declines with an angry rebuke.

But on the occasion of the momentous encounter between John and Jesus, who baptized Jesus? It has to have been John, doing something *more* than just a simple water baptism. John baptized him, he then went into his prayer – presumably a deep and silent period of inner communion – and then the light of heaven appeared to him followed by the endorsement of God himself. Jesus was now 'full of the Holy Spirit' and was able, after his time in the wilderness, to begin his own work.

The mystery here is that John, to give Jesus his uniqueness, has to say one is coming who, unlike him, can baptize in the 'Holy Spirit'. But the first instance in the New Testament of such a baptism is Jesus' own. Did Jesus baptize himself? Was he an auto-baptizer? If so, why did he need to go to John in the first place?

The inference has to be that – notwithstanding his regular baptisms in water and the words put into his mouth that he cannot baptize in spirit, but someone is expected soon who can – John also has the power to perform the spiritual baptism, and, if so, then yes, he has to be given the kudos of being Jesus' predecessor. Luke's birth narrative of John says he is destined to lead people into the light, to show them the divine pathway, and Paul later found disciples of John who had been "instructed in the way of the Lord" – all formulae that could equally well apply to Jesus. But by the time the gospels are being written, the deification of Jesus had already made great progress and the Baptist's role has to be down-played. It has to be made clear that it is not John the Baptist but God himself who is endowing Jesus on this occasion with his unique power.

Thus two versions of the story are laid out before us from which to choose. One has Jesus first being hailed by John as the special one, and then receiving a 'water' baptism from him, this in some way being a signal for the heavens to open and the 'Holy Sprit' to descend upon him. And in the other, John simply gave Jesus the baptism in 'Holy Spirit', which at some subsequent point, most likely after a period of time during which Jesus had manifested as John's star pupil, led to John announcing that Jesus was indeed the one who could succeed him.

Because of the language of the gospels, employing phrases such as 'a light from heaven', an understanding has grown, especially once the great Italian artists of the Renaissance started depicting the scenes, that these powerful 'conversions' took place outdoors, and heaven must mean the sky. It is much more likely, however, that both Jesus' 'baptism in the spirit' at the hands of John, and Paul's at the hands of Ananias, took place indoors, or at least privately, as we will see in due course was Jesus' own *modus operandi* when performing the baptism on others.

Recently, as part of the attempt to de-mystify the miraculous content of the Bible, it has been suggested that, as 'heaven' could also mean 'sky', the 'voice of God' might therefore have come 'through the air', possibly from the people gathered there. Someone in the crowd had heard John's statement that Jesus was 'the one' and had shouted out, somewhat euphorically, "At last our savior, the one sent by God, has arrived". So, instead of a sonorous baritone voice booming its beautiful words from the clouds in the manner of a film starring Charlton Heston, we have just this human intervention. We are reluctant to let the Biblical account go, so rich is it in imagery and significance, but if we want to strip the story down and get to the essential truth, we have no choice in the matter. Of one thing we can be sure: no voice came from the sky, and, plausible as the 'voice from the crowd' theory is, it is far more likely that no voice of any kind was heard. As in the Old Testament, the idea of God speaking to people from heaven is a device used to give legitimacy to a course of action, or, as in this case, to an individual needing to be endowed with divine authority.

We should be warned; such embellishments indicate something added later to convince a future audience of Jesus' 'Son of God' persona. The fact that a few years later Paul also heard a voice bellowing from the sky, this time the voice of Jesus himself, suggests a metaphorical device and should fuel our sincere skepticism of the situation. Although John's gospel, striving to give every credential to Jesus, says that the Baptist himself saw the heavenly light descending on Jesus, the other three make it clear that only Jesus saw it. John would not himself have 'seen' anything, as whatever took place during the procedure must have constituted an internal experience only accessible to the person being baptized, in this case Jesus.

We should also bear in mind that the entire vignette of John baptizing in the river Jordan could have another meaning altogether. Nobody before John had actually done any baptizing. Far from being a well-worn tradition, it was something entirely new, and not associated with the purification rituals of ancient religious practices, the ignoring of which later landed Jesus in trouble with the Pharisees. Yet John had a large number of followers clamoring for his baptism. Why should people be lining up to be immersed in the River Jordan at the hands of someone who was making a far-fetched promise that by being submerged momentarily in the river they would be forgiven their 'sins'? One expert has suggested that since no payment was asked for by John, people found it a more cost-effective way of pleasing God than the usual method of having a lamb or goat slaughtered by the priests in the Great Temple of Jerusalem, for which a fee was charged. But we know that whatever John was doing, it did not have the official approval of the religious police, the Pharisees, who came to investigate him, and most orthodox Jews would therefore be wary of engaging with him, unless something else hitherto undetected was being given to these many followers.

The notion that John was in fact leading people into the river, presumably waist or chest deep, and submerging their heads whilst calling on God to bless, forgive and accept the 'sinner', has never been questioned. The gospels seem to make it quite clear that this is what John was doing. But we shall see during the course of this book that on several occasions they use analogies to tell their story. Increasingly, modern Biblical study is becoming aware that allegory played a much greater part than previously supposed either to make their stories and meanings more vivid, or to draw a discreet veil over matters they would rather have remain confidential. We have to give consideration to the possibility that the daily immersions in the river Jordan did not take place in the way we have been assuming, but were a metaphor for the kind of inner transformation we are in due course going to suggest was to become Jesus' own stock-in-trade – an inner baptism into an inner 'river'. Maybe Jesus was not the only one to receive John's baptism in the spirit, whatever it may have consisted of. Certainly the little giveaway passage in *Acts* about followers of the Baptist having been shown the 'way of the Lord' indicates a teaching in how to approach or commune with the divine, rather than a simple ritual conferring a 'forgiveness of sins'.

The evidence against this theory is considerable, mainly the references to water in the story of the Baptist, and the information that after his meeting with Jesus, he went somewhere else to continue his baptisms, in a place where 'water was plentiful'. But if I were a neutral inquirer, I would prefer to keep an open mind. Could 'water' be a metaphor used in the gospels to indicate something else: a flow, an ocean, of grace, of 'divine presence'? It is a thought we need to bear in mind as we take our new look at the life and work of Jesus.

In this version of events, Jesus has not gone anywhere at all during his 'missing years', but is a man in waiting for his destiny to unfold, storing up a sense of inner power, until he hears of somebody – John – turning people inwards and revealing in some way the Kingdom of Heaven in an initiation process – possibly involving an immersion in water – that is beginning to be widely talked about.

Jesus makes the journey one day to visit him and receives the inner experience, which has such an immediate and galvanizing effect on him that he finds he now has a clear channel which allows him to reach and communicate directly with God. Little wonder he has to go off into the wilderness to commune profoundly with the divine and come to terms with what has been revealed to him, possibly returning from there to John, who at *this* point, rather than immediately after the initiation or baptism, proclaimed Jesus as the one to succeed him.

* * *

Hollywood should consider posthumously inducting the four gospel writers, Matthew, Mark, Luke and John, into their illustrious academy, for their accounts of Jesus' life are filled with lurid scenarios, ready-made for cinematic interpretation. Their 'scripts' have found acclaimed expression in both the 'serious' films about Christ, full of solemn deference, and in Monty Python's *Life of Brian*, mocking some elements of Christian belief. A more accurate version of the subject would probably fall between these two extremes, and is still to be made.

Regarding Jesus' time in the wilderness, however, we have to take the evangelists to task for their depiction of

Jesus' confrontation with the devil, providing later film directors with a ready-made array of arresting images – haggard face, wind-blown deserts, thirst and deprivation, gigantic struggles with an unseen enemy, and the final victory of good over evil. The reality would far more likely be that he found a quiet place where he spent a period of profound contemplation and meditation until he emerged, like a butterfly from a chrysalis, as a fully developed conduit to the inner kingdom.

We cannot tell if Jesus had previously known his first disciples, Simon and Andrew, then James and John, the sons of Zebedee, although it is quite possible that he did. There is some evidence that James and John were, in fact, cousins of Jesus. A.N. Wilson speculates that they had all, Jesus included, been disciples of John for some time and it was not a complete stranger who commanded them to follow him, rather someone they could already see had reached fulfillment, had accrued compelling authority, and was indeed worthy of their discipleship. The gospels tell us only that Andrew, the brother of Peter, and one other, unnamed, had been disciples of John and had been present when he endorsed Jesus as 'the lamb of God'. But that is sufficient for the connection to be made: Jesus had some prior association with his first followers before he began his astonishing period of mastership. It is therefore unlikely that his coming across them by their fishing boats some time later was a chance encounter, as the gospels clearly imply. It might also be the case, as a new theory has persuasively argued, that Jesus had been brought up not in Nazareth but in Capernaum itself, and so possibly knew the fishermen from earlier times.

This mention of the first disciples provides an appropriate opportunity, before we arrive at the central questions of Jesus' 'mission' and his work, for us to take a look at the unusual and fascinating group of young people who attached themselves to this charismatic leader who suddenly appeared amongst them, effortlessly commanding their loyalty.

Chapter Five

Jesus' Men...and his Women

Once the mythology of the birth is eradicated, and the conundrum of John's 'baptism' looked into, all we are left with is the appearance in the vicinity of the Sea of Galilee of an unknown person, probably in his mid-thirties, who quickly gained a reputation for a series of acts and statements during a brief period of a year, or maybe two or three, until he was put to death for reasons that are still not clear.

The statements were a mixture of comments about the 'being at hand' of something no-one had so far heard of, the Kingdom of Heaven, which it was possible to 'see' or 'enter', and a very personal god he addressed by the Aramaic word for 'dad' or 'daddy': *abba*. They also included moral teachings of a fundamentally different nature from what anyone had previously heard, based on extreme selflessness. There was also a series of allegorical stories, called parables, which he said contained hidden meanings only understandable to some, mainly about something special, such as a highly-priced pearl, which could be given to those who deserved it – presumably referring to entry to the Kingdom of Heaven. His acts appear to consist of a large number of instantaneous cures of the sick and 'possessed', and some miraculous activities which defy the laws of nature and gravity, such as walking on water. These we know did not happen literally and likewise, since instantaneous cures would count as miracles, we need to find out what was really meant by these references.

Whatever he was doing was sufficient for him to have been, from all accounts, something of a sensation. People flocked to him as teenage girls besieged the Beatles on their arrival in New York. Even the staid language of the Bible cannot hide the excitement, the clamor, Jesus' appearance and his fast-growing reputation caused: Matthew tells us, "His fame spread throughout all Syria....great crowds followed him from Galilee and the Decapolis, and from Jerusalem and Judea, and from beyond the Jordan...". Mark adds that they also came "from around Tyre and Sidon", in such numbers that "he told his disciples to have a boat ready for him because of the crowd, lest they crush him, for he had healed many". Nowhere in history can there be found such an instantaneous word-of-mouth success. Some of the places named were neighboring countries, requiring several days' journey. What were the people hearing that made them hastily pack a bag and head for the land of Galilee? It could not be that a new teacher had arisen who spoke wonderful words of truth delivered

with 'authority'. That would be impressive, but not
enough to cause migrations. It could not be because of
his healing of the sick, for the crowds described were
not, it seems, gatherings of invalids as if at Lourdes. Nor
would it be the anticipated Messiah, promising to drive
the Romans back into the Mediterranean, for not all
these lands were necessarily Jewish. Jesus' words did not
in the slightest refer to a reclaiming of territory, a defeat
of the occupying power, a fulfilling of Old Testament
'prophecy'. Something more was going on, something
more powerful was being whispered urgently on the
street corners and in the meeting places of these distant
lands and cities.

* * *

During this period he acquired a number of adherents
we could call followers or disciples. How many is not
revealed but it seems there were gradations involved
which indicate first of all his three closest male colleagues, Peter, John and James, and his closest female
disciple, Mary Magdalene, and around them an inner
group of totally committed members of both sexes who
had given their all to Jesus and regarded him as having
a direct pipeline to an inner truth – a veritable master
worthy of the utmost dedication and loyalty. We do not
know if this group all traveled with him on his many
teaching excursions – probably not as it would have
been logistically unfeasible. Not all of his close followers would have given up their livelihoods; there was

probably a sliding scale of those who did whatever they could to help the cause and be in attendance as often as their circumstances allowed. The full-time group might have consisted of the twelve or so named as his apostles together with a handful of personal attendants: mainly the womenfolk, who were not able to go out 'on the road', and also some males either needed by Jesus to be close to him or possibly not sufficiently mature or capable for the robust front-line work of traveling and teaching on their master's behalf.

Occasional clues in the New Testament indicate that Jesus may, like many famous people, have had something of a private life away from his own circle, dining with tax collectors, or possibly nurturing private contacts amongst the Essene group, whose teachings we shall look at presently.

We know the inner group included a number of women, some of whom are named: Mary Magdalene, Joanna and Susanna, for example, names we feel comfortable with today for their simple familiarity. There was also a Salome – not the daughter of Herod, although as Joanna is named as the wife of a senior palace official, there was no reason why wealthy and influential women could not be followers of Jesus. There is also some evidence that this Salome might have been the mother of two of his first disciples, James and John. We are told the women were 'providers' for Jesus' close group, meaning either they cooked and looked after the domestic arrangements or were wealthy enough to offer financial support. It would be enormously interesting to know how these women came to be in Jesus' inner circle; how they first heard of him, how they made the decision to dedicate themselves to him, whether any of them – and presumably there were others – knew each other, or were, like the sisters Mary and Martha, related, and passed on this urgent good news that a man was here who could really set fire to their hearts, and who deserved their devotion. Knowledge of this period of intense excitement is denied to us, but however they came together in those early days and weeks of Jesus' ministry, a picture emerges of a close mixed-sex group of intelligent and real people working in support of their master and his teachings.

It is now generally accepted that there was no sexual discrimination either in his work or in his following, and the anti-female slant of the Catholic church was something inaugurated by church fathers some time in the future. It is easy to overlook the deep significance of this feature of Jesus' ministry, at a time when women were treated as no better than chattels, when Peter himself was to dismiss them as empty-headed, and when even the priests of the Temple regarded them as objects of possession. When Jesus selected twelve apostles to travel around in two's representing him, we can probably refute the notion that he was thinking of the legendary twelve tribes of Israel, as modern pedants have declared. No doubt he knew the history of his people as well as anyone, but would not have based his 'new beginning' on historical precedent. Moreover, we can dismiss the idea that only men were favored enough to do God's work. It was simply against the mores of the time to have women going it alone; it would be dangerous and impractical. Like most societies until relatively recent times, divisions of labor between men and women were strictly adhered to.

Jesus however appears in many respects to be closer to his female disciples than his male. The British historian, Professor Maurice Casey, after a detailed examination of the role of women in Jesus' ministry, concludes: "All the evidence indicates that Jesus was emotionally and administratively more dependent on a small group of women than the gospels tell us". To understand this we need to put ourselves inside that little coterie of people who were around him on a daily basis. We might then realize that his was a mission not *essentially* of teaching, or of 'healing', but of devotion, of loyalty to the man himself, of recognizing his significance – even his *preciousness* – and caring for him in a personal way. The women might not be involved in the nightly discussions, after an evening's teaching, over which would be the best route to take on the next day's journey, or the increasing threat of the authorities, but *would* be waiting afterwards to serve him refreshments, wash his feet, and afford him some moments of relaxation. They would make sure he had a comfortable bed at night, his clothing cared for and his food prepared to a high standard.

They might have been responsible for sending a young male as a runner at daybreak to let the next town's disciples know the plans and approximate time of arrival, and any special requirements for Jesus' care.

When the disciples sat around Jesus for the evening teaching session, there would be no rule of 'men in front, women behind'. Both sexes were equal, and from the segments of dialogue reported in the gospels between Jesus and his disciples, we can discern that with the women there is an easier rapport, a more fluid exchange of conversation than is generally found with the men, who are more the butt of his instructions, orders and more solemn declarations.

* * *

What are we to make of the suggestion that has caught the imagination in recent decades that Jesus might have been in a relationship with Mary Magdalene? It is clearly hinted at in the Gnostic gospels, where it is reported he kissed her often 'on the mouth', arousing some jealousy in other disciples. The Gnostic writings in general appear to give Mary a very senior position amongst the apostles in the aftermath of the crucifixion, and for this reason she aroused the enmity of Peter whom it is assumed was the senior male disciple. Some of these tracts are considered to be contemporary with or not much later than those which found their way into the authorized Bible, in which Mary is not given a great deal of prominence. Of these, the gospel of Mark was the earliest to be written, Matthew and Luke making it a template for their accounts. Mark is known to have been the secretary and probable traveling companion of Peter. His version of events, relying on Peter's personal evidence and memory, would, if such enmity had indeed existed, have downplayed Mary's role.

Much of the theory that Jesus was single and celibate comes from an assumption that the Son of God would be above the need for female company. But even if Jesus were the son, carrying his father's banner, doing his father's work, all the indications are that he had come as a full human being, not the saintly otherworldly person of much Christian mythology. He defined himself, when contrasting his lifestyle with the austere one of John the Baptist, as someone who liked his food and drink, and accepted invitations to dinner from tax collectors and other wealthy people. We can read into the accounts of his life that he possessed a formidable personality and sense of self-worth, as well as a powerful charisma, and was able to face down any challengers: he was the indubitable leader of his own followers. Today he might be called an *alpha male*. Such a man is naturally inclined to attract female admiration and company; if he enjoyed his food and drink, why not also the pleasure of female companionship or even a sexual relationship? We simply do not know the truth of the matter, only that there is no reason why Jesus should not have been 'in a relationship', and the significant words about his kissing

Mary Magdalene are difficult to get around, and will be looked at again later in our investigation.

There is one extra and telling piece of evidence in support of Mary's role as 'wife'; it was she, along with Jesus' mother, who was watching as he was crucified, close enough, according to John, for Jesus' words to be heard. It was also these two who watched him being entombed and then, on the third day, went early to wash Jesus' body with fragrant oils, to find the tomb empty. Mark adds the extra note that they were accompanied by Salome, possibly as the oil bearer, or in the role of an attendant, almost a lady-in-waiting, to the queen of Jesus' world, Mary Magdalene. It is instructive that none of the male disciples came to pay these personal and intensely private acts of respect and devotion to the body of Jesus. Few will argue that the two most important women in any man's life are his mother and his wife. The story provides almost overwhelmingly strong evidence for Mary to be given the benefit of the doubt; it is very likely she was Jesus' partner.

Her importance is also reflected in the fact that she was the first to have a vision of the 'risen Jesus', telling the riled Peter: "I am only telling you what I saw, why are you angry with me?" So much store is placed in later church history on the absolute authority of those who saw the resurrected Christ as the founders of the church that it is a great embarrassment that the first amongst these, the first to 'see' the risen Christ, was a woman, and Mary's role has been consistently downplayed in church annals. Even now that the papacy accepts she was probably not, after all, a prostitute, as she had been portrayed, the case is not finally closed. It must be the longest official inquiry ever held.

We sense that, while pre-eminent amongst the male disciples for his unshakable loyalty to Jesus and incisive insight into who he thought his master really was, Peter was a strong, egotistical man with a short fuse. It would have taken a woman of considerable quiet strength to stand up to him. We can wonder what would have become of Mary after the crucifixion, this woman bereft not only of her man and master, but also her protector, cut adrift so suddenly in the maturity of early middle age. Would she have stayed with the Jerusalem set, now led by Peter and later her brother-in-law James, set up home with one or more of the other women, or possibly have forged a new relationship with one of the male apostles, living lives in mutual self-support and shared memories of their deceased leader? She would not have become an apostle, spreading the 'word'. More than the others – or at least more then the menfolk in the inner circle – she would have known that the great game that had been played out was one of devotion to a living master, and now that he was gone, the game was over.

There is perhaps another clue about Mary's role, relating to the last supper, and Jesus' pronouncement that one of those present would betray him. This is portrayed as an example of Jesus possessing the power of

knowing the future, although he would have known by
now from his anxious complaints that Judas was having
a crisis of conscience and his loyalty had been stretched
to breaking point. Jesus might also have been tipped off
by one of his contacts amongst the authorities that Judas
was already talking to the Pharisees. We are told in the
traditional Bible that one disciple, 'whom Jesus loved',
was leaning on his bosom – new translations prefer to say
'reclining close to him', taking away any hint of intimate
physical contact. The following sentence in the Biblical
account has this special disciple being asked by Peter to
find out who Jesus meant: "Peter beckoned to him, that
he should ask who it should be of whom he spake". If a
special disciple whom 'Jesus loved' had their head resting
on Jesus' bosom, the indication would be that this was a
woman, but the thought is put out of mind by the disciple
being identified as 'he' in the very next sentence. Yet if
we go back to the original literal translation of the text of
the gospel, we find the word 'he' does *not* appear, and the
gender of this specially close disciple is left undisclosed.
The words are: "Peter motioned to *this one* to inquire who
it might be," almost as if the gender were being deliberately concealed. If Mary Magdalene were his girlfriend,
this episode makes perfect sense, and of course explains
why, in da Vinci's painting of the last supper, the disciple
on Jesus' right resembles a woman.

We need also to acknowledge the discovery, in the
summer of 2012, of a 'business card' sized piece of
papyrus with four lines on either side which include

the words: "Jesus said, 'My wife…' " and Jesus' assertion that a woman called Mary is indeed "worthy to be my disciple". The provenance of the item is not yet clear, but is assumed to have come from the excavation of an ancient Coptic Christian rubbish dump, the source of many torn pieces of ancient parchment from the Biblical era, and appears to be a fourth century copy of a second century original, which if verified would make it as ancient as almost any early Christian writings. Besides acknowledging he had a 'wife', the quote appears to show Jesus fighting the corner of sexual equality in face of patriarchal opposition, and that even during his life he had to use his rank to silence Peter on the question of Mary's credentials.

Whether Jesus was married is beside the point. It would have no bearing on either his teachings or his works, and is only a hot topic these days because of the challenge the possibility poses to the position of the Catholic church, which answered the discovery of the fragment not with a "Let's look into this," but with a "Jesus was single, there's nothing more to be said". It is a statement which might one day have to join "The sun goes round the earth, no doubt about it" as a previously irreversible declaration which later required the eating of humble pie.

We also have to bear in mind when discussing the possibility of Jesus being in a relationship that one of – if not *the* – most enigmatic people in the New Testament is the unnamed 'disciple whom Jesus loved'.

This personage appears time and again, and it seems to be accepted amongst the apostles that one of them – or someone else with a similar degree of closeness – is especially dear to the master. We feel instinctively, from the clues we have found, that this might well be Mary Magdalene herself. Yet it is Mary who, according to John's gospel, after finding the tomb vacant, ran to tell both Peter and 'the other disciple, the one who Jesus loved' that the tomb was empty, whereupon they both ran themselves, the unnamed one reaching it first. Luke, in his account of the drama, does not mention the disciple whom Jesus loved; according to him only Peter ran to the tomb. Mark and Matthew, on the other hand, while acknowledging Mary was the first to see the empty tomb, do not mention anyone else, neither Peter nor an unnamed lover, going to verify her story.

As with so many incidents in the gospels, we are left with similar but contradictory accounts. Speculation on the identity of the mysterious 'lover' has been, as can be imagined, intense. Likely candidates have been Lazarus, the youth whom Jesus allegedly raised from the dead, and John himself, who in the last chapter of his gospel appears to claim the role. However, the last chapter of John's gospel is generally thought to have been a later addition in someone else's hand, and in any event, if John had been a contemporary of Jesus, since his gospel is dated at 110 C.E., he himself would have been around a hundred years old when he put stylus to papyrus. On these grounds many observers believe the John who wrote the gospel could not have been a contemporary of Jesus and would not therefore have been a candidate for the 'one whom Jesus loved'.

It is also John, and only John, who tells of Jesus on the cross looking down on his mother and the 'disciple whom he loved' and saying, "Mother, behold your son!" and to the disciple, "Behold your mother!" "And from that hour", we are told, "the disciple took her to his own home". It is assumed Jesus was telling his mother to accept the disciple as her own son and vice-versa, although, if we are to believe Mark's account, Mary Magdalene and other women were only able to watch the crucifixion 'from a distance', meaning such conversation would probably not have taken place. In any event, both John, paradoxically, and the other evangelists only mention women as witnesses to the crucifixion – Mary his mother, Mary Magdalene and another Mary, the 'wife of Clopas'; no man appeared to be present. Could John in his gospel account be trying to hide what really happened, which would present a much more believable scenario: Jesus asking his partner Mary to take care of his mother? The notion that John, in an effort to demonstrate that Jesus, as a 'divine being', did not have a female consort, deliberately gave Mary and the 'one he loved' separate identities, when in reality they were one and the same, has gained currency in recent decades, but the evidence is speculative. It is yet another example of insufficient or contradictory information giving us a tantalizing but insoluble mystery, though the discovery of the Gnostic gospels, with their many references to Mary as Jesus's special companion, has tilted the search for the identity of the 'one Jesus loved' strongly in her direction.

If, on the other hand, Jesus did have an especially close male companion during his ministry, it opens up the suggestion that he might have been gay. Again, it would make no difference to Jesus' status, his identity or what he accomplished. The chances of him being gay are the same as for any other human being then or now, and in today's open-minded society it would not necessarily cause raised eyebrows, except possibly in the homophobic churches of Africa. But the evidence in favor of Mary Magdalene, a strong and constant presence close by Jesus throughout his ministry, even if the relationship between them might well have been platonic, is daunting.

There is another reason why, notwithstanding the mystery of the 'disciple whom Jesus loved', we can be quite sure Jesus was not a homosexual. It is that if there had been the slightest suspicion of it, we can be certain that that arch defamer of Christ, the second century Celsus, would have had a field day of salacious gossip.

At the same time as acknowledging that Jesus and Mary were possibly 'an item', we must also note that Jesus was clearly against sexual infidelity, and that to him even having lustful thoughts was a form of adultery, but this was in reference to behavior – almost certainly male behavior – within marriage, in a society where women had no conjugal rights to protect them. Looking at the world around him, Jesus might well have identified the dehumanization of women, and the right of a husband to divorce his wife if he found her behavior 'displeasing', as one of its most offensive aspects. We know he did not require his disciples to be unmarried, for since we are told Peter – and for a time Jesus too – lived in his mother-in-law's house in Capernaum, we can take it that he had a wife. The attitude of Jesus to marriage needs more investigation, especially in view of his controversial assertion that loyalty to him supersedes loyalty to family, presumably including husband and wife. The 'marriage' in which he was really interested appears to be the one between himself and his disciples.

* * *

Beside the inner group of men and women intensely bound to Jesus, there would have been a wider set still who did not travel and live with him, who had their own lives, homes and families, but nevertheless had enjoyed some kind of interaction which bound them together in devoted loyalty. They may include the centurion whose servant he cured, the tax collector, the woman cured by her faith and especially, because he seemed so close to them, the two sisters from Bethany, Mary and Martha and their younger brother Lazarus. This group might number two or three hundred. These two categories would merge into each other in a gradually changing spectrum; there would not have been a hard and fast division.

Then there appears to be a further grouping of thousands who come when they have the opportunity to hear Jesus speak. They like his words, they accept that he is a great prophet, empowered by God, but have not necessarily been instructed in the 'inner teachings' that Jesus often says those closest to him have been privileged to receive. These included the 5,000 who were fed with apparently inadequate supplies of victuals, the 4,000 who were also similarly fed, and if those groupings were mainly of people of, say, a day's journey from the speaking engagements, we can assume over the whole area of Jesus' perambulatory teachings, about ten or twenty thousand could be included in this number. This group must have included a large minority who had traveled from much further afield, even outside the boundaries of Israel, who had heard of him and his miraculous deeds, had packed up a few items and set off on a journey that might have taken several days, to see if the instinct that here was a true representative of God – a new prophet – was actually well-founded.

These three groups of followers were not what could be called Christians, a title that did not appear until a century or so after Jesus' death. The name by which his followers styled themselves during his teachings and in the early years after his death was as followers of 'the way'. Once Jesus had left the scene, it would not be possible for anyone else to become a disciple, what would later be called a Christian, in its original sense, for his was a very personal form of teaching and interaction with those who followed him. After his death, this interaction could no longer take place, and was replaced by devotion to his memory and a continued teaching of his message.

In this light, it is likely that Jesus did not intend any organized religion to develop after his unexpected death – his mission was for those who lived at the same time as he: "as long as I am in the world, I am the light of the world". The person who started and molded the early Christian *religion*, Paul, became an adherent of his own interpretation of Jesus' message, based on an event that was as spurious as the virgin birth – the 'resurrection', and what it signified. Paul himself had no time for the life of Jesus, and little time for what Jesus actually taught, shown by how little space in his copious writings was devoted to Jesus' life, actions and teachings. He had his own agenda, which Jesus, had he really returned to earth after twenty or thirty years, might not have recognized. The word 'crosstianity' has been coined to describe this post-crucifix variant of the original message, which interprets Jesus' purpose as 'to die for our sins'. It is a very different teaching from that of the living Jesus, for whom sins were not a major concern.

Since we are focusing on Jesus the man rather than Christ the Messiah, it does not matter that Jesus was not called 'Christ' – meaning the anointed one – until after his death, and the scriptures, written in primitive Greek, adopted this Greek word as an appropriate title. But it is instructive that the earliest dated *inscription* relating to Jesus, found on a Syrian house-cum-place of gathering, an early 'church', dated 318 C.E., uses instead of *Christos* – the term referring to the notion of a Jewish Messiah – *Chrestos*, almost identical in spelling but very different in meaning, indicating one who had become 'perfect', complete, sanctified; someone who had achieved the highest human state. We might recoil from the word 'perfect' to describe any human being, especially one whom we know was prone to temper and the other human qualities shown by Jesus in the New Testament, until we recall one of his most famous, not to say challenging, injunctions: "Be perfect, as your father in heaven is perfect". This indicates that he believed that there is a process, a journey, that a sincere person can undertake from their present 'imperfect' state to a state of 'perfection', not the superficial ideal the word has been taken to mean in our own age, but in its true sense of completion, fulfillment, of having achieved the goal of human life. The presumption is that at least some trends of early Christianity saw Jesus in this way, rather than as the 'anointed one' expected to lead his people to freedom that the word *Christos*, the Greek translation of the Hebrew word *Mashiah* – in English, Messiah – implies.

Long before the light of research into early Christianity fell so strongly and dramatically on the

Gnostics, and revealed the battle that raged between their view of Jesus and the church's preference for a Messianic Christ, the great early twentieth century Christian scholar, G.S. Mead, suggested that *Chrestos* was probably a common word used to describe Christ in the early days which was gradually replaced, when documents were copied after older ones wore out, from ignorance rather than malice, by the Messianic term *Christos*. Hence the dearth of references to *Chrestos* in Christian writings. Inscriptions in stone, however, could not be so easily altered. To quote Mead:

> "In early times there seems to have been much confusion between the two titles. *Christos* is the Greek for the Hebrew Messiah, Anointed, and was used by those who believed Jesus was the Jewish Messiah. This was denied, not only by the Marcionites (the sect to whom the building belonged) but also by many of their Gnostic predecessors and successors. The title *Chrestos* was used of one perfected, the holy one, the saint: no doubt in later days the orthodox, who subsequently had the sole editing of the texts, in pure ignorance changed *Chrestos* into *Christos* wherever it occurred."

Jesus, of course, was never anointed, as David had been when he became king, so this vision of him as the anointed one is a case of making him conform to Old Testament precedents. The only anointing we are aware he undertook was the emotional washing in expensive oil of his feet by Mary – either Magdalene or Mary the sister of Martha – at the sisters' home in Bethany, followed by drying with the woman's long hair, and this was not the kind of anointing that would bestow kingship upon its recipient. 'Christ' – the Messiah expected in the Old Testament – was not a healer or miracle worker, but a strong king who would drive out the Romans; not a savior of individual souls but of the nation of Israel. Therefore, the title 'Christ' was inappropriate when used to describe Jesus.

But does this debate over nomenclature matter? We can quote Shakespeare's declaration, "a rose by any other name would smell as sweet". In any event, we are today so used to the striking phrase, Jesus Christ, that we might gloss over the theological implications and be secretly pleased the word for Messiah won the day: *Jesus Chrest* just doesn't have the same ring. We need only take issue with Professor Mead's kindly opinion that later transcribers *mistakenly* changed 'Chrest' to 'Christ'; it sounds like a very deliberate ploy in the attempt by the Jesus deifiers to undermine Gnosticism.

In his own life Jesus would have been Jesus of Nazareth or Yeshuah Bar-Yoseph – Joshua Josephson – but his disciples had no qualms in giving him titles such as 'Master', 'Rabbi' or 'Teacher'. They did not share the obsessive interest of future generations of followers in whether he was Christ or Jesus, God or man. To them all such concepts were subsumed into one reality: to use a modern romantic term, he was their everything. He was their touchstone, the center of their focus: compared to this real sense of mutual belonging, titles and definitions were redundant.

Chapter Six

The Embarrassments

The work of scholars over the past few generations has been a search for the real Jesus, the historical Jesus, not the one shrouded by a religion or smothered by Christian preconceptions but the simple first century Palestinian itinerant preacher; not the Christ of later worship but Jesus of Nazareth. On the one hand we have those who deny such a figure ever existed but is a construct created from a mishmash of theological concepts and superstitions of the time to fulfill the strong belief that a messianic figure was about to turn up and lead the Jews, as Moses had reputedly done, out of subservience and towards their promised destiny. On the other are those who very much accept his existence but differentiate between the simple, 'human' Jesus of the pre-crucifixion era and the great 'living god' Messiah whom the original man gradually became after the new, previously unknown, ingredient of resurrection had come into the mix, sucking the energy from the simple 'miracles' and teachings of the earlier Jesus.

For the most part, the idea that the man did not even live is discredited. Even taking into account the natural bias of the gospels and the frequent occasions where later additions and embellishments are incorporated into the original story, it is accepted that there is enough historical truth in the four gospels and supporting evidence from other observers to be sure of the man's existence. This much is widely acknowledged, even if the only certain facts are that he was tied in, in some way, with John the Baptist at the beginning of his ministry, he gathered a group of dedicated disciples, he performed 'works and signs', and he was arrested before being tried and crucified by the Roman governor, Pontius Pilate for no clear reason. Anything else is open to conjecture.

Amongst such supporting pieces of evidence, pre-eminent is that of the contemporary Jewish chronicler, Josephus, who reported most of these basic facts in his account of Roman-Jewish life in first century Palestine, and additional sparse references in the writings of other Roman historians. An interesting way our modern-day forensic researchers agree on what can be added with some degree of certainty to the essential facts about Jesus are what are sometimes called 'the embarrassments'. These are incidents in the gospel accounts of Jesus' life that one might think would have been edited out by the evangelists because they do not reflect well on him. The fact that they remain included supposedly testifies to their truthfulness.

We have touched upon an outstanding example of these, the relationship with John the Baptist and in particular the agreement in all the gospels that Jesus was baptized by him in the River Jordan at the very start of his ministry. Why should this have happened? Theories abound, but none are convincing. Shouldn't it have been the other way round – John being baptized 'in spirit' by the man he had just proclaimed was the 'Lord'? The implication is that Jesus was originally a follower of, or at least subservient to, John, who was therefore Jesus' predecessor, and the baptism was a passing of the torch from the one to the other. It is an opinion which is accepted by a surprising number of experts. But this mysterious, and possibly embarrassing, interaction between the two men is not the end of the story.

One would think that John, having done his proclaiming, would now join Jesus, or at least retire from his own line of prophesying: it would be a case of 'mission accomplished', otherwise we have two important ministries incongruously overlapping. But John continued with his work, and Mark tells us that Jesus did not begin his own ministry until John had been arrested: "after John was arrested, Jesus came into Galilee, proclaiming the gospel of God". No time period is given; it could be any number of weeks, months or more, although the implication is that it was not very long after Jesus' baptism. In this reading of the story, it seems Jesus waits until John's enforced resignation before beginning his own ministry, and we are left with the tantalizing but unspoken possibility that between his time in the wilderness absorbing what he had received from John and John's arrest, he was still with John as one of the Baptist's disciples, and only took up the leadership of the followers of 'the way' when a vacancy became available. Put simply, if John's true 'Lord', "the strap of whose sandals I am not worthy to untie", had finally appeared, why did he carry on his independent mission instead of becoming Jesus' follower? This was the second embarrassment. The third also concerns John, after he has been thrown in jail for criticizing Herod's adultery with his sister-in-law.

By now Jesus is making waves and John sends his emissaries to ask him: "Are you the one who is to come, or shall we look for another?" The fact that, even after, according to the gospels, seeing the dove landing on Jesus' head at the time of baptism and hearing God's voice speaking from the heavens, the Baptist seemed to have doubts about Jesus does not really represent a ringing endorsement. And Jesus does not appear to give a clear response. Instead of telling him, "Yes I am," he replies, "Go and tell John what you hear and see: the blind receive their sight and the lame walk, lepers are cleansed, the deaf hear, the dead are raised up and the poor (meaning poor in spirit) have the good news preached to them". A few cures, the odd 'miracle', and a rather strange teaching about a God very different from the Jewish concept, a gentle, loving and most importantly, a non-violent God, the argument goes, probably constituted the kind of report that might give John in his cell cause to reflect on his earlier endorsement. John of course was not to be around to show his future devotion to or rejection of his nominated successor, or, indeed, to continue his own work, never regaining his freedom but being unjustly beheaded at the request of Herod's daughter Salome in exchange for her entertaining dance display at a palace party. But John's questioning of Jesus' credentials, one senses, is a vibrant and real exchange. His message, and Jesus' reply, have the strong ring of an actual historical event, and far from being an embarrassment, the episode provides a missing link, a 'smoking gun', showing the similarity of the teachings of the two men, Jesus appearing to expect his mentor to understand clearly what he was talking about. The incident is only 'embarrassing' in view of the gospels' earlier story of Jesus' baptism, and the strength of John's endorsement at that time.

A further 'embarrassment' is said to be Jesus' poor view of his own disciples. He often berates them for their petty pride and their lack of understanding, and we cannot entirely disagree that this opinion is deserved. Even after two or so hectic years living almost full-time in his company, when he hints at the last supper that he might be leaving them, "a dispute arose among them as to which of them was the greatest". It is hardly credible. 'Who are these people?' we feel like asking. Of course, Jesus has to rebuke them with an obvious truth: "Let the greatest be the one who serves", for, "he who is least among all of you is the one who is great", reflecting his constant theme: the children, the innocent, the poor and the humble will be the first to be welcomed into the Kingdom of Heaven.

We then arrive at the moment where he calls his chief disciple, Peter, 'Satan'. Was Jesus a liar? Presumably not, yet Peter evidently wasn't Satan. Jesus must have been exaggerating for effect; after all, he had called Herod 'a fox', and his disciples were not to throw their pearls before 'swine'. He had possibly learned this line of invective from the Baptist, who was quite his equal, if not in spiritual power, then in the field of vituperative insults, calling the Pharisees who came to interrogate him 'vipers'. Be that as it may, it shows Jesus, whilst loving Peter and apparently relying on him, could sometimes vehemently rebuke him; hence another 'embarrassment'.

Then we have the apparent bluntness demonstrated by Jesus in his encounter with the Canaanite woman who asked him to cure her daughter. "It is not right to take the children's bread and throw it to the dogs", he replied – 'children' being generally understood to mean Israelites. The woman is not cowed by this crude put-down, saying even dogs are entitled to a few scraps from the master's table, and he looks at her with a new eye, admiring her spirit, and "her daughter was healed instantly".

There are other embarrassments, such as his apparent rejection of his own family, his own rejection by the population of his home town, and his subsequent need to escape from them when they try to throw him from a cliff top, before we come to the biggest one of all: the crucifixion itself. Now that the death on the cross is universally regarded as some form of triumph, it is strange to realize that this is not how it was seen at the time. How, it was felt, could someone sent by God to save humanity, or at least the Jewish people, suffer the humiliation of being caught and crucified like a common thief or murderer? It is now accepted that Christianity as a new religion, with Jesus dying on the cross to redeem sinners as its central tenet, was not something that came about in his lifetime but was created later, with the subtext that his whole ministry was building up, in a predetermined way that he was fully cognizant of, to its dramatic and tragic climax. Such a re-telling makes the crucifixion seem like a glorious crowning moment of his life, rather than the utter disaster it at first appeared. As the great expert in the post-Jesus period, Professor Murphy-O'Connor, says, to his followers, Jesus "was dead and that was the end".

Jesus appeared to have been so confident in his teachings, so sure that a new beginning was at hand; how could he have walked into the jaws of the lion and found himself so clearly outwitted by those he had goaded and made fools of over the previous couple of years – the priests and Pharisees? At the same time, for those of his following who really believed he was the leader who would usher in God's kingdom, his ignominious end was a bitter blow.

In the Far East today, the blazoning of the crucified Christ in Christian iconography, in neck pendants and above the altars of churches, is viewed with quiet distaste. It is considered unnatural to have a corpse, or even just the gallows – the cross – as some kind of religious symbol. It was viewed in a similar way at the time it happened, Paul himself quoting the prevalent belief, "cursed be him who hangs from a tree". It would be several centuries before images and statues of the crucified Jesus began to take their place in Christian iconography.

This incredulity that the worst possible thing had taken place, and the deep desire to put some kind of meaningful interpretation on the tragedy, created a climate for the visions and ethereal visitations apparently experienced by the distraught group of the closest disciples in the days and weeks after the dire event. It was fuelled all the more by the story of the empty tomb, with many more plausible explanations for the removal of Jesus' body – the most likely one being that his family had taken it away for burial – being overlooked in favor of the most fantastical one: he had risen from the dead.

Something had to be made of this critical collapse of Jesus' reputation, and it was Paul who turned the disaster into a remarkable, joyous triumph; Jesus had come back to life. It is tempting, even today, to wish this had really happened. What a sweet ending it would provide to a dreadful drama. From tragedy, triumph. From failure, success. From death, life. Few Biblical scholars today, however, believe a physical resurrection actually took place.

But it had *almost* happened. People *thought* they had seen him, that they had experienced a visitation that in some cases seemed preternaturally real. Even Paul, who was persecuting the followers of 'the way' until his own dramatic conversion on the road to Damascus a couple of years after the crucifixion, claimed to have seen the living Christ. And in such powerful circumstances of suspended disbelief, a convincing sense of presence could be just as good as the real thing. For Jesus, after all, had been talking throughout his teachings of the victory of life over death, the need for a new birth, the possibility of a 'life eternal'. What better symbol for this essential message than that he should himself have physically conquered death and come to life again?

Now, the resurrection lies at the very heart of belief in Christ. It is so deep-rooted that it has become even more emblematic than the man himself and his teachings while alive. The image of the cross is everywhere. It is as meaningful as the stars and stripes to Americans, as sacrosanct as the *Koran* to Muslims. In the 1970's, the theory was propounded that actually Jesus might not have been crucified but was more likely to have been stoned to death – the more usual form of execution at the time for Jews, as shown in the story of the woman saved from stoning by Jesus himself. It was the manner by which Jesus' brother, James, was put to death some thirty years later. The strong evidence in the gospels, not to mention the importance of the cross as a symbol – for without it there would be no religion – soon restored the traditional view, but the consternation widely expressed about this possibility was considerable and heartfelt. How could the universal symbol of love and eternal life, the crucified Jesus wearing his crown of thorns, be replaced by a pile of stones? It was unthinkable.

So the legend grew that Jesus had survived his execution and with it demonstrated that for his believers death held no fear. How and why it grew we will address at a later juncture. For now we can observe that this is an area where the speculative functions of theologians and academics, so rife and prolific in every other aspect of Jesus' life and teachings, turn into near silence. As Diarmaid MacCulloch says, "The New Testament is a literature with a blank at its center, yet this blank is also its intense focus". The 'intense focus' has become not what Jesus did and taught while alive but what he is supposed to have done after his death, namely, returned to life. Yet, even Professor E.P. Sanders – 'the most distinguished scholar in the field of Jesus research today' – suggests, "The reader who thinks that it is all perfectly clear – the physical, historical Jesus got up and walked around – should study Luke and Paul more carefully. The disciples could not recognize him; he was not 'flesh and blood' but a 'spiritual body' ". He does not, however, regard "deliberate fraud as a worthwhile explanation" for the visions. The people who had an experience of the risen Christ were, in Sanders' opinion, telling the truth. What is in question is what exactly had they had an experience of.

By the time the stories were written down, except for the claim of Paul, who had never encountered Jesus while alive, the accounts were already second or third hand, while the last chapter of John, containing the most post-resurrection appearances, giving Jesus the chance to issue instructions about the future direction of his teaching, is, according to Sanders, "an appendix probably by a later author," writing after all the disciples had died. The most recent 'neutral' expert to evaluate the evidence, Professor Maurice Casey, is quite categorical, even consigning the story of the empty tomb to later embellishment: "Jesus did not rise bodily from the dead, leaving an empty tomb behind. He was probably buried in a common criminals' tomb, where his body rotted in the normal way". Even Matthew, he points out, admitted that amongst the first apostles who were supposed to have witnessed a risen Christ, "some doubted". The stories of resurrection, so tentative in the aftermath of the crucifixion but building in certainty the further the distance from the event, especially in the fourth gospel, Casey concludes, "have been written for the needs of the churches for whom the evangelists wrote".

The disciples themselves were not initially sure of what they had experienced. Even the first to have the 'resurrected Christ' appear to her, his special friend and possibly his partner, Mary Magdalene, had her doubts as to what she had seen and was flatly disbelieved when she told the others what had happened, especially by Peter. The weakest portions of the New Testament are those tentative chapters and verses which describe sightings of, and visitations by, the deceased Jesus. Mark, the author of the first gospel, does not include any resurrection sighting at all, while Matthew, whose gospel was the next to appear, is noticeably brief and dismissive in his reports of the post-crucifixion appearances of Jesus. His final words, "Jesus said...go and make disciples of all nations, baptizing them in the name of the father, son and holy spirit", are ideas and phrases never touched upon by the living Jesus, and seem more likely to be assertions added as the original disciples died to justify the continued growth of their work.

In the two remaining gospels it is as if we have encountered a series of hazy passages of wooden prose. The life has gone out of the story. Those who apparently meet the risen Jesus do not at first recognize him. He does not have the same appearance as when he was alive. He floats like an apparition in an out of rooms, in MacCulloch's words, "regardless of doors or any normal means of exit and entrance", yet he eats some grilled fish with the apostles, a claim Vermes tells us was a later addition to the legend to give it legs, as were apparent hints that the pre-crucifixion Jesus had foretold his fate; "the predictions by Jesus of his death and resurrection are inauthentic", claims Vermes. It is not really surprising that modern psychologists have no hesitation in putting this central lynchpin of Christianity, if indeed such apparitions did take place, in the drawer labeled dreams and hallucinations. To them, it is a classic case of a profound sense of shock, loss and grief causing a conviction that the recently deceased has been sighted.

This aspect of the resurrection story has been well-covered by the late Professor Michael Goulder, who, in his book, *A Tale of Two Missions*, concludes, as do most scholars, that a physical resurrection did *not* take place. The original apostles knew that their visions of Jesus in the days after his death were more like spiritual visitations. This, he says, is why the verb 'appear' is repeatedly used in the gospels whenever a sighting occurred. 'Jesus *appeared* to Peter': 'he *appeared* to James', implying a kind of vision, or apparition, rather than an actual presence. He also points to the examples of people 'seeing' their deceased spouse in the period of time after their death as a comparable phenomenon, although when we discuss presently the possibility that *inner* visualization formed part of the 'secret' teaching of Jesus, the notion of Jesus 'appearing' to his closest disciples after his death begins to be seen in a more plausible context. As a post-script, the story of Jesus eating with the disciples and inviting them to touch his wounds is, Goulder says, a later addition to the verbal tradition, made under Paul's growing influence, to make the resurrection seem like a physical one.

Paul, who made up for his late arrival in the Christian world, some two years after the crucifixion, by the fervor and dynamism of his proselytizing, had not been there at the time of the apparitions, and had never been part of the Jerusalem fraternity, but worked hard to transform these stories of vague sightings of the deceased master into an actual physical resurrection to make it absolutely clear that if you joined the new religion, one of the benefits would be triumph over death. He was so successful in this that he had to put a stop to a practice amongst some new converts of enrolling their dead relatives posthumously into the Christian faith, so that they too would benefit from the promised physical re-emergence at 'the end of days'.

Jesus did not rise from the dead, but something did happen, as suggested by Shusaku Endo in his 1978 *Life of Jesus*:

> "If we do not believe in the resurrection of Jesus, then we are forced to believe that what did hit the disciples was some other amazing event different in kind yet of equal force in its electrifying intensity...Without some sort of a new beginning (after the crucifixion), whatever it might have been, there would have been no Christian faith and no Christian movement".

We will look presently at what this "amazing event... of equal force" which led to a realization by the apostles that they were not emasculated by the crucifixion, but dynamically motivated to carry on their master's work, might have been.

We can also add that, quite apart from considerations of implausibility, the story of the resurrection creates a problem even greater than if the accounts of Jesus' life had ended at his death. It is that the subsequent religion has to say that Jesus will return to complete his work, and to 'save' his true believers: the much talked about, even to this day, 'second coming'. But the essence of the resurrection story is that he did indeed return after death: it *was* the second coming; it had already taken place. He had proved he could transcend death. What was anticipated now was the 'third coming'. Whether second, third or twenty-third, however, is beside the point. The problem is that, as there seems to be no evidence of Jesus actually 'saving' people while he was alive, it is necessary to believe that he will be doing so at some future date.

* * *

It is a light-hearted but interesting speculation to wonder what the Nazarene teacher would have made of all this were he to 'return', as many Christians hope and in many cases fervently believe he will. It could be that he would be aghast at the adoption of the cross and his emaciated body as symbols of his time on earth, and be equally challenged by the many variants on his original teachings that have been incorporated into the religions bearing his name over the past 2,000 years. But wouldn't it be the same if any founder of a major institution were magically to reappear, a Mr. Hewlett, visiting HP today, or Henry Ford, not to mention the founding fathers of the United States?

Wouldn't the present-day directors of the concern say, "We appreciate what you did in inventing the product and setting us up in business all those years ago, but you are now out of touch. Adaptations have had to be made to adjust to modern times and conditions. If we had kept it as it was when you left, it might have not taken off at all, or still have been a small Jewish cult, without proper rules, dogmas, liturgies and rituals, not to mention the vast amount of theology we have had to develop, since you left us with so little. These innovations have paid off, because look how big and international the business has become. So, thank you for what you did, but you are no longer needed, you can return to your retirement home in the sky". And a confused Jesus would be unceremoniously escorted through a side door lest the faithful congregation and priestly management class be put off by this strange and unsavory character from the distant past.

Chapter Seven

What We Know

Having questioned the evidence supporting the story of Jesus' birth and cast a sprinkling of doubt-dust on the credibility of the resurrection, we are left with the nub of the story: what happened in-between. And what did happen in-between? No wonder so much Christian academic research and theology prefers to avoid this contentious area. Because, as the controversial American politician, Donald Rumsfeld, put it, in relation to another matter: "There are things we know that we know. There are things that we know we don't know. But there are also unknown unknowns – there are things we do not know we don't know".

This mysterious – and in its original context quite meaningless – quote is well applied to the life of Jesus. There are certain clear and undisputed facts. There are also a lot of 'known unknowns', missing areas such as his early life and many little gaps where we can only speculate on events and their background. But running beneath the entire story is a sense that something else is happening here which we simply do not know about. We vaguely detect an aroma of something more profound but intangible. It is this area that in our revisiting we will try to gently probe.

It has already been proposed that we remove from the story anything that is patently untrue, namely, accounts of miracles. Let us also take out of the equation something else that, common sense left at the door, are accepted as an unquestionable part of Christian belief: prophecies. The future cannot be known; Jesus had no more power of predicting the future than you or I. The predictions he is said to have made, whether about his own death, the destruction of temples, or the future course of world history, we know he did not make, not because of the obvious change in language or tone when these passages appear in the gospels, indicating 'later addition' or 'reworking of the original story', but because, not having any special gift of knowing the future, he would simply not have made them.

By prophecy we also do not mean the kind of prediction some might have made to him, if they were brave enough to risk a sharp rebuke: "If you don't stop attacking and insulting the Scribes and Pharisees, you might find yourself in serious trouble". No, we mean prophecy along the lines of: "He will be great, and will be called the Son of the Most High; and the Lord God will give Him the throne of His father David", or "The Son of

Man will be mocked and flogged and crucified. On the third day he will be raised to life". We need to accept such embellishments for what they were – colorful additions to the rapidly growing legend of Christ the king rather than Jesus the man. To understand the true meaning of prophecy we have to revert to its original definition, 'divinely inspired words' coming from a prophet, defined as 'someone who speaks on behalf of God'. Predicting the future is not prophecy but fortune telling. The Old Testament is full of predictions, which are usually spoken in the context of warnings of what will happen to a people or a civilization if a particular course is not followed. If, as Dr. Johnson ventured, patriotism is the last refuge of a scoundrel, then prophecy is the last refuge of those who cannot find other means to persuade people of the value of their case.

The Christian church through the ages has placed great store in prophetic fortune telling as a cornerstone of its faith, especially in the circumstances of the birth of Jesus and again of his death. The latter is the more serious, for the foretelling of his death and resurrection by Jesus is at the heart of the later misinterpretation of Jesus' message, while in fact, as Geza Vermes has clinically demonstrated, no such clear predictions were made, accounting for the surprised stupefaction of the disciples when his crucifixion did happen, and their initial disbelief when tales that he had survived the experience began to circulate. Nothing had been further from their minds.

Within a few years of the crucifixion, a Pharisee called Paul had a sudden, blinding conversion and began to power forward with the creation of a new religion, based on worship of Jesus, which spread widely around the Mediterranean over the coming decades. It is easy to forget that apart from Judaism, people at that time were still, as far as belief in the supernatural was concerned, worshipping multiple deities, but were now ready psychologically, had developed a level of social maturity, for the great step forward to accepting that there must only be one God, one creator. The Jews themselves had reached this point several centuries prior, but had 'invented' their god as the kind they thought was the ideal: a military leader meting out rough and often compassionless justice on his creation. The tribes in the desert lands south of the Middle East, on the other hand, would not reach the crossroads of abandoning their multiple deities in favor of one God until some six hundred years later, with the messenger and divine spokesperson, Muhammad, providing the catalyst.

For the Mediterranean populations, however, the monotheistic message of Jesus, as interpreted and promoted by Paul, resonated deeply. It was the missing piece for which they had been waiting. The idea would not overtake Rome itself, with its system of multiple deities, including the emperors themselves, for two or three centuries more. But when it did, the message of Jesus presented Romans with a ready-made religion that fitted their needs, only requiring some degree of stability and organization to make it worthy of such a great and far-flung empire. The new Catholic church was enormously fortunate in being handed the reins of spiritual power just as the temporal authority was crumbling; it filled a vacuum which allowed its writ to spread relatively unimpeded over Western Europe. However, it owed its position to the earlier work of Paul himself and the equally fervent contemporary promoters of the new religion.

We noticed earlier a parallel between the beginnings of Christianity and those of the soft drink, *Coca-Cola*. In the latter case, on the one hand the drink with *the* taste, the elixir, had been created. On the other was a potentially willing market of millions waiting without realizing it for the thirst-satisfying product that was on its way. All that was needed were the mechanics of connection: the logo, the advertising, the retail outlets, the publicity and, last but not least, the means of distribution. With these in place the beverage was ready to conquer the world, ironically, in the twentieth century, taking over the very idea of Christmas itself by appropriating the image of Santa Claus.

In the first and second centuries a similar dynamic was in place. On the one hand a new religion that pushed all the right buttons: one God, an invisible, omnipresent, all-seeing and most of all *benevolent* power, and a messenger representing the God who had sacrificed himself to bring the religion to people and who

101

could himself be worshipped as the great bridge – the go-between – whose grace, once bestowed on believers, could vouch eternal life. On the other, a million yearning souls, frustrated by the void of existing beliefs, waiting without realizing it for the new elixir of life. It was a felicitous meeting waiting to happen. All that was needed were the means to bring the two parts together. Would it have happened without Paul? Probably not, or at least not in the form that finally emerged. He unwittingly created the foundations on which would be built the framework of liturgy, beliefs, instructions, hierarchy, rituals, saints, and the last pieces in the puzzle: relics and pilgrimages. Eventually of course, a vast international structure was in place, dominant, powerful, led from a global headquarters, with at its heart the product that could not be challenged…and of course a logo that could not be beaten for its simplicity, its universality and its symbolism.

Without wanting to be unnecessarily provocative, it might not be a profitless speculation to wonder if, circumstances demanding, the church could manage without Christ, and, with a few medium-sized adjustments, the answer might be in the affirmative. Jesus' main task, the introduction to, and teachings about, God, has been completed. One of the Trinity might be gone and, of course, without wanting to cause any offence, it is hard to harbor any personal feelings of warmth toward the mysterious third part, the 'Holy Ghost'. But at least the Father himself, revealed by Jesus' teachings, would still be in position, the recipient of prayers, hymns and acts of worship.

* * *

In the first decades after the crucifixion, Paul's letters to the newfound communities in Corinth, Thessalonica and Rome itself do not dwell on Jesus' teachings, much less on the details of his life, but on his self-sacrifice as the 'lamb of God', able after his death to offer forgiveness and eternal life to those who believe in him. This set of beliefs, with little in common with what Jesus had actually taught, became the foundation of the new religion.

It is natural that Paul knew nothing of Jesus' life and teachings, for he had not lived through it. The gospels, recounting the familiar narrative we know so well today, were to appear decades in the future, and Paul spent very little time anyway in the company of the original disciples in their Jerusalem community, with whom he felt little sympathy. All he had to go on was his knowledge of, and possible presence at, the crucifixion, the powerful inner experience of his road-to-Damascus conversion, and the certainty that he had been given a command to bring the news of Jesus to the wider world. But these ingredients were enough for him to concoct a powerful brew.

Initially, it was the original group of bereft personal followers of Jesus, based in Jerusalem and led by first,

Peter, then Jesus' brother James, who were the heart of the Jesus remembrance movement, until the city was destroyed in 70 C.E. by the Romans following the Jewish rebellion of 66 C.E. It is generally accepted that until this point there had been a division between this group, which saw itself closely tied in with Judaism, and the determination of Paul to spread the new teachings to the world of the gentiles.

Until then, only Paul's letters provided written evidence of the existence of Jesus, but towards the end of the first century three versions of Jesus' life were committed to papyrus: the gospels – the 'good news' – followed, some time later, by a fourth. Much speculation has gone into who wrote them and why. The consensus has generally been a mixture of the Christian communities, after the destruction of Jerusalem, thinking the end of the world was indeed at hand, and deciding a record of their teacher should be left behind, and, rather contradictorily, that Jesus' alleged promised return had not yet taken place as expected, so in the meantime they should commemorate his life with written accounts. Even more potently, as the people who had lived with him were dead or dying, the word-of-mouth stories they had told of Jesus' sayings and actions would soon lack the authenticity of eye-witness testimony, and something should be set down to remind the world of this illustrious life before it was forgotten. These reasons appear rather simplistic, and we need to take cognizance of the new theory which has developed, and been widely accepted, over recent years, that in the decades after Jesus' death, a new religion was rapidly emerging which positioned him as a divine savior figure, worthy of worship, at its heart, and needed a back story which would support and emphasize this message.

As a result we have the gospels of Mark, probably written around the year 70 C.E., Matthew and Luke some ten years later, each of them telling a very similar story, often with identical phrases, hence being called the synoptic gospels (syn – same, and optic – eye), and John with a more distinctive take a further thirty years down the line. While the synoptic gospels are almost cheerful, chatty and vernacular in style, John's is more sonorous, portraying Jesus not so much as an itinerant teacher but more as the 'word made flesh', a living embodiment of God. John's gospel is also at variance with those of the others evangelists in content, emphasis and language itself. 'His' Jesus, for example, hardly ever uses the terms Kingdom of God or Kingdom of Heaven, but replaces them with a phrase seldom used by the others, 'eternal life'.

A difference already noted lies in the length of Jesus' 'ministry', which is calculated by how many Passovers – the annual Jewish celebration for which a visit to the Great Temple in Jerusalem was mandatory – are mentioned. The synoptics have Jesus only present at one – the one that leads to his death – but John has him in Jerusalem for three Passovers, hence making his ministry appear to be spread over three years. Among other discrepancies is the incident of Jesus throwing over the money-changers' tables in the outer courtyard of the temple. In the synoptic gospels this is the trigger of the events that lead to his arrest. In John, however, it occurs at the very beginning of his work, and is regarded by many Christians as the very act of changing the world order and ushering in the Kingdom of God.

It can be argued that these differentials, while significant, are not really game-changing. What is widely considered to be of greater importance is the distinct difference in tone between the three early gospels on the one side and that of John on the other. Some forty years had passed between the first of the synoptics, Mark (even though Matthew comes chronologically before Mark in the Bible), written about 70 C.E. and John's gospel, believed to have been written around 110 C.E. And whereas the synoptics tell more or less the same tale, John's stands out for being altogether more philosophical, theological and, not to put too fine a point on it, verbose, than its predecessors. It is full, according to Geza Vermes, of 'ambling monologues', portraying Jesus as not only the Messiah, but, for the first time, as God himself in human guise.

All commentators remark on this strong difference in style, coining the phrase Johannine Christianity to describe it. Geza Vermes says John's Jesus is 'lordly, transcendent and authoritative', and 'far above all others'.

He is not at all shy of stating who he thinks he is – "I am the way, the truth and the life", 'the way' being the key element, the path by which his disciples can reach the truth and the life eternal: "He who has seen me has seen the father". John never mentions the parables of Jesus that are such a striking feature of the synoptic gospels and never calls the 'miracles' by that name, preferring the word 'signs'.

He also quotes Jesus at much greater length than the synoptic gospels, having him utter long monologues about his divine identity, Old Testament prophets, and his own purpose, which don't sound at all like spontaneous speech, certainly not the pithy, to-the-point, style of speaking we are used to hearing from Jesus in the earlier accounts.

Why is John's gospel so intent not on providing simple biography, complete with miracles, but on portraying Jesus in a light that the other gospel writers did not? Elaine Pagels, the expert on Gnosticism, believes that the gospel was not written primarily to set the stories down before they were lost from memory, but to contradict the Gnostic tradition that appeared to be giving priority to the experience Jesus had apparently bestowed on his disciples, at the expense of the man himself. It was the man, more than the experience, that was important, claimed John, setting a marker for regarding Jesus as a divine being worthy of worship. It is a view supported by Michael Goulder, who says that as the generations passed, and Jesus became more of a memory, the experience of the 'holy spirit' was beginning to take his place. This tendency had grown even more since the earlier gospels were written, and the time for Jesus' expected return had long passed. John's powerful 'Jesus is Lord' gospel was pulling out all the stops in its attempt to redress the balance, and it was successful, for his blueprint for a Christ figure worthy of deification and worship became, in centuries ahead, the accepted model. The more 'human' Jesus was gradually consigned to history.

We must now also be aware of, if not include under the title 'scripture', the cache of writings that have been discovered in the intervening years, and most famously as recently as 1945 in northern Egypt, which are generally called the Gnostic gospels, since they talk of Jesus teaching his followers to have an internal experience – or *gnosis* – of the divine. Amongst them is the *Gospel of Thomas*, not an account of Jesus' life at all but a list of his sayings, some of which are replicated in the established gospels, some of which are new, which has been portrayed by Professor Pagels as the spark which led to John's gospel, since the two show the beginning of a serious split between the Messiahists, if we can so refer to people who worshipped Jesus as God, and the Gnostics with their focus on inner experience.

It is well-chronicled that these Gnostics were vilified by the church hierarchy, especially after its adoption by the Roman Empire, when orders went out for their writings to be destroyed. They represented a rival approach to Christianity which seemed to assert that no hierarchy, no intermediaries such as priests and bishops, were needed at all to have an experience of God. These Gnostics gathered, said their main opponent, Irenaeus, the Bishop of Lyon during the last two decades of the second century, not in officially designated places of worship but in each others' homes, speaking in turn, if so moved, of the experience of *gnosis*, and with lots drawn to decide who was to be the meeting's master of ceremonies. This persecution is why so few of their writings remain. We will see if they have any bearing on the Jesus story in due course, but we must not conclude that the new church was unnecessarily authoritarian. In its infancy it was remarkably tolerant of variations of belief and activity within its walls. But what it could *not* tolerate was a way of interpreting the Christian message that in its very heart carried an existential threat to the new religion, and in claiming the church was misrepresenting the very message of Christ, the Gnostics were sealing their own fate.

Chapter Eight

The Beginning of his Teachings

It was probably not a coincidence that Jesus, setting out to begin his teachings after his home town neighbors had given him such short shrift, causing him to complain that prophets are not honored in their own country, came across the two fishermen, Simon whom he renamed Peter, and his brother Andrew. Much more likely is that he sought them out – people his own age from his own locality, at least one of whom, Andrew, had been present at Jesus' baptism. It is not explained why this particular disciple had been with John by the River Jordan, close to Jerusalem in the south of Judea at the time of Jesus' baptism, when his place of work was on the northern rim of the Sea of Galilee at the opposite end of the country. A suggestion has been made that he was delivering fish to Jerusalem, near where John was preaching, and somehow came across the events happening by the nearby river. More likely, John's reputation was growing enormously. People wondered if he, not Jesus, might be the Messiah. His first appearance in the Bible came at a time when church elders had made the journey to his riverside headquarters to investigate this new variant on Judaism, and young men from far and wide, seeking a new beginning, were flocking to his colors. Possibly Andrew – and maybe Jesus also – was amongst them.

In considering this and the general presentation of Jesus' travels, it might be helpful to have a picture in mind of the geography of his homeland. Israel, as it is now called, was not then a unified country and did not have fixed borders. The area we are looking at is a long, north-south strip of land loosely similar to California, Florida, Portugal or Great Britain, although much smaller. In the north is the country called the Galilee, around the inland sea of that name, with many surrounding towns. A hundred or more miles to the south is the kingdom of Judea, also Jewish, with its capital Jerusalem, also surrounded by several towns and villages. Between them is Samaria, from where came the Good Samaritan of the parable, and also the woman who chatted to Jesus by the village well. There is possibly a comparison between Jesus' territory and nineteenth century England, in that the north was a hive of activity around the Sea of Galilee with several busy towns, while the south, beside the capital Jerusalem and the largish town of Jericho, was not populated to the same degree. People from the north, like Jesus and his companions, would have been easily recognized in the cosmopolitan capital by their regional accents.

With a hundred miles between the two ends of the country, and traveling being on foot, mule, or camel, the journey would take three or more days, and would not therefore be made over-frequently or without purpose. John has most of Jesus' activity take place in and around Jerusalem in the south, while the synoptic gospels locate him primarily in the north.

It is not clear how much time had lapsed between the baptism and the point when Andrew and Peter became Jesus' first disciples. Mark says it followed John's arrest, indicating it was quite some time after the baptism, possibly several months or longer, while John's gospel makes it appear to be almost immediately. We are told Jesus started his mission in his hometown and, after meeting rejection, headed for Capernaum, where he met the brothers.

From Nazareth to Capernaum was a journey of around fifty miles, with the large city of Tiberias between them, indicating Jesus had a specific destination in mind, or he would possibly have found his first followers there instead of Capernaum. He would also have had to pass through the busy fishing town of Magdala, where research has shown there was a fish-pickling factory. While there he may have befriended his future disciple, Mary, whose surname Magdalene indicated this was her hometown. The original gospels name her Mary of Magdala, as Jesus was named Jesus of Nazareth. Fish-pickling is traditionally a woman's task, employing most of the women of a fishing community, so possibly Mary worked at the local factory. With their childhood homes being so close, he might already have known her and her family. Perhaps she offered him the night's accommodation he would need before heading off for Capernaum, knowing he would find the brothers there. She might have decided to accompany him, making *her*, not the brothers, the first disciple, something that would not necessarily have been mentioned in the later gospels, anxious to give Peter his right of primo-geniture. Certainly Jesus would have had little time for courtship after his meeting with the brothers, the spot-light of history now, briefly, holding him in its glare. If he had encountered this most important of people in his retinue while his work was at full steam, we would have expected it to be mentioned in the gospels: the fact that she had as many as seven demons removed by Jesus, and then became his closest female disciple, should have merited some coverage. But if she were already with him, as a friend, personal assistant, wife, partner or just a loyal follower, there is less reason for her to be introduced into the story of Jesus' life.

Later in this book we examine the possibility that Jesus might have been a member of the monastic sect, the Essenes, during the years prior to him beginning his work. If not, we have to observe that at the age of thirty-three or so, it might be expected that Jesus could have been with Mary for many years before his emergence into the spotlight of history. But the fact that Mary Magdalene was first and foremost a disciple, from whom, we are told, he had 'cast out demons', indicates she was not someone from the ancient past of teenage life in the Galilee area, but a more recent acquaintance, someone he had met while he was already a master. That said, the late Professor Murphy-O'Connor draws our attention to the Jewish religion requiring a young man, especially a rabbi, to marry and procreate, and this would be expected of someone already in their thirties. The popular recent pseudo-history, *The Holy Blood and The Holy Grail*, by Richard Leigh, Michael Baigent and Henry Lincoln, based on the legend that Jesus survived his crucifixion and settled in the south-west of France, assumes that he would have been accompanied by Mary Magdalene and subsequently raised a family, on no more evidence than this traditional Jewish expectation that its rabbis marry and procreate.

If it were not a chance meeting with the brothers in Capernaum, how did Jesus know where to find them? Possibly Andrew had spoken to him after the baptism by John, and, learning that they came from the same northern end of the country, invited him to visit them by their fishing boats, where he found them washing the nets, just as fishermen do today on any working beach. Possibly a more profound connection had already been made. One version of the fateful meeting – Luke's – has Jesus using Simon's boat from which to teach the throng, which might explain where the bond between the two started, with Simon, soon to be renamed 'Rock', or 'Rocky', taking a leading position amongst the disciples. This story, although possibly completely true, leads us to another unanswered question – why, if Jesus was already so famous crowds hemmed him in so that he had to deliver his teachings from a boat, did he not have any existing disciples?

There are many ways of speculating on this huge series of events between Jesus being baptized by John and recruiting Andrew and Simon, and soon after, James and John, the sons of Zebedee, who left their boat in the hands of their servants: they were evidently not poor people. We simply do not know the facts, but we can be sure that much did happen: once he had begun his work, Jesus was not proceeding at a leisurely pace.

Whatever their former relationship, we are told by Mark, his account being closely followed by Matthew and Luke, that he invited them to join him, to become 'fishers of men', and they immediately put down their nets and followed him. This is arguably the most important point in the entire Bible: Jesus recruiting his first disciples. Later there would be a track record based on the fact that he was giving some very persuasive and revolutionary sermons, spoken with 'authority and power', and he was already performing his miraculous 'works' that in some way convinced people he had divine powers, that he was the 'Son of God'.

On this first occasion, nothing along these lines had yet materialized. The fishermen had nothing to go on. Why should they suddenly throw in their lot, in effect, their entire lives, to follow Jesus? We learn in short order that Simon was married. Was he going to give up his family also? Were the gospel writers glossing over inconvenient truths here in order to show that the first apostles entertained not a moment's qualm before changing their entire lives? It requires an unrealistically wide stretch of the imagination to accept that it happened this way.

There is certainly an essence of truth in the story. The phrase 'fishers of men', which is such a delightful one, showing a light wit and intelligence, also gives us a first real insight into the personality of Jesus. In the emphasis placed on Jesus' suffering and death by the later church, we tend to see his whole ministry as doom-laden and heavy-hearted. One of the more difficult discoveries of recent times has been the *Gospel of Judas*, implausibly implying Jesus welcomed his crucifixion, but which nevertheless paints an authentic picture of a Jesus who laughs often at his apostles' shortcomings. This reminds us that here was a well-adjusted man, able to command loyalty effortlessly while staying on light-hearted friendly terms with his disciples.

* * *

Jesus' work can be broken down into certain categories: actions, about which we have no need to dispute – "he then went to the next city" – miracles, which we know did not happen, meaning such stories were allegories making another wider point, and a further form of miracle, cures. The fact is that if a miracle *were* needed to believe in Jesus, then belief in him is founded on very shallow ground indeed. Even if he had performed miracles, it would be no different from those portrayals of a human God by someone like Jim Carrey, George Burns or Morgan Freeman in a Hollywood film, who might make it rain indoors as proof of his divine identity.

But beside his actions, there are his actual teachings, which are focused on two areas: talks and parables about the interaction between God and man and the role of the master, and preparing people for, or actually showing them how to experience in some way, the Kingdom of Heaven. This appears to be the clue. The theory has increasingly been mooted over the past fifty years that Jesus was able to show people an inner experience that gave them some awareness of a new way of seeing things, in some cases actually believing they have 'seen' the Kingdom of Heaven. Yet these teaching sessions – the central part of his work, one would think – are simply not recorded.

In this scenario, Jesus might have been saying, "I have become one with the divine which is within each of us. I am a link to that divine being. I am in partnership with it. I can speak on its behalf, with its authority. I do not need previously written scriptures to tell me about that inner realm for I am there with it. I need no form of intermediary and neither do you. You just need to be shown that inner 'kingdom' by someone with the gift to do so, and the proof will be not what I say but what you yourself experience". If this possibility holds water, as is becoming accepted, although with many caveats and much skepticism, then we should look again at the clues that might have led to this conclusion.

Let us first return to that initial meeting with Simon and Andrew as they tended their nets. As usual the synoptic gospels – those of Mark, Matthew and Luke, which are almost identical in their accounts – tell the same story, even recounting the same 'fishers of men' conversation. In John's version, the initial coming together takes place not in Galilee but at John the Baptist's riverside headquarters, possibly to avoid the inference that it was not until much later, after John's imprisonment, that Jesus began his independent mission, with its implication that until that point he had been a disciple of the Baptist. John's account involves not Andrew and his brother Simon, soon to be renamed Peter, but Andrew and one other, who is *not* Simon, as he is recruited by Andrew *after* Andrew's acceptance of Jesus' invitation to join him in his work. These are the kind of relatively minor discrepancies that accompany the gospel accounts of nearly every episode in Jesus' life.

But John's gospel then adds an interesting extra detail: the two men asked Jesus where he lived and requested he show them. We are told John the Baptist saw Jesus and said, "This is he who baptizes with the Holy Spirit...The two disciples heard him speak and they followed Jesus. Jesus turned and saw them following and saith unto them, 'What seek ye?' They said unto him: 'Rabbi, where dwellest thou?' He saith unto them, 'Come and see'. They came and saw where he dwelt, and they stayed with him that day...". The next thing we are told is that they began to spread the message, Andrew going to find his brother Simon with the life-changing information: "We have found the Christ". Something must have happened during that day 'at home' with Jesus that convinced them of his identity, but we are not told what that is.

John's inclusion of this intriguing snippet of dialogue concerning Jesus' 'home' sets a little bell ringing. Why should he mention it at all? Undoubtedly it happened for there would be no ulterior purpose in including it if it were untrue – it would almost qualify as an 'embarrassment' as it does not show the disciples in a particularly good light. This is a momentous occasion, possibly the most dramatic of the New Testament narrative. It simply makes them look like dullards if, after hearing Jesus out, or alternatively after having heard the identification of Jesus by John as the 'lamb of God', the first thing they ask him about is his home. Why would they do such a thing? It is incongruous. It would be tantamount to asking Martin Luther King, after his 'I have a dream' peroration, where he had purchased his suit.

There could be another explanation; that these first disciples were asking him to give them the baptism in the Holy Spirit, as John the Baptist had claimed he could, using the simple metaphor, 'home'. They follow him, he turns to ask what they are looking for – "What seek ye?" evidently meaning more than merely "What do you want?" – and they in reply ask him to show them where he lives. There was no importuning on his part – he was already walking away from them – but they were urgent in their request. They wanted him to show them his 'home', and he simply said, "Come and see". It is a quote never mentioned amongst the many sayings of Jesus which have become almost part of the language, but it could be that this simple three-word expression is the most powerful he ever uttered. They then spent the rest of the day together, after which they were convinced that they had found their true master, enough to bring their friends, brothers and mothers to him; the 'fishing' had already begun. They immediately shared the same commitment. Something had been shown to them, something had happened in those hours 'at home' that made all the difference in the world. If it did not, then it leaves a gaping chasm in our understanding of why they suddenly identified him as their master and began to follow him. Even a practical, no-nonsense commentator like Professor Maurice Casey admits that something

For Christ's Sake

more than just hearing Jesus' teaching had galvanized his first followers: a transformation had taken place.

The alternative account, in the other gospels, also has a reason why the fishermen 'fell down at Jesus' knees' and became his disciples. They had witnessed the miracle of their two boats, after an unproductive night's fishing, being suddenly filled with fish, so much so that 'their nets were breaking'. As so often, we have to make our own choice: a physical miracle, with its allegorical meaning that countless 'men' will be caught as a result of their 'fishing', or a practical process where Jesus shows or teaches them how to access something utterly life-changing within themselves by giving them the baptism in the Holy Spirit.

There is a comparison here with the story of Gautama, the Buddha, some six hundred years earlier. He had searched for enlightenment with a group of colleagues, called his *bhikkhus* – 'companions' – but in frustration at not achieving the *realization* he wanted he left them to spend time alone in contemplation. The tree under which he sat for forty-nine days, achieved an inner experience of *nirvana* and then became the Buddha – 'enlightened one' – still supposedly exists. Under this tree Sujata the milkmaid gave him a bowl of milk pudding, which led to the scales falling from his eyes. Traditionally the bowl of milk pudding is considered a metaphor for the secret of enlightenment, with Sujata as his teacher. It is more likely that Gautama was initiated into a 'direct experience' of the 'truth' some time before by his first teacher, Alara Kalama, but did not realize the immensity of what had been given to him until his time alone under the *bodhi tree*. This tree deserves its own place in history for its repeated appearances in the scriptures of many religions, not least with reference to the Garden of Eden and Moses' encounter with a burning bush. As Karen Armstrong comments in her book, *Buddha*, "This is not a physical location" but is "a common feature of salvation mythology", the point where the divine, the absolute, encounters the human. It is the 'axis of the universe', the 'immovable spot', the 'point of perfect balance', in which any human who has achieved inner oneness with the divine, whether he be Buddha or Christ, Gautama or Jesus, has to locate himself, in order to receive 'the supreme insight'.

Be that as it may, as with so many scriptural stories, the allegory is much more attractive than the philosophical explanation, and conveys the same meaning, so we will leave Gautama under his tree, really wanting to stay there forever, until he realized he now had a gift he must share with humanity, and returned to his friends to tell them what had happened. To say, as he apparently did, that he had now transcended ego and deserved their devotion sounds paradoxically like a demonstration of hubris – and may well have been a 'later addition' – but not if it were no more than the truth. At first they were suspicious but after he delivered his first talk, called a *sutra*, and then *showed* them the secret of inner experience, which he called *stream-entering*, they realized that one of them had been elevated to the status of a truly 'realized soul' and began to call him not friend – *bhikkhu* – but 'master'.

In the same way that we are suggesting that the first disciples of Jesus did not become totally committed to him from his words alone, but had been given some kind of direct inner experience by him, Karen Armstrong says of Buddha's companions, his *bikkhus*: "(They) could not have become a stream-enterer and gained his special 'direct experience'…simply by listening to a sermon and accepting its truths on hearsay". Because of this supposition that a long period of understanding would be required before the *bikkhus* could consider themselves fully immersed in the stream, she postulates that "the instruction of these five *bikkhus* almost certainly took longer than a single morning" before they could become 'stream-enterers', a single morning having been given as the time it took for the initiation to take place. Not necessarily. Jesus began his stream-entering session with his first disciples 'at the tenth hour', and the Bible tell us they spent the rest of the day closeted away while Jesus showed them his – and *their* – home. It appeared to have taken not much more than half a day. Buddha also initiated three of his *bikkhus* into his 'special yoga' while the others went to town to buy some food for a meal. When they returned they were also initiated. This is the difference. A revelation does not involve mental activities – learning, explaining, memorizing, which may well need to extend over a long period and require some degree of intelligence or mental ability. The only qualities apparently required by Jesus, and presumably Buddha also, were sincerity, love, and trust.

The phrase *stream-entering* ought to ring a bell. It brings to mind the image of a rushing stream of fresh water, and stepping into it to be immersed into its life-giving powers. Stream is also interpreted as *river*. Buddha was showing his colleagues how to access and then enter a river of life experience. The incident took place near the holy Indian city of Benares, at a point of the river Ganges where pilgrims flock to immerse themselves into the holy water, to wash themselves clean of sins and renew their spiritual life. But nowhere is it claimed that the newly-enlightened Gautama led his friends to the river's edge and performed a kind of baptism. The stream-entering was internal. It might lead us to ask, in the comparable Biblical story of Jesus beginning his teaching: could we find a similar reference to a process of immersion into a water of life, a river of enlightenment?

If this is what happened in the two cases, it means that ironically the later students of both Buddhism and Christianity made a similar simple error. In the former case they downplay the revealing of an inner experience by Gautama to his companions, the *bhikkhus*, and believe instead that it was Buddha's first talk to them – his first *sutra* – that made them realize he had become enlightened and they needed to follow him. Likewise with the Christian interpretation. Jesus just had to say, "Follow me," and without further ado, they did. Yet it is most unlikely that they would leave their livelihoods, their homes, their families, on an uncertain path with no income, facing possible persecution and death at the end of it, unless they had undergone the most profound inner transformation. What is being suggested is that the three men spent the rest of the day together, undergoing the initiation, or what John had already termed 'baptism in the spirit'.

It is this phrase of course that gives a clear clue as to what was really happening in Jesus' ministry. Almost countless times there are references in the gospels to this mysterious process: 'baptism in the spirit'. John himself has already made it quite clear: "I baptize you with water, but he who is coming will baptize you in the Holy Spirit". Running through all the gospels like a strong thread is this story of an inner revealing of an internal 'heaven', an experience of the place 'within' where God resides.

The question is, was Jesus really doing this, or was he merely placing people in a hypnotic trance, which made them believe they had had the experience?

Chapter Nine

The Secret Gospel: The Controversy

No miracles of Jesus carry the full potency of divine power like the raising of the dead, the bringing back to life of those who are deceased. Whoever can do this must surely hold sway over the very essence of existence, the ebbing and flowing of the life current – life and death itself. It lies at the core of Jesus' divinity. Paul declared it to be the very foundation of Christian belief, and according to the four gospels in the New Testament, he performed this miracle no less than three times, not counting his own auto-resurrection.

Two of those occasions are simply narrated, and both have a feature in common; the apparently deceased were children. The third also was either a youth or a young man. Jesus did not revive elderly people. First was the daughter of the ruler of the synagogue, to whom Jesus uttered his famous words, "Tabitha cumi," meaning,

"Girl, arise," which, taking his hand, she did. There is something strange about this miracle; according to Jesus, the girl was not actually dead but 'sleeping'. It was the hysterical people outside the house, crying and wailing loudly one moment, laughing the next when Jesus said the girl was not dead, who claimed she was. If we are to believe Jesus, rather than the mob, we have to accept nothing untoward happened here, certainly not a raising of the dead. The story is more like an episode from *House*, the television series about the unconventional doctor who goes against everyone else's diagnosis, and is invariably proved right.

The second resurrection also involved a child, or young man, apparently dead before his time, the son of the widow from Nain. Jesus touched his coffin, using the same phrase he used with the girl – "Boy, rise" – and he came back to life. This time there is no room for doubt, as far as the reported facts of the story go. The boy was in the coffin being taken for burial. The only snag with this story – apart from it obviously being allegorical since no raising of the dead took place – is the strange fact that it is almost identical to a similar event reported in the Old Testament Book of Kings, when the prophet Elijah likewise brings a boy back to life, using the same language as the New Testament account of Jesus' miracle. Both stories, for example, end with the identical sentence, "He gave him back to his mother". It is likely, and fairly well-accepted amongst our scholastic friends, that the story, true or not, is told not so much to demonstrate Jesus' power over life and death, but his similarity to the great prophet Elijah. It is Elijah who features in the 'Transfiguration' incident, where Jesus appears to three of his apostles in a strange cloud-like light on the top of a 'high mountain' alongside the two great personages of Jewish history, Moses and Elijah himself. The gospel writers are apparently at pains to make sure people understand Jesus is the natural successor to these legends.

Of the three resurrection occasions recounted in the New Testament *before* Jesus' own, none is more poignant, more human, in its coverage than the raising of the young man Lazarus, the brother of the two sisters Mary and Martha who lived in Bethany, close to Jerusalem, and who can be counted amongst Jesus' most intimate disciples; he is a prime candidate for the title, 'the one Jesus loved'.

The story is full of incident and drama. Jesus delays on his way to help Lazarus, and the grief-stricken sisters chastise him bitterly for not coming sooner: "If you had arrived earlier, he would not be dead", they sob. Jesus tells them, as he had done with the young girl, that they are mistaken, he is not dead, and they become even more censorious for this callousness on the part of their master, for their brother has been in his tomb for four days, and by now his body will be malodorous. Indeed, in the vernacular of the Bible, 'it stinketh'. Jesus ignores their pain, orders the stone to be rolled back from the entrance to the tomb, calls to Lazarus to 'come out', whereupon the youth emerges dressed in the white linen sheet used as a shroud to wrap the dead. In countless frescoes and church paintings, it looks comically as if an Egyptian mummy is ambling forward out of the tomb.

The story holds many mysteries and contradictions. If Jesus did raise Lazarus from the dead, why did he say beforehand, "He is not dead"? If he were not dead, how could he have been in a tomb for four days without calling out to be rescued? If he were dead, and his body was already decaying as his sisters had said, how did he emerge in full health, intact, with no apparent ill effects? This is the most important miracle of Jesus' brief career, yet it is not even mentioned in the synoptic gospels. Why did they omit it, while including many more minor incidents in Jesus' life? Also, why does the last gospel, John, go into considerable detail about it, adding statements from Jesus that seem to be stilted, and altering the facts of the story as it is related in another source we are going to examine by changing the claim that a voice called out from within the tomb into one saying it was Jesus who did the calling? We also cannot avoid the evident comparison with Jesus' own resurrection with its story of a rock rolled back, somebody surviving after being considered indubitably deceased, and funerals shrouds left in the tomb.

A popular view is that with many lapses of memory over the decades after the crucifixion, the four gospels mix up and conflate stories and names. The names, and exact number, of the twelve apostles are notoriously at variance from gospel to gospel, and the events after the crucifixion are likewise very disparate, with someone who was not even an eye-witness, Paul, adding his own 'memories' to the mix. Professor Sanders gives as an example of this well-meaning unreliability of the gospels the varying accounts, with different locations and characters, of the story of Jesus being anointed by a female disciple, either over his feet or his head, with expensive oil. The stories "probably rest on memories, although details have been exchanged and possibly confused". Similar differences of memory and opinion of what actually happened probably came into the confusions and variations in the stories of the raising of Lazarus from the dead and Jesus' own resurrection.

Yet, the discovery of an unusual letter in 1958 seems to put the entire incident in a different light. The find was made by the late American professor, Morton Smith, and led him to the conclusion that at the heart of Jesus' work was an ability to initiate those worthy and prepared into an experience of new life. Let's not dwell too long on this, for every person with an interest in New Testament scriptural matters is very familiar with the discovery. The reference, to a 'secret gospel of Mark', was in the form of an excerpt from a letter sent by the influential second century Christian scholar, Clement of Alexandria – the major city of northern Egypt – to some early Christians in a community in Judea. The letter was in answer to one they had sent to him, of which there is no copy, where he was asked about the purported existence of a secret, longer, gospel of the apostle Mark, which they had heard about from a local Gnostic group. Yes, he had replied, such a gospel did exist but it was only to be used for those being prepared for the initiation into the mysteries of the inner kingdom, and there is a clear reference to such an initiation being performed by Jesus on a boy whom he had recently raised from the dead, who is evidently the same Lazarus as in the gospel of John, as the accounts are nearly identical.

Morton Smith made his discovery in the dusty ancient library of a monastery called Mar Saba (St. Saba) in the desert not many miles from Jerusalem itself. The letter was not the original but a seventeenth century copy. This is not surprising because it was common practice for old texts of value to be copied when the originals were becoming too old to handle. Alexandria was the capital of Egypt, one of the two great cities of the Eastern Mediterranean, the home of not only one of the wonders of the ancient world, the great lighthouse at its port (the *Pharos* of Alexandria), a celebrated library and a very large Jewish Diaspora, but also of a prominent grouping of this new religion following the teachings of Christ. Clement was highly respected as an important early Christian writer and authority, living and working in the last decades of the second century.

The excerpt, in Greek, was quite long, perhaps representing three or so pages of modern text, and much of it was a strong attack on the Gnostic sect his correspondents had complained about, the Carpocratians, who under its leader, Carpocrates, were apparently following a hedonistic lifestyle, in keeping with the belief of some Gnostics that since the 'inner being' is the truly immortal part of a person, the outer, mortal, body is entitled to indulge itself.

Clement, being asked about the rumors of an extended version of the gospel of St Mark, not only confirmed its existence but revealed that it was kept in Alexandria, where Mark had relocated after his time in Rome, which after the execution of Peter had become too dangerous for the leading apostles.

These are the relevant quotes from this mysterious letter, translated from the Greek:

> "Mark came over to Alexandria bringing both his own notes and those of Peter, from which he transferred to his former book the things suitable to whatever makes for progress towards knowledge (the Greek word is *gnosis*). Thus he composed a more spiritual gospel for the use of those who were being perfected…".

> "When he died, he left his composition to the church in Alexandria, where it is even yet most carefully guarded, being read only to those who are being initiated into the great mysteries."

So much for the references to an initiation or secret teaching. In particular we can note in passing the phrase 'being perfected' as a reference to the process of becoming perfect which Jesus in the gospels had instructed his close disciples to undertake. Clement then appears to answer questions about one particular Biblical story, that of the raising to life of a dead man – presumably Lazarus – at the request of his sister. But an extra section is added to the original story, with Clement quoting directly from the 'secret gospel':

> "The youth, looking upon him, loved Jesus and began to beseech him that he might be with him. And going out of the tomb, they came into the house of the youth, for he was rich. And after six days Jesus told him what to do, and in the evening the youth comes to him, wearing a linen cloth over his naked body. And he remained with him that night for Jesus taught him the mystery of the Kingdom of God."

This was incendiary stuff. The two Scottish sisters, Agnes Lewis and Margaret Gibson – the 'Sisters of Sinai' – had at the end of the nineteenth century discovered a fourth century copy of the four gospels, which naturally caused a sensation. But here we have, if true, an actual *addition* to one of the four gospels, giving out vast reams of extra insight and factual information. It had to be too good to be true, said the critics, and they were helped in their claim by the mysterious disappearance of the document just as the world was becoming interested in it, leaving only the photographs Morton Smith had taken.

The authenticity or otherwise of this letter has become a mini-industry in itself lasting to the present day. The nay-sayers point out that the quotes from the 'secret gospel' indicate Jesus might have been a homosexual, as Smith might have been, and he wanted to cause trouble for the church on the issue, and, strangely, that a 1940's novel related the story of a long lost secret manuscript being found in the monastery of Mar Saba. Coincidence indeed, indicating that reading the novel might have given Smith the idea of using a blank page pasted to the inside cover of a seventeenth century book to forge the letter from Clement and the quotes from the 'secret gospel'. The fact that many discoveries of ancient texts, such as that of the Scottish sisters, were taking place as western academics searched the dusty libraries of ancient Christian monasteries in the area, does not entirely mitigate the strange coincidence of the 1940's novel.

The supporters point out that the document's disappearance had nothing to do with Smith. It was apparently removed from the library by protective monks when it was beginning to attract unwelcome attention to their monastery – some scholars had already made the trip to examine it – and deposited in a private library owned by the orthodox church of Greece, to which access has not since been granted. The photographs, however, are sufficiently detailed and clear to show the full text of the discovery. Secondly, there arises the question, if Morton Smith were going to perpetrate a hoax for whatever malevolent personal reasons he might have entertained, why should he have written something of such obscure content? An attack by a prominent Christian scholar, Clement, on a Gnostic sect with hedonistic tendencies, a reference to secret teachings, and a reworking of the Lazarus story with an additional sentence suggesting Jesus taught him the mystery of the Kingdom of God, although enormously interesting and significant, hardly represents the kind of new revelation a forged scriptural discovery might have been expected to contain. "Not very much there", might have been the reaction of people first coming across Smith's discovery. Something far more revealing about Jesus might have been expected.

Smith's own conclusion from studying the extract, as we shall see, was that Jesus was considered in his time to be a magician, and he spent the remainder of his academic life working on this hypothesis, producing numerous books and articles. He simply would not have done this, in effect wasting his whole career, if he knew that the very premise all his work was based on was a hoax of his own making. Lastly, and most tellingly, a detailed forensic analysis of the handwriting of the letter, completed in 2008, comparing it with Smith's own handwriting, concluded that the two are not by the same hand. The result is that while many experts remain skeptical, holding to an unwritten law of Biblical research that if a new early Christian scripture is discovered, given the scarcity of such material, it must be a forgery, the criticism has become much more muted and a grudging acceptance of the secret gospel's authenticity had settled over the affair. It is possible that at some future date the original letter in its Greek library might come to light, and the matter settled once and for all.

We also have to consider the fact that over the rest of his life, Smith worked occasionally with a heroine of modern Christian research whose credentials are beyond reproach: Elaine Pagels. She would simply not have joined forces with him if she had entertained the least suspicion that he had perpetrated such an outrageous hoax.

Chapter Ten

The Secret Gospel: The Conclusions

So, with an awareness of the doubts about its authenticity, let us now look at what Clement's letter reveals. While the letter itself must have been written around 180 C.E. when Clement was active in Alexandria, the quoted extracts from the secret gospel of Mark, if genuine, are thought to be of an equal age to the synoptic gospels of Matthew and Luke, and therefore earlier than the gospel of John. It is undisputed that John was written some time, maybe thirty or forty years, after the other three, which are so similar – in many cases identical – in content that they were considered to be based on a previous account of the life of Jesus, now missing, which was given the name 'Q', from the German word *quelle*, meaning 'source'. Now this theory has gone out of fashion in favor of considering that Mark's was the first of the gospels, and the authors of Luke and Matthew used it as a basis for theirs.

It is easy to see that the young man raised from the dead was Lazarus, for the story fits exactly with that already recorded in John, with Mary complaining that had Jesus hurried, her brother might not have died. Morton Smith suggests John used Mark's account as a basis for his own, altering it to suit his own purpose. For example, the 'secret gospel' says a voice called out from the tomb before Jesus opened it, whereas John has Jesus do the calling, because a voice coming from within the tomb might have indicated that the person inside was not in fact, dead, and throw doubt on the miracle. Also, where Mark has Jesus himself roll away the stone, in John, Jesus orders someone else to do it, as menial manual work like this would be too demeaning for the supernatural Christ of John's gospel. But this is the kind of detailed discussion the experts have been having for over a hundred years on the various accounts of the life of Jesus, and it would be very easy to become lost in the fascinating maze of their opinions and interpretations. What is really new in the secret gospel is the story that Jesus, at the young man's request, subsequently taught him 'the mystery of the Kingdom of Heaven'. Once again we come across this enigmatic phrase that occurs throughout the synoptic gospels without ever being explained.

What has added significance are the words that the youth was 'wearing a linen cloth over his naked body' – not because, in tandem with the phrase '(the youth) loved Jesus', they give rise to a possible homoerotic implication, but because one of the enduring mysteries of the study of the gospels is the little detail in the story of Jesus' arrest in the Garden of Gethsemane, recounted in the Mark we are familiar with, of the unexplained presence of a naked young man who stood his ground when the disciples fled and appeared to try and protect Jesus. The story goes: "And there followed him a certain young man having nothing but a linen cloth cast around his naked body. And the young man laid hold on him. And he left the cloth and fled from them naked". The story is strange. Theologians have not discovered a plausible explanation, some thinking the youth's presence was just a case of a bystander being in the wrong place at the wrong time. But if so, why should it be mentioned? And if this young man was indeed trying to protect Jesus after the others had abandoned him, such an explanation does not give him the honor he deserves.

Morton Smith puts two and two together and comes up with a new theory. Jesus was able to show some people of his choosing an inner experience of the mystery of the 'kingdom'. This is the famous baptism in spirit, which differentiates what Jesus can do from the water baptism of John. And this is what he was doing with both Lazarus in Bethany and the near naked youth in the Garden of Gethsemane.

The idea did not come to him straightaway. At first, he assumed a water baptism was taking place, similar to John's, but doubts immediately arose. One is that nowhere in the four gospels is there a reference to Jesus conducting any baptisms, of any kind. It appeared he had left them behind. Why should he start doing them now, towards the end of his work? It would seem like a step backwards. Moreover, just a few months into the future, after the crucifixion, we find the apostles and, a few years further on, Paul, baptizing people most mysteriously, not with water but in the 'holy spirit', in a kind of process which seemed to emulate the death and resurrection of Jesus and which would join the person being baptized with Jesus in an inner union of 'new life'. This baptism gives a powerful experience. Once you have had it, says Paul, human differences are blown away: "There is neither Jew nor Greek, slave nor freeman, male nor female, for you are one in Messiah Jesus" – letting us know in the process that women had just as much right to what was being offered as men. Morton Smith assumes that this special and rather mysterious baptism by Paul must be similar to the one Jesus performed while alive, and could not then be the same as John's, which provided no more than a symbolic cleansing of one's sins. We have already, of course, cast doubt on the water baptism of John, but are recounting here Morton Smith's line of conjecture.

Consequently, Professor Smith reaches the momentous conclusion that Jesus was able to conduct a kind of initiation that produced some form of inner experience, and this is what he was doing both with Lazarus and with the anonymous young man in the Garden of Gethsemane: "He could admit his followers to the Kingdom of God, and he could do it in some special way so that they were not there merely by anticipation, nor by virtue of belief and obedience, nor by some other figure of speech, but were really, actually, in". Or were they? Unfortunately, according to Morton Smith, they were not. This would be too much to take on board. Jesus must have been using "some form of hypnotic technique by which men could give both themselves and others the illusion of having experienced such an ascent (into the 'kingdom')".

In both the case of Lazarus and of the unnamed youth, they were wearing what presumably was the garb Jesus required them to wear for such a sacred event, a linen cloth and nothing more, although 'naked' might not have precluded an undergarment or loincloth. It could be that the candidates had to attend their initiation naked under a sheet to replicate how they were attired when they came into the world, this being their 'second birth', or, as A.N. Wilson speculates, they were required to wear the kind of linen shroud used for corpses, as the initiation was, indeed, a 'resurrection', not meaning the resuscitation of a corpse, but the bursting into to life of something so far dormant – a raising of people from 'death' to 'life' in a spiritual sense.

Quite possibly, since everything we know tells us Jesus had little time for symbolic gestures, neither of these theories is correct, and the sheet was only used as a kind of covering, to provide privacy and retain secrecy. If it had been an indoor initiation, it might not have been needed. At a time when the privacy Jesus required for his initiations was not easily come by, the erection of a simple tent or covering made of a large sheet of linen might have been one of the tasks the disciples closest to him, Peter and James, were used to performing before they retired to a position a short distance away to stand guard while the process was taking place. If this were the case, it is not the only instance in the gospels where a tent to provide Jesus with privacy is mentioned. In the story of the Transfiguration, Peter asks Jesus if he should erect a tent for his mystical reunion with Moses and Elijah. The story of the youth in his linen sheet trying to protect Jesus at the moment of his arrest has another resonance in a chant performed some two hundred years later by early Roman Christians, meeting in the catacombs or 'house' churches, which contains the words, "Wrap a naked boy in linen, and face him to the light", a fascinating piece of evidence from a time when the Gnostic tradition was gradually being subsumed into one of external worship.

Morton Smith is right in one respect. Nowhere else in the New Testament can references to Jesus baptizing be found. John claimed to his followers that Jesus would baptize not with water but in spirit and with fire. But no evidence can be found in any gospel of him doing so. All we have are the frequent mentions about him having revealed the mystery of the Kingdom of Heaven, or, in the language of John's gospel, the secret of eternal life. All scholars up until this point had taken it for granted that in making such claims, Jesus was speaking allegorically. Merely by the presence of Jesus and hearing his words about God – his teachings – this entry into the 'Kingdom' had been achieved. But when asked why he spoke in parables, he made it clear that the close disciples had received something more than his presence and his teachings, which were, after all, available to everybody who came to hear him speak. They had, he told them, received a gift it was in his power to grant and which was so valuable he would only give it to people who would truly recognize and treasure it; the pearl of great price must not be thrown before swine. This idea of a special object of great value – in this case the key to the Kingdom of Heaven – makes sense of the parable of the farmer sowing his seeds. Only some will fall on fertile soil, take root and grow. Thus, the importance of guarding it carefully and giving it only to those whose fields have been prepared.

Almost like a great scientific discovery, it dawns on Professor Morton Smith that this giving of a gift refers to an inner opening of an inner door, an initiation into a previously unseen 'mystery', the baptism in spirit which only Jesus was able to bring about. Now he turns his attention to what the baptism in the spirit might have consisted of.

He does not have to look far, for he is already aware of the strong tradition of magic spells and secret initiations in the ancient world, and has no problem assuming that this is what Jesus was up to. He was, no less, a magician, and the initiation he was able to give included techniques and sounds from ancient Egyptian magical practices, resulting in a form of self-hypnosis where the recipient profoundly believed that he had been transported into an inner 'kingdom', the Kingdom of God.

This, he concludes, was the reason for Jesus receiving a sentence of capital punishment, for practicing magic was punishable by death in Roman law. It is an educated guess, since there is no clue of this in the detailed account the gospels provide of Jesus' trial, but it does again raise the conundrum of why exactly he was executed, given that he had not committed any crime that, under the strict Roman legal system, deserved capital punishment. But practicing magic? There was no question for Morton Smith that Jesus had been doing this for he had been caught red-handed, in the very act of an initiation with a near naked young man.

What kind of initiation was taking place at night and in secret, under a linen sheet? It seems the garden where the second initiation took place was a regular venue for this event, for in John we are told, "Jesus often met there with his disciples," again, if true, providing evidence that Jesus was frequently in the Jerusalem area. It was on the Mount of Olives, and one can imagine Jesus with his subject, huddled together between olive trees while conducting his initiation: meantime, three of his stalwarts, Peter, James and John, stood 'a stone's throw' away, keeping guard. Privacy was of the essence. "We are told", says Smith, "that before performing a cure (Jesus) took the sick man aside, privately. Or, if he went where the patient was, he shut out everyone and took with him only his closest disciples."

Once the candidate had been prepared – we are not told what the preparation consisted of, but we can assume it would not be any book learning or scripture study – Jesus initiated him or her. This would be accomplished not by a simple 'laying-on' of hands, or making a sign of the cross – for obvious reasons – or by reciting prayers and promises together. We can probably assume it was superficially the same kind of initiation available in the west over recent decades from one of the new groups importing meditation teachings from the Hindu or Buddhist traditions. A very common one involves close proximity between teacher and student, the student sitting cross-legged, or kneeling, before a kind of altar on which a symbolic offering such as fruit has been placed, the teacher kneeling close by him. With eyes closed, the teacher begins to quietly chant a sound. Professor Pagels also concludes, as a result of her investigation of the Gnostics which we shall examine presently, that Jesus was performing initiations, possibly using as a mantra a sound which resembles the syllables, *zza–zza*. Let us assume this is a common mantra that is taught in the kind of initiation available today that we are taking an example. The teacher, after telling the student what is to happen so there are no unpleasant surprises, begins to chant the sound *zza, zza*, after some time asking the student to join in. When they have been doing it together for a short period, the teacher will stay silent, leaving the student to continue alone. The student is then instructed to gradually make his or her repetition of the mantra silent, so it becomes an internal recitation. After ten or fifteen minutes or so, the teacher will alert the student by gently placing a hand on his or her shoulder and the student will come to a halt and gradually open his or her eyes. After pledges of secrecy, the 'initiation' is then complete. By now the student should be experiencing a sense of inner calm which is the object of the exercise, and is then expected to repeat the practice regularly, once or twice a day, in his or her daily life.

But Jesus' initiations, although apparently similar in form, seem to be much more than this. Not only was the experience, from the examples we are given, life changing but recognition of the teacher as an actual bridge to an inner divine is a requisite. We are reminded of Jesus' stirring declaration: "I am the way". It is not a claim made by modern day teachers of meditation.

His initiation is, according to Smith, something much more visceral than a gentle mantra repetition, involving actions and techniques that make the process seem more like an hour or two of torture rather than a calm approaching of a place of stillness, truth and light within one's own being, or maybe behind one's own mind. Searching the gospels for occasions when Jesus has performed otherwise inexplicable actions, often during his 'healings', Smith comes up with an array of strange procedures and techniques, which include "touch, manipulation, looking upward, sighing or groaning...use of spittle in a salve, conspicuous use of the hands, touching the tongue, claiming to use 'the finger of God'...requirement that the 'patient' have faith, secrecy...in some cases interference with breathing".

Whatever is happening, it sounds like very hard work, and not one, we would think, conducive to being put in touch with the home of God, the Kingdom of Heaven, the place of eternal life. If the God Jesus has introduced is compassionate, caring, a God of love, we should expect that any kind of approach to him would contain elements of these ingredients, along with a growing sense of awe and wonder. The calm solemnity of worship in a cathedral, with soaring rafters, inspirational artwork, ethereal singing, solemn ceremony and beautiful intonations of devotional words, could be said to be an outer equivalent of the closeness of God into which Jesus might have been able to induct his disciples.

Jesus' initiation was, as far as we can tell, a gentle but serious process. If it were something akin to lurid exorcisms, a holding down of a frenzied person while Jesus commanded an evil spirit to leave the affected one's body, candidates to receive it would be few indeed, certainly not the crowds at the door of the house he might be staying in, as we are told.

Morton Smith is trying, of course, to prove that Jesus was a magician and hypnotist, and his description of the induction process may for that reason appear over-dramatic. But for most of these ingredients of an initiation, the evidence is clearly there in the gospels. As far as interfering with breathing goes, we do not find clear references, but the importance of breath, and its connection with the very concept of the 'spirit', which underpins all of Jesus' miracles, is touched on later in this book. It is at least clear from the gospel accounts of his curing of blind and mute people that Jesus uses such manipulation, but Morton Smith is raising the ante here by suggesting that these occurrences were not 'cures'; they were initiations.

If Jesus *were* conducting an initiation at night in a quiet part of a small orchard, and if Morton Smith is right in his conclusions about the process taking place, we can see that Jesus was concerned with the recipient's senses: sight, hearing and, possibly, taste: eyes, ears and tongue. We do not know what he was doing but we might inquire why this should be the case. And here we have a clue given at the very beginning of his ministry, his baptism at the hands of John – repentance, the need to repent, in the sense of turning around. Later Jesus makes a famous pronouncement; the Kingdom of God is within you. If it were in the sky – addressing people who believed God lived beyond the stars – birds would get there first, he joked. It is not in the world around; it is within. It is possible that to begin the process of knowing, of approaching, or even of entering, this inner place, senses had to be turned away from the external world to face, in some way, inwards. Looking at it this way, the inexplicable magical ceremony of Morton Smith, or what A.N. Wilson terms a 'bizarre ritual', might be very simply explained, if not understood.

It is Wilson who, unlike the more serious theologians, dares to think the impossible, and makes the link between the secret gospel and John's account of Lazarus being raised from the dead. What was really happening, he says, was a 'rite of initiation', "in which the newly-admitted catechumen would be dressed up in grave-clothes and then called to 'new life' in the Spirit". John's later account provides "a narrative in which the inner meaning of the ritual has been translated into an event, a 'sign'. The catechumen in his grave-clothes becomes an actual dead man in grave-clothes, coming forth to be initiated into the Baptism of Spirit, the Baptism of Eternal Life".

We will leave the late professor, for now at any rate, with his wealth of outlandish theories about what Jesus was doing with his baptisms in the spirit. We are indebted to Morton Smith, even though, like Columbus believing to the end of his life that he had discovered India by sailing west, he missed the obvious clues. Nevertheless, the few sentences he discovered at the Mar Saba monastery in 1958 throw an interesting new light onto the notion of an initiation, and more especially on the possibility that the stories of Jesus raising people from the dead were allegorical. It was not physical death that was ailing his patients but one much more serious and, paradoxically, life-threatening – death of the spirit.

With the help of Morton Smith's discovery, we have a new and far more credible explanation for one of the New Testament's enduring mysteries; the rebirth into the spirit via an initiation as the cornerstone of Jesus' work. In this interpretation, he was dealing with the business of bringing the dead back to life, but in a much more real way than a physical resurrection. He was offering *life everlasting* – a concept we will have to look at more closely in due course. Without it, true life had not even commenced. It commenced with him teaching the mysteries of the Kingdom of Heaven.

It is not so much that there was an initiation involved in the teachings of Jesus that is so surprising. This has been suspected for centuries. It figured prominently in the few writings discovered from the heretical early Christian sect, the Gnostics, which we shall look at presently. It would be a surprise if such a theory were not widely known in the Catholic church, for they after all were the ones who suppressed such heresy in the third and fourth centuries to give themselves a firm grip on power in this new and fast-growing religious movement. They knew what they were fighting against: a philosophy that had no need for bishops, hierarchies, intermediaries or even churches, for to them the home of God was not churches or cathedrals but the human body itself. It is now generally accepted that if Gnosticism had not been suppressed, we today might know very little of that teacher from Nazareth, and there may well have been nothing like the world–wide following and multifarious religions which circle the world with such great influence, providing succor and support in many people's lives. But if the principles of today's great Christian religions are based on something that is far from the truth of what Jesus was actually teaching, we might well ask if the trade-off has been worthwhile.

Again, it is not therefore the possibility that there had been a secret initiation into heavenly mysteries that is particularly noteworthy, but the notion that this really did need to be kept secret. Clement's letter is at pains to stress that certain things are not to be written down: "not all true things are to be said to all men". Is it because they are too sacred? If so, why should the sacred be secret? Why should there be a mystery that only the teacher and certain others know, to the exclusion of many others who could only hear about it in parables? Could it be dangerous knowledge? Surely not. The entire essence of the divine and the hope of finding a closer experience of 'him' are, one would surmise, steeped in the purest form of goodness and joy. The mystery cannot be kept secret because something bad might happen if it were in the open. There must be another reason.

Chapter Eleven

The Secret behind the Secret

Clement's letter, in dwelling so strongly on the need for confidentiality, reveals something much more than the existence of a secret knowledge. From this revelation comes the reason why, in any of the gospels, so very little is said about the initiation. It is likely the authors wrote their accounts independently, but something colored all their writings; an immovable, unshakable conviction that the secret teachings of Jesus could be alluded to, but not revealed. Why did they do this? It is not as if they were going to be punished if they did break confidences. Nothing would happen.

While alive, Jesus performs his 'signs' behind closed doors. He orders people he has 'cured' not to tell anyone what has happened to them. Could the 'curing' have been, in some way, a metaphor for the initiations, and the injunction to confidentiality felt so strongly by those around Jesus that long after he had died, his surviving followers maintained this bond, this promise to their deceased master? And even if, as is widely supposed, the gospel writers had not themselves been alive during Jesus' ministry, for they would have been in their seventies, eighties and nineties at the time they decided to write their accounts, but instead formed a second generation of disciples, imbibing the stories passed down by word-of-mouth from those who actually had been there, the respect surrounding the secret teachings of Jesus permeated them also just as much as it had Jesus' closest associates and apostles. Elaine Pagels alludes to this by pointing out that Paul himself, while being the author and originator of the newly evolving church of the Christ, was himself a Gnostic who had received the initiation – the epiphany on the road to Damascus – but who felt it needed to be kept secret. It was simply too much of a hot potato to deal with in open forum.

Here we are touching on something vitally important and essential, and the reason why Morton Smith's conclusions about Jesus being a magician – one amongst many, who just happened to have a sect formed in his memory, which by historical accident prospered for centuries – do not ring true. Even a skeptical reading of the story of Jesus cannot mistake the extraordinary loyalty and devotion amongst those who followed him. They did not regard him as the Son of God, or heir of David, in some mystical or grandiose way. But something developed between them, a bond of loyalty, trust and recognition that ran deeper than such questions of nomenclature. They *belonged* to him. It is as if they recognized something profound in him, something inexpressible; they seemed to know that he was a supremely special human being, their own true master, in a very personal, human way.

We get a taste of this in the stories where the sisters Mary and Martha figure, one of them, by chance, being the very one which Clement uses to demonstrate that Jesus did in fact give a secret initiation. There is such a familiarity, such a deep respect, such a knowing, such an acceptance, it goes far deeper than Peter and others trying to answer Jesus' question, "Who do you think I am?" These women have a living reality that punches us, through the centuries, in the solar plexus. They argue and complain. They tell Jesus off: "If you'd arrived sooner, he wouldn't be dead". They sit at his feet and hear his teachings – not to chat with him, as Wilson says, but to hear the words only he can speak, truth from the heart of truth, directly from the *abba* he asserts he is united with, or, in the modern expression, *channeling*. It is because of this recognition, this understanding, that he is one with the father, that they wash his feet in expensive oil, which causes Jesus to commend their devotion, reprimanding Judas for complaining that the money should have gone to the poor with his comment, "The poor will always be with you", which proves the final straw for the troubled disciple, who then decides to betray Jesus to the authorities.

In this little seven-word sentence lies the clue to the entire mystery. Jesus' very existence, his presence amongst them, is the great reality of their lives, more meaningful that anything else, and should be savored to the full while they still have him there. It explains the enormous buzz when he first began his teachings, his initiations and his recruitment of followers. We sense the people running here and there to tell others about this special one who has arrived amongst them. People flock to hear him and 'be cured'. Some – men *and* women – have an immediate recognition, as if an old and loyal friend has suddenly returned after a long absence and, without hesitation, throw in their lot with him. There is a palpable 'Oh my God, he's here' feeling about those early days.

In the early twentieth century, the poet laureate of England, Robert Bridges, broke his promise to his close friend, Gerard Manley Hopkins, that he would never publish his poems after his death. But Bridges knew how good they were, and felt he owed a greater duty to the world by revealing them. In his justification he compared existing poets, including himself, to chaffinches amongst whom a brilliantly-plumed creature 'of far wonder and heavenward flight' had temporarily settled. Jesus' disciples had had a similar experience, and, it appears, also made a non-disclosure vow. But in his case it was easier to keep, for they knew that it was the relationship with him that made the experience come alive. In other words, if they betrayed Jesus' wishes, the magic of their relationship would be broken. You can detach Gerard Manley Hopkins from his poetry, but, it appears, you cannot detach Jesus from his personal involvement in an individual's salvation.

Take this a step further and we can see that the secret initiation itself is the bond that binds them. One would think that the opening of an inner door, if this indeed were what took place, would be the greatest of gifts. But compared to the fact of Jesus' living presence, love and companionship, it was not of great significance. It might be that its value lay, besides providing an inner experience of the divine, in the fact that it allowed them to recognize who *he* was – their special one, their master. It would almost be blasphemous to try and divulge the details of the initiation and the resulting experience he was able to bring about. It was something else, a personal recognition, which was at the heart of true devotion to this Jesus. And, as a corollary to this unbreakable loyalty was the promise he extracted from them at the time of initiation: "tell no one". Was he protecting himself from attacks and accusations that he was claiming divine provenance from the Jewish thought-police of the day, the Scribes and Pharisees? Or was he simply acknowledging that the initiation could only be effective if conducted by a *bona fide* master – himself? Without his guidance the 'baptism' didn't work: it was the personal element that brought it to life.

The master-student or master-devotee relationship has never taken root in western Christian tradition, precisely because there has been no-one qualified to assume Jesus' role; no 'master' has presented himself. But in the more esoteric traditions of spiritual growth, a master-student relationship is more common. There are many stories in Zen Buddhism of a student traveling with and learning from his itinerant master. A typical, and delightful, one recounts an occasion when, coming across a woman hoping to cross a river ford where the waters were too high, the elder monk offers to carry her across, and they all go on their ways. Hours later, the young monk speaks. "I can hold it in no longer, master, we are forbidden to touch women, yet you carried that one across the ford." "My son", answered the master, "I put the woman down on the other side of the river, I see you are still carrying her".

This kind of monastic lifestyle, with its rules, is far removed from Jesus' approach. As Paul was later to claim, there is no male or female in the world of the 'way'; all have become one. But the story does give a flavor of the personal loyalty and interaction to be found in a devotional relationship between teacher and student, and also gives a clue about the much-debated assertion that by being in touch with the Kingdom of Heaven, one is 'above the law'. The real 'law', it would seem, is what your inner state of 'grace' defines it to be. It appears, in this case, that the master broke the laws of his order, but the moral of the story is that it was the student who broke the more serious law of maintaining his connection with the inner divine.

Likewise, the path Jesus taught was not one of creating and following a religious structure but of an inner awakening underpinned by profound personal loyalty. In India such a dynamic has given rise to an aphorism, which says, "Devotion without *gyan* is blind. *Gyan* without devotion is dry", *gyan* meaning divine knowledge in the sense of an inner experience. In Jesus' case, his disciples were not necessarily looking for a master, but when they came across him there was an undeniable recognition that here was someone who had to be followed, who demanded and deserved loyalty, obedience and love.

* * *

Could it be, then, that the gospel writers were following the lead of their elders who had been with Jesus in recognizing that the story here was not Jesus' initiation, nor his cures and miracles, but the man himself? The *gnosis*, if we can use that term for the inner experience, was the golden chain that locked them in mutual love. But without the presence of the master, its efficacy was weakened. The great secret, then, was not the fact – if we are to accept the hypothesis – that Jesus performed an initiation, or what that initiation might consist of. The great secret was that, for those who lived with him and recognized him, that small band of brothers and sisters sometimes lost behind the sonorous Biblical language, that Mary and Martha, that Peter and Andy and Peter's mom, that Phil and Jim and the women, Susanna, Salome and Joanna, and the one – possibly Lazarus himself – for whom Jesus had a very special love, and Mary Magdalene, and for others whose names have not been commemorated, something truly amazing was happening. It was a fulfillment not of prophecy but of life itself. They were in no doubt that the master, the one who was one with 'the father', lived amongst them and had called them to him. To talk about the great work he was doing – showing people the Kingdom of Heaven – would be an unthinkable betrayal.

This is the kind of relationship that is bulging through the pages and lines of the New Testament gospels, waiting to burst through its dry words and sometimes impenetrable prose. Whether we accept it or not, those people really did believe, "This is it. How fortunate we are!"

This line of conjecture calls into question the very purpose and meaning of Jesus' time on earth. It indicates he was not in the business of creating or ushering in an earthly kingdom ruled by God – a task much of modern Christian thinking still believes will be accomplished at some future date – but was rather about creating a personal dynamic of love between his disciples and himself, cemented by the initiation. It was not a case of "Heaven is just around the corner," but, "Heaven is here now".

This was not the work of a 'magician' who could hypnotize people and convince them they had enjoyed a trip to heaven, someone Morton Smith envisages as a kind of warlock with his spells accrued from ancient Egyptian and Jewish manuscripts. Morton Smith falls foul of that well-known condition amongst Biblical scholars, not being able to see the wood for the trees. They can't sense the real magic that Jesus represented. This was the true secret.

Of course, Morton Smith had little choice in the matter; he was driven to his conclusions by the sheer power of logic. If the disciples were utterly convinced that they had an experience of the Kingdom of Heaven, there were only two possible answers; either it *was* true – Jesus had wrought some inner transformation, had given them access to a realm not otherwise in the field of human possibility – or it was not true but they were convinced it was. They sincerely believed that they had actually been in the Kingdom of Heaven.

The first is beyond the ability of Morton Smith, and maybe many others, to envisage or contemplate. Just listen in to any debate or discussion on the existence or otherwise of God by a group of high-minded philosophers or theologians, their nit-picking, their deft footwork as they nimbly trip between the ontological theories of Anselm and the arguments of Descartes and Spinoza. Such discussions are academic, noted for their dryness, far away from any attempt to acknowledge the love, the joy, the possibility of a communion with a divine presence, wherever it may be found. Could this experience be bestowed, as Jesus claimed, by the touch of a finger? If so, it would have enabled the recipient to pass through to an apparently self-sustaining inner world, a chamber of inner life, an ineffable dimension. It would simply be beyond the comprehension of human minds, no matter how sophisticated, how intellectually complex, those minds might be. Even to thinking-outside-the-box trailblazers such as Morton Smith, this scenario of *heaven-entering* – comparable, it seems, to the *stream-entering* bestowed by the Buddha – cannot be contemplated without immense difficulty.

But the second option is completely plausible. If the experience Jesus led them into was as good as the real thing, if it convinced its recipients they had entered an inner world, an inner 'kingdom', it had to be by an amazing power of hypnosis, delusion or some mystical feat of inner channeling. There was no other explanation. Jesus was a magician par excellence, a hypnotist to match the very best that today's prime-time television can offer.

I propose that there is enough evidence now from the discovery of the Gnostic gospels, the more detailed knowledge of other religious and spiritual traditions, and mainly from the New Testament itself, to give serious credence to the theory that Jesus was able to lead or induct his followers, or some of them, without hypnosis or magic, spells or incantations, into an inner experience of another dimension, characterized by luminosity, possibly an inner version of other normal senses, and the presence of a loving resident: 'god'.

Chapter Twelve

The Healings

Let us now return to the real story, the Biblical evidence itself; knowing that the gospel writers were delicately drawing a veil over certain important aspects of Jesus' work.

Jesus was becoming celebrated and notorious both for his words and his deeds – his teachings *and* his healings. In addition, besides these healings he was showing people how to enter the Kingdom of Heaven within themselves. It was the main thing he talked about. The vast majority of his words, his parables and his teachings were not about the importance of being cured of illness or disability, but about the urgency of entering the Kingdom of Heaven, so it ought to have been the main thing he actually *did*, as well. But it is never mentioned. We never appear to have any instances of situations described where Jesus actually revealed to people the mystery of the Kingdom of Heaven, or baptized people as John had predicted he would. Instead we have a huge catalog of healings. What is going on here? It is a strange mismatch. Not only is he constantly healing, but when he finds his work is too much for him alone, he has to empower his apostles to go out and cure diseases, to heal the sick and raise the dead, on his behalf. It was all about curing the sick, the maimed, and raising the dead. After he performed one 'cure', people would come in their droves to be cured themselves or to have someone they know cured. It happened very quickly after he started doing his work – immediately after he had cured Peter's mother–in–law 'of a fever' in her home, where it appears Jesus had taken lodgings: the crowds came pouring in to also be healed. "The whole city was gathered together at the door", we are told.

The answer has always been assumed to be that by the very acts of miraculously curing people he is revealing the Kingdom of Heaven. It is a central pillar of Christian belief that has proved so challenging to modern scholars trying to divest the Jesus story of its miraculous content, for if Jesus was not performing miraculous cures such as allowing the blind to see or the dead to return to life, there would be no way for his contemporaries to gauge that he was indeed sent by God. Yet the growing consensus, from the lone voice of David Strauss in the nineteenth century to universal agreement within the scholastic community today, is that the miracles did not happen, they were metaphors and they need to be taken out of the equation. But in doing that, what is left?

If Jesus really had come to heal the sick, the blind, the lame and the possessed – not to mention raise the dead – as his primary purpose, we might ask why they are not mentioned in his great statement of intention, the Sermon on the Mount, and in particular the Beatitudes, where he lists those who need divine help. We have the poor in spirit (translated in the modern Bible as 'those who recognize their need for God'), those who mourn, those who hunger and thirst for righteousness, the merciful, those persecuted for righteousness's sake, the meek, the pure in heart (the ones who shall 'see God'), and the peacemakers. It is a long and comprehensive list. We can understand why he does not include the Scribes and Pharisees, or the people he was often accused of befriending, the sinners and tax-collectors. But why does he not include the people the gospels put at the center of his teachings, the sick and the maimed, the blind and the mute?

The answer requires us to recalibrate our perception of what was happening and drag our focus away from the deep-set idea that some kind of physical curing was taking place. In the light of the new knowledge that Jesus was enabling people to have an inner experience of 'heaven', we can now see that it is not the miraculous cures which are a sign of Jesus' identity and role. It is the initiations into the Kingdom of Heaven which are themselves the signs by which he is recognized, and it is these initiations, these baptisms, which are being camouflaged in the cloak of not just physical healings, but *miraculous* physical healings.

The conclusion is clear; the healing and the revealing were one and the same thing. The more we consider this, the more evident it becomes. John the Baptist announces dramatically that he only baptizes with water but one is coming who baptizes with fire and spirit, words which could be translated as 'with light and with breath'. Jesus then progresses at a fair speed throughout the territory of his ministry teaching the people in general, and to some giving instruction in how to witness the mystery of heaven. To these he says they are privileged. The least amongst them is greater than the greatest who has not had the mystery revealed. They believe as a result of the initiation that they have had a powerful experience of a divine reality within themselves, and consequently identify Jesus himself as being a special servant of God, a link between God and man, or at the very least someone with unique ability. Jesus himself makes no bones about his special power, claiming that nobody can come to the father except through him.

But this unveiling is not for everybody. The key to making it take place is to believe that Jesus can indeed do it. Any doubt will cause the 'miracle' not to happen. The word Jesus uses is 'trust', which is now usually translated as 'faith'. It appears that if you trust Jesus and ask for his special gift, you might be in line to receive it and be admitted to the Kingdom. The act of initiation was not just a sequence of physical interactions, of instructions, leading to an inner revelation, but a powerful bonding of trust and love between a teacher and a supplicant during which a profound inner transcendence took place. It was a private and confidential affair, which is why Jesus repeatedly told those he had 'cured' to keep quiet about it.

Now we have a sense of why the initiation work of Jesus is camouflaged in the gospels. It cannot be that the evangelists themselves did not understand that they were drawing a veil of secrecy over this central part of Jesus' work. Writing between forty and eighty years after the crucifixion, they were very much second-hand witnesses of Jesus' life, hearing the word-of-mouth tradition of the various memories before committing the stories to papyrus. Jesus' work of revealing the inner mystery would not only be remembered. We see from many references in the New Testament books covering the post-Jesus period that it was still being carried out, in his name – possibly, in a fervor of evangelism, more than had happened even during Jesus' lifetime – and would continue to be, as we shall see, for many generations to come.

Those first writers of the story of Jesus' life and work would have known the importance of discretion, and therefore omitted, or were charged to omit, direct references to the initiation. They might well have received, at second hand, the initiation themselves. But why did they choose to camouflage this central aspect of Jesus' work in acts of healing, allowing their master centuries later to be hailed as a physician, a healer, an exorcist or even a magician? Jesus himself set the pattern when he taught in parables, using examples and metaphors that even his closest disciples did not sometimes understand. And in the only reference in the gospels to him being a physician, we find it is he himself who uses the word, telling the Pharisees who complained he was consorting with tax collectors and sinners, "Those who are well have no need of a physician, but those who are sick". He is making it clear that he is not actually a physician who cures illnesses, and the people who need him are not actually in poor physical health, but that he is a different kind of healer, 'curing' a different kind of ailment. His dining colleagues were not physically ill, but nevertheless needed his 'cure'. "I came not to call the righteous," he continues, "but sinners" – again no mention of physical illnesses: just his clear use of the term 'those who are sick' to indicate those who really need 'the physician'. He knows full well that he is talking, as in his parables, by means of a metaphor that might be confusing for some, for he challenges his critics to make an effort to understand him: "Go and learn what this means".

In considering the episode where he tells John's disciples to inform the Baptist in his prison cell that he is giving sight to the blind and raising the dead, we have here a verbatim conversation which shows that he knew very well that the terms were allegorical. He had no sense that John would not understand precisely what he was talking about. This was a metaphor not unique to the two men; it was also employed by the mysterious sect, the Essenes, to describe the pathway of inner experience and also by the prophet Isaiah himself, as well as by teachers of other spiritual traditions. It would have been an accepted convention with the later gospel writers that Jesus' fundamental analogy should continue, and that allegory should play a central part in the telling of the stories of his actual 'cures', as it did when he was alive. It is not so difficult to see, that in showing people the life, the mystery of heaven, the light – to use just some of the words Jesus himself employed for the experience he bestowed – he was in fact healing and curing them in the simple sense of making them whole, of filling in the missing link, of joining the circle, of 'becoming perfect' in its original meaning of complete.

The Chinese scripture, *The Secret of the Golden Flower*, where it is made clear that the golden flower is a metaphor for the 'inner light', makes much of this completing of the circle of life's energy. Until we can turn in on ourselves, it says, and focus our consciousness on our source rather than letting it all flow away through the outer senses, we are losing our 'chi', or life force. No doubt Jesus had no knowledge of any such Chinese teachings – more than likely he had no knowledge at all of the existence of the great civilization in the east – but the sense that he is completing people, fulfilling them, by his initiation bears a direct correlation to what is described in the *Golden Flower*, where "the practitioner will see a bright image in front of the middle point of their two eyes". When this inner visualizing begins to take place the practitioner is, according to the scripture, entering "the beginning of the immortal essence".

In several respects we see a close similarity between Jesus' initiation and the Taoist version; both the inner visualization comparable to Jesus' healing of the blind, the act of healing referring not to physical curing but to completing the circle, and not least by the reference in the Chinese scripture to an immortal essence, which might reasonably be compared to Jesus' description of the experience as offering 'eternal life'. If we came across such oriental sounding terminology in the New Testament we would be suspicious indeed, yet in both the language as well as the processes it describes we find remarkable similarity. We think we know the name of the author of this Chinese equivalent of 'the way', as the Taoist path was also called, but know nothing more about him. Perhaps he too was a 'revealer' or 'savior' for his people, as Jesus had been for his.

* * *

An essential preliminary part of this healing procedure might have been preparation; smoothing away those elements in a person's make-up that prevented a clear access to the heavenly kingdom. Today we might call them projections of the mind, mental blockages or egotistical traits that would manifest as doubt, skepticism, hesitation or simple fear, preventing the development of the faith or trust necessary in the operation. The busy mind, the ego, had to be abated, replaced by a trusting heart. But there may well also have been more extreme cases of deranged minds which needed his 'cure', not egotistical people but genuinely troubled souls; giving these the solace of his initiation may well have been behind his reputation as an exorcist.

There is a mysterious passage in Luke's gospel, which has defied every explanation. Jesus is 'curing' a mute; the phrase used, tellingly, is: "He was casting out a demon that was mute," indicating the muteness itself was seen as the demon. We know immediately that no miracle took place here; Jesus was not enabling someone suffering from total dumbness to speak. This is an extremely rare condition resulting from serious damage to the brain or the organs of speech. Less rare is 'elective muteness' where someone is capable of speaking but does not do so for psychological reasons. We can imagine this was not necessarily an unusual condition in Biblical times, and Jesus might have induced such a startling experience from his initiation that the recipient suddenly started volubly expressing his joy and gratitude. This could not be classed a miracle in itself. Certainly a sudden and noticeable transformation in the 'patient' had taken place, for the bystanders commented on it in terms they would understand – a 'demon', a curse, or to use the Greek meaning of demon, a blockage, had been removed, or 'driven out', by Jesus.

More likely, however, is that the reference to muteness is completely allegorical, as are the other occasions when Jesus is said to have effected a miraculous cure of a physical affliction.

Some onlookers suggested Jesus must be in league with 'Beelzebul, the prince of demons,' Beelzebul being the normal Palestinian name for Satan. Jesus points out – exasperation oozing, over the centuries, from his words – that if he is driving the demon out, how can he be considered to be in league with the said demon? Presumably turning to the person he has just 'cured', he then pops up with the remarkable phrase, "But if it is by the finger of God that I cast out demons, then the Kingdom of God has come upon you". Biblical commentators look at the Old Testament's description of the finger of God inscribing the Ten Commandments for a possible reference point, or the New Testament mention of Jesus writing with his finger in the sand. Some Bible translations replace finger with power, thinking this makes more sense. An account of the same incident in Matthew's gospel uses the word spirit instead of finger, the author of Matthew evidently not wanting to give too much away.

For an assessment of what this passage means we now have Morton Smith's suggestion that during his inductions into the Kingdom of Heaven, Jesus used his hands, or 'the finger of God', to touch the recipient in ways that are not clear. Of greater interest, however, to a modern observer, than Jesus' reference to the finger of God, or the criticism he had to face, or him having, with some degree of impatience, to justify himself to his critics, is the remarkable final statement that his driving out of the demon is actually the very act of leading the person being cured into the Kingdom of Heaven; he, or she, is not being healed, but being reconnected. Jesus tells us the Kingdom of God has 'arrived on' the person being initiated; there is no mention here of the kingdom being 'nigh', or waiting at some future juncture for those worthy of it. It has actually happened; the man or woman is now in it, thanks to his unique ability.

We cannot so easily believe that Jesus' Galilee was overrun not only by lepers and the blind, but people whom today we would think have just escaped from the set of *The Exorcist*. Such people were more likely to be ordinary men and women, psychologically damaged by the harshness and desperation of their lives. It could well be that in the society Jesus inhabited, with life for many being short, unjust and cruel, there were indeed those with what we would today call mental problems which he was able to overcome by giving them his special curative remedy, his revealing of the inner 'kingdom', and these more dramatic 'cures' have come down to us as 'exorcisms'.

This is not to say that Jesus himself did not believe in 'possession by demons'. It was the normal way of understanding mental illness, or epilepsy, at the time, and Jesus would probably have shared that point of view: we must beware of the tendency to put a twenty-first century mind on first century shoulders. If Jesus saw the calming of a troubled mind as the 'driving out of demons' or simply an act of 'cleansing', it does not affect the essence of what he was doing – enabling people to overcome inner blockages and barriers, and from there leading them into the inner experience of the 'kingdom'.

Explaining Jesus' miraculous cures has become something of an obsession for modern scholars. Their conclusions generally fall into the area of attempting to demonstrate that they did take place but were not necessarily miraculous. Maurice Casey articulates this point of view quite thoroughly by assuming that the 'many' blind who had their sight restored were probably people suffering from cataracts which Jesus knew how to remove by rubbing saliva into their eyes. Along the same lines, he shows, as is now accepted, that the word leprosy did not refer to the incurable deforming illness of that name but to any form of skin complaint, which Jesus could have cured, at least temporarily, without resorting to miracles. Similar short-term relief from mental disturbance might account, says Casey, for the 'exorcisms': temporarily cured by Jesus, the subjects "might have relapsed into demonic behavior at a later date". This still leaves the case of the actual resurrection of the dead, which, he claims, simply did not happen: the daughter of the synagogue official was not dead, the boy's story was 'lifted' from the Old

Testament to provide Jesus with more credibility, and John simply made up the story of Lazarus to convince his readers that Jesus could perform the resurrection miracle. "The authors of the fourth gospel", says Casey, "deliberately produced miraculous events as part of the process of rewriting Jesus tradition to meet the needs of their largely gentile community in Ephesus (where, it is believed, the book was written) at the end of the first century."

The idea that the healings were not miraculous might well be easier to accept than that Jesus did indeed perform miracle cures on very many people, but this much more low-key scenario does not account for the sensational effects Jesus' work had on the wider population, nor match his claim that by his 'wonders and signs' his divine credentials will be recognized.

It is interesting to observe that, while most modern *Christian* scholars tend to consider those miracles of Jesus which defy natural laws, such as walking on water, quelling storms or feeding the five thousand, as events that almost certainly did not actually happen as described, they tend to accept the miracles of Jesus that appear to be healings of one kind or another – lepers having their disability removed at a stroke, people's deformities remedied, the sight of the blind restored. Even modern day skeptics have an open mind when it comes to people being cured in a way that defies conventional medicine; perhaps some forms of faith healing did exist, is the unspoken thought. It is this line of reasoning that allows the view of Jesus as some kind of miraculous doctor to remain a possibility for many modern Christians.

But to those first century gospel writers, Jesus was indeed restoring health to the sick. It was just not the kind of health or the kind of sickness we today readily associate with the terms.

Chapter Thirteen

A New Birth

In today's evangelical or charismatic churches, the idea of being 'born again' is commonplace, meaning a renewed acceptance of Jesus into one's life, and is achieved by a baptism in water – usually by full immersion in a river, lake or swimming pool.

When Jesus says you have to be born again, however, he is not offering a water baptism but this new phenomenon, baptism in the spirit, which enables people to turn inwards and have an experience of a 'heaven' within themselves. These are entirely new concepts. The word 'heaven' hardly appears in the Old Testament – the idea of God having a location as a 'home' was beyond the confines of Jewish thought. And when demand for his services increased to a level Jesus could not manage alone, he nominated twelve 'apostles' to go out on his behalf, in twos, to replicate his baptisms – not water baptisms but this new phenomenon, baptism in spirit. This spiritual baptism is not a symbolic act like John's, nor is it equivalent to the laying of hands practiced today to admit people into God's world or to convey divine blessing, but is apparently giving the recipient access to an experience of God, heaven, or 'eternal life'.

What do we know of this word 'spirit'? In the Old Testament the term used is the Hebrew word, *ruach*, or *ruah*, which also means breath, or wind, or an invisible moving force. The New Testament, written not in Hebrew but in Greek, does not use *ruach* but the Greek word *pneuma*, which again means breath, or when translated into Latin, *spiritus*, also meaning breath. We use the words today in regular speech as the roots of such commonplace terms as pneumatic, pneumonia, respiration, aspiration, and so on. If English had been the mother tongue at the time of Jesus, 'breath' would probably be the word we would find being used instead of *pneuma* or *spirit*.

This line of reasoning does not present us with a solution, however, but with even more of a conundrum. Why is breath, which is the most commonplace action, performed by every human being throughout their lives, given such importance in the teachings, and presumably the initiation, of Jesus? We know the importance of breath; that life begins with the first and ends with the last. We also know that in many mystical traditions it is considered the life force, the gift from God who 'blows' his breath into his creation, giving it life. In Hinduism there is much reference to *prana*, not the breath itself but the power behind it, which draws it in and out of the living body. It is the fundamental meditation technique of many forms of yoga, which in turn means union, in the sense of union with the divine. But how does this relate to Jesus' teachings, the possibility of him giving his disciples a heavenly experience, and the growth after Jesus' death in recognition of the Holy Spirit as a mystical power which can visit a location, touch people and eventually take its place as one of the three aspects of the divine?

It is a dilemma we will look at in due course. For now we are probing this newly-established phenomenon in our approach to Jesus – the possibility that he was initiating people into some kind of inner experience, and that his miraculous cures may have been metaphors for these acts of initiation. 'Spirit' is certainly part of the equation, but are there any other clues we can glean from these short and almost identical accounts of the period of teachings of Jesus called the gospels, bearing in mind that so little is revealed in their brief pages that 'exasperated' is not too strong a term to describe the attitude of most scholars and writers on the subject?

There is one, of course, that stands out for the frequency with which it crops up, the idea of an inner visualization. Direct quotations from Jesus can sometimes sound quite forbidding, even when he is making relatively anodyne statements. When we see that, as reported by the evangelist Mark, he says, "There are some who will not taste death until they have seen the Kingdom of Heaven", he makes it sound quite threatening, more like a pirate captain hissing to his heroic prisoner than a promise of something beautiful to those who dedicate their lives to a search for God. Even when John reports him as saying something similar: "Unless one is born again he cannot see the Kingdom of God", we cannot avoid an image of Middle Eastern market places and cutlass-rattling derring-do.

Take those images away, however, and we are left with quite a simple statement which appears to mean nothing at all, certainly not in the later Christian context that entry to 'the kingdom' might be granted, if deserved, *after* death – and possibly a long time after death – but not before. And once again, we learn that the process of being 'born again' will lead to the 'seeing' of the Kingdom of Heaven.

We then have the various accounts of Jesus actually enabling blind men to see again. In one we have the simple narrative of Mark: "They brought a blind man and begged him to touch him...He spat on his eyes and laid his hands on him. 'Do you see anything?' Jesus asked. He looked up and said, 'Yes, I see men like trees walking.' Then Jesus laid his hands on his eyes again; and he opened his eyes, his sight was restored, and he saw everything clearly".

If we look at the original Greek text, however, and its translation as used in traditional Bibles, we find that in recent versions the wording has been tampered with. There, we find the last sentence was: "He put his hands again upon his eyes, and made him look up; and he was restored, and saw every man clearly." In this original text, it was not the man's sight that was restored but the man himself, and the interesting comment about Jesus *making* the man 'look up' is omitted from the newer versions. We also find the phrase "he opened his eyes" has been added, because of course, unless he opened his eyes, how would he be able to know that his sight has been restored? Similarly, he told Jesus he now sees 'every man' clearly, which might not necessarily mean people's physical forms, but something more to do with life's essence; modern interpretations have changed this to 'everything'. The learned translation committees might have possessed great erudition, but it seems they fell into the simple trap of making an assumption, by taking it as unquestionably obvious that Jesus was giving physical sight to a blind man, when it is clear something else altogether was taking place here.

In another 'miracle', recounted by John, "He spat on the ground and made mud with the saliva. Then he anointed the man's eyes with the mud. 'Go wash,' said Jesus and he came back seeing".

In both these instances, Jesus told the men, as he usually did after performing a 'miracle', not to tell any-one what had occurred, but they immediately did so, the second one blurting to the Pharisees a line immortal-ized in the beautiful hymn, *Amazing Grace*: "I was blind but now I see".

We also have Mark's account of the curing of another blind man, named Bartimaeus, who asks that he might receive sight, 'and immediately he received sight'. In this case again, all Bibles add the possessive pronoun 'his' before the word 'sight', when it is not in the original Greek, while the most recent translations have replaced the word 'receive' with the word 'recover'.

There are two other giving of sight miracles recounted in Matthew where it is said Jesus touched the men's eyes. Presumably he used the same mixture of spit and earth to form a kind of mud. Why would Jesus do this? The implication is that for an inner illumination to be experienced, it would be necessary to block out all external light. Whatever else Jesus did is left undisclosed, but the result is that some form of inner vision appears to have taken place. Again, in the original Greek of the Biblical account, we are told that the moment Jesus 'touched their eyes', they 'received sight', a phrase which has been changed in the more recent translations to 'recovered their sight', it being mistakenly taken for granted that a restoration of physical sight, rather than the opening of an internal 'eye', had taken place. We are also told that these two men, and Bartimaeus also, immediately began to 'follow' Jesus, implying they became his disciples, not something they would necessarily have done had the 'healing' been a physical one. If the two first disciples of Jesus, who had asked him to show them his 'home', had undergone a comparable experience, it would explain why they also, without hesitation, became his followers.

The Secret of the Golden Flower, sometimes translated as *The Secret of the Golden Light,* is only one of several mystical texts in the Buddhist and Taoist traditions that mention a light appearing in the forehead. Does this apparition require a blanketing out of all external light? It appears so, but something else must presumably take place to give rise to an outburst of golden light or some other form of heavenly vision. Is something further done by Jesus, maybe some form of manipulation, as Morton Smith surmises, perhaps activating the 'inner eye'; or is it, as Jesus constantly tells the people he has cured, or made whole, a matter of their trust, their faith, their absolute belief, and it is this alone which makes the ember of divine light suddenly burst into flame? Certainly the blind men in the Bible begged Jesus to 'heal' them, ignoring the people telling them to 'hold their peace'. "Have mercy on me," cried Bartimaeus desperately. He was begging for something more than his sight; he was begging for his life.

Could the 'anointing with mud' be a part, maybe the central part, of the initiation, which led the recipients to believe, rightly or wrongly, that they had seen God? And if so, what were they now seeing that could be simply characterized, as it was by the blind man in Mark, as 'everything'? The evidence would seem to be 'light', a word Jesus uses many times to describe the inner experience. The idea of an inner eye is widespread in religious iconology, and it is not denied that Jesus frequently mentioned it, but modern opinion has focused on the interpretation that the light referred to is not an actual light but is, metaphorically, a light of reason or a light of understanding. This would make it far easier to accept, for if not what we are confronted with is an explanation that does not fit easily with our rational processes – that in some way Jesus was able to activate an inner trigger that allowed the recipients to actually see a light or believe they had seen one.

Can we be satisfied with this, when there is strong evidence that Jesus meant an actual, visible, light? In one of his pronouncements, he refers to this phenomenon, saying, "The light of the body is the eye. If your eye be single, your whole body will be full of light". It seems that he is speaking of an actual inner 'eye' which either allows an inner light to be witnessed or is itself a source of light. The irony is that all modern translations of the Bible have reinterpreted this famous quotation from the King James and other earlier versions using the word 'healthy' instead of 'single', on the premise that 'healthy' has a clear and obvious meaning, while a 'single eye' is meaningless. Meaningless, that is, unless the teacher was referring to inner sight and an inner eye.

When the New English Bible was finally released to the world some forty years ago, replacing 'single' with 'healthy', a similar judgment had to be made about a reference to a single eye in the Book of Psalms. In this case the translation committee was helped by the fact that the psalm in question was, as is quite common in Jewish sacred literature, couched in language that could indicate love for a woman as well as the deity. In their research they found that because of the frequent sand and dust storms in the Middle East, women often covered much of their face with their shawl, so that only one eye was exposed, the other protected by the shawl, providing justification for the word 'eye' being singular.

But when Jesus spoke of a single eye, the choice of words could not rely on any such alterative meaning, therefore it would only make sense if 'single' were translated as 'healthy'. For what else could he have intended?

There is a further clue in trying to come to terms with this unwieldy concept – the notion that Jesus was trading in an actual light – namely, his assertions that this inner light is no ordinary light but actually is the light of God, or even God himself. Seeing light is one thing, but to associate it with heaven, God, or eternal life is something else. Yet somehow the recipients of Jesus' gift, or many of them, had this conviction. They emerged from the experience not only 'seeing everything' but with a certainty they had been in the presence of God. It must have been an exhilarating, euphoric, life-changing rite of passage and it must have been extremely frustrating for outsiders, people like the Pharisees, who were denied the opportunity of subjectively having the same experience because of their natural skepticism. Jesus was only interested in enlightening those who were truly sincere, who had faith and trust in him. The very fact that the priests were convinced *they* were God's representatives on earth, and therefore this man with the startling claims an imposter, made it impossible for them to have the trust and sincerity necessary for them to request the experience for themselves. This is why the Roman centurion who asked Jesus to heal his servant is such an important figure in the New Testament: he was that most rare specimen, somebody on the other side of the fence to Jesus' authority who 'came over' in any case because he recognized something in Jesus others like him could not. And the same in reverse, witnessed by Jesus saying to him: "Truly I tell you, with no-one in Israel have I found such faith". Faith was the key.

The priests were particularly put off, as many were, by Jesus' self-assurance, sometimes bordering, in their eyes, on arrogance. The 'faith', the trust, was the Catch-22. If you had it, the experience worked, if you didn't, it didn't. But how to get it? Some saw what was happening, and their hesitations were washed away, they were caught up in the euphoria and excitement around them; a real prophet, a real messenger from God, had appeared. Others may have had a more solemn recognition, an inner attraction to this charismatic teacher which, over a period of time, waived doubt aside. However it came about, trust was the prerequisite to being shown the Kingdom of Heaven within.

It is known that many religious traditions see God as dwelling within the life-form, within ourselves, as the power of life, a kind of energy within us, which when we die, departs and possibly merges with a greater source. In Indian religious philosophy, we find an infinite soul – which we could call God – named the *Param Atman*, meaning highest soul, and within each living creature is a small spark of this, called the *Jiva Atman*, meaning the individual soul. The latter is compared to a drop, which has separated from the infinite ocean of the former, and has as its destiny to rejoin it. Buddhism in particular holds the theory that the soul is from the outset on a journey to discover itself, passing from 'incarnation' to 'incarnation' until human birth is attained, when it can achieve the desire and the wisdom – the Buddhist word for this is *discernment* – to begin the return journey, not outwardly but inwardly, until enlightenment and a joyful reunion occur. A similar belief exists in Hinduism, where an ancient story compares the soul to a blind man perambulating the wall of heaven and tapping it with a stick in the hope of finding a gap, until, having achieved the rare prize of a human birth, there is, instead of the wall, an open gate. Unfortunately the soul is distracted, looking outwards instead of in. When the tapping recommences, the wall is again in place. The clear inference is that an experience of heaven is available not after life has ended but while it is still being lived.

This is of course an unprovable theory, and also relies on something not taught by Jesus, reincarnation, although there are sufficient references in the gospels to people thinking Jesus was a returned Elijah, or 'one of the prophets of old', for it not to have been a totally alien notion in first century Palestine. But the entire concept of a 'divine' energy, a soul, within our being, lends itself to the speculation that Jesus in some way had it in his power to turn people's focus inwards so that they became aware, for however long the experience lasted, of this inner world. If its physical quality was one of a light that could be visualized, its experiential quality must have been one of love, an actual feeling of heart-warming that left the recipient in no doubt that he or she had not only 'seen' the inner world, but had felt, had experienced, the 'love' it seemed to consist of. Jesus then had no need to ask people to believe that God was light and love: he could demonstrate it.

In his book on the meaning of the Dead Sea Scrolls, Hershel Shanks suggests Jesus' earliest disciples were psychologically unstable, and easily persuaded that they had had an experience of the inner kingdom. This is fanciful thinking, borne out of an agreement with Morton Smith that the inner experience was not a real one, but the result of some form of hypnosis. There is no evidence for such speculation. If anything the close disciples seem like a remarkably well-adjusted group of men and women. A great 'miracle' *had* taken place in their lives, much more meaningful than any future rising from the dead of either themselves or their teacher, and they handled this astonishing occurrence, from all accounts, with maturity and consciousness.

Chapter Fourteen

Into the Light

Inner visualizations of light are phenomena beyond the realm of most people's experience. This is why Morton Smith, Elaine Pagels, and other students of the Gnostic tradition who mention such experiences, consider some form of powerful hypnosis might have been at work. Yet the relatively recent ability of modern medicine to resuscitate people who are clinically dead has opened up a line of speculation demonstrating that the inner light theory might have some grounding in reality.

We are all familiar with the stories that have emerged over recent decades of people having what are called 'near death experiences'. These people had been clinically dead for a period of time before being brought back by resuscitation or some other process, to report that during their 'dead' time they had a strong and vivid experience of a light, usually in the form of a tunnel, along which they seemed to travel toward what they felt was a benign or welcoming destination. They were then pulled back, as it were, into their physical bodies to find themselves once again on the operating table, or wherever they were positioned. Sometimes a variant of this experience would take place, where the patients find themselves 'out of their body' and see themselves as if from a higher point – as if on the ceiling for example – on the bed while a medical crew try their best to bring them back to life. Again, if their attempts are successful, the patient suddenly finds him or herself once again 'in the body', no longer 'up there' but back in the real world. A recent advance in scientific research into this phenomenon is that totally brain dead patients report such experiences on their 'return', challenging the prevailing theory that consciousness exists as a result of brain activity. Consequently, what is now being considered is that consciousness is pre-existent, is 'everywhere', and is 'filtered' though the brain to become life as we know and experience it. It is a coincidence that in Eastern mystical traditions, the term 'supreme consciousness' is often used for the divine, leaving us to question whether at the foundation of existence is an infinite consciousness of which a small sliver makes its way into the individual human being.

The religious interpretation of near death experiences – that in some way this is a heavenly light beckoning people to a heavenly destination – is understandably treated with great skepticism. It could well be that if the patient actually does die the light will disappear immediately and all consciousness lost. The light is not necessarily the gateway to some kind of eternal heaven. The point is, however, that whatever the reason for the experiences, and whether they were real or illusory, the patients who had them are convinced they were real. To them they were certainly genuine. In the same way, the people to whom Jesus might have been giving some kind of inner experience of light were convinced they had received it, and that Jesus was indeed the master of the light.

In this line of reasoning, Jesus was the bearer of the gift of inner vision, of light, and was himself seen as the personification of the light of which he seemed to be the custodian. "I am the light of the world," he proclaimed, whilst making it clear that this state was temporary – "as long as I am in the world". John's gospel has Jesus say unambiguously, "I have come into the world as light, so that whoever believes (or 'trusts') in me may not remain in darkness".

We find Jesus claiming, "God is light, and in him is no darkness at all", while his disciples were exhorted to "believe in the light, that you might become sons of light". If Jesus were able, by some power unique to himself, to physically initiate a person so that a 'eureka' moment of inner illumination was granted, then it is little wonder that the notion of light is made so much of in the gospels.

Jesus, however, whilst claiming that he *was* the light or the bearer, or the bestower, of the light, was also

197

keeping this fact something of a secret affair. He did not perform his miracles – his initiations – in public but appeared to take his supplicant into a remote or private location. And time and again, he tells the recipients of his miracle to keep quiet about it. To his disciples, asking him why he spoke in the riddles of parables whose meaning was not easily discerned, he makes it clear that he is talking to two categories of people, those like the close disciples who have 'seen the mystery of the Kingdom of Heaven', and the rest who haven't. It might seem like nit-picking, but Morton Smith draws attention to a discrepancy at this point in the gospels. Whereas Mark, the author of the earliest gospel, uses the phrase, "To you the mystery of the Kingdom of God has been given", Matthew and Luke, writing a decade or two later, have modified it to, "To you has been given to know the mysteries of the Kingdom of God" – a more diffused interpretation. The distinction between 'given' and 'given to know', and pluralizing the word 'mystery', says Smith, indicate Matthew and Luke had "changed the text in order to conceal the reference to the mystery". Apart from that minor dispute about the wording of Jesus' sentence, both versions carry a similar meaning; only certain people have had the mystery revealed to them.

Again, the active ingredient in this potent mix appears to be that the individual has to have genuine trust that Jesus can lead him or her into the light. There could be no skepticism, no element of doubt or withholding of trust in the bargain, no attitude of "Let's see if it works". God would give his all to you but in return you had to give your all to him, seemed to be the unspoken equation. The more open you were, the more your heart was 'as a child', the more this flow from one to the other, from higher to lower, could take place. This is the clear meaning of Jesus' constant references to the need to be as guileless as a child, not in one's daily business – as an adult you could not conduct your affairs childishly or chaos would ensue – but in one's heart. None of the promoters of the Christian faith after Jesus' death picked up and carried forward this position, which was central to his message. Paul praised adulthood; that was the time to 'put away childish things'. But perhaps Jesus was not kidding when he said that entry into the 'kingdom' required one to be as innocent as a child.

Maybe, as we suggested earlier, the doubts, the sense of suspicion, the questions and reservations, which would act as dams and blockages in this flow of grace, or divine favor, that allowed the light to manifest, were the devils and evil spirits which Jesus seemed so adept at quelling, especially in those whose inner battles were affecting their very sanity. For the most part we can assume that most candidates would need these doubts to subside, the trusting inner child resuscitated, before being ready to receive the gift.

Now, what happened to this situation after Jesus died? With the master gone, we can imagine his followers were distraught beyond measure. If Jesus had been the only one giving the initiation, that would be the end of the affair, no further revelation, no further gifts of light, no rebirths in the spirit. But Jesus had during his life empowered twelve apostles – followed, we are told, by a further seventy-two – to go out and initiate on his behalf, so strong had the tide of demand become. From this basic information we can hazard a rough guess as to how many had been initiated during Jesus' ministry. The instances described in the gospels are of one-to-one initiations, but many might have taken place with larger numbers to account for the great following he accrued. Crowds pursued Jesus, to such an extent that he is often on the run to escape them, jumping into fishing boats, or taking off suddenly to travel and teach in different cities. We have enough evidence from the gospels to indicate that in many places he was treated to a rapturous reception.

Jesus makes it clear that not all these followers had received his special gift, but over a teaching period – a 'ministry' – of around two years at most, if he could only initiate one person at a time, and if he did this work most days or possibly, if Morton Smith is to be believed, nights, we would only have a total of a few hundred initiates. If we accept, however, that the episode known as the 'Transfiguration', where three had the inner vision, was an initiation, we have a clue indicating that one-to-one sessions were a rarity, and groups of two, three or more were the norm. Once he had authorized his close disciples to initiate on his behalf, this number might double or triple. It is significant that he instructed them to work in pairs, possibly to give each other moral support. It is also interesting that the gospels say Jesus did not himself 'perform any miracles' once he felt confident the disciples could do it on his behalf, although this was not strictly held to if Morton Smith's theory holds water that Jesus was performing an initiation in the Garden of Gethsemane the night he was finally arrested.

The speed at which the Christian message spread after the crucifixion to areas and cities beyond Israel itself indicates that people from those cities had already, during Jesus' lifetime, heard of the miraculous Kingdom of Heaven work this apparent messenger from God was performing in the Galilee and Jerusalem areas and had made the journey to see him, received the inner baptism, and returned to their home towns. Once these local groupings of followers of 'the way' realized that Jesus' death was not the end, but that his surviving apostles were willing to accept invitations to teach and give the same baptism, growth in the following could be guaranteed.

How long did the procedure take? If Jesus were indeed performing an initiation when he showed those first disciples his 'home', it took several hours, for it says in John, "They stayed with him that day". The nocturnal initiations detected by Morton Smith, where the garb of a linen sheet was necessary for the process, seemed to take some time also, for lookouts were posted nearby to ensure privacy. Yet the blind people given their sight by Jesus seemed to have the inner eye opened almost instantaneously, although these 'miracles' might also in reality have taken a matter of hours. We are not told.

It is possible, from the huge numbers asking to be 'cleansed' or to be 'made whole' that the initiation could include several people at once, maybe a room full. A rare insight into what a teaching session with Jesus would be like comes to us in the incident of the man having to be lowered through the ceiling, so full was the chamber where he was speaking. We see a crowded room, with people hunched together spellbound, while the master, standing or probably sitting, is giving out his unique inner understandings, acting as a channel for the inner divine. Possibly at the end of such a session, the crowd would be reduced by a selection process of those beseeching him to show them the inner Kingdom.

Taking all this speculation into account, we could assume that several thousand people had joined the ranks of those who had been taught the secrets of the Kingdom of Heaven during Jesus' lifetime, and maybe many more, providing the foundation for the later spreading of the faith.

* * *

Having the ability to pass on the inner experience did not automatically confer divine status on Jesus. The story of the Transfiguration, where Peter, James and John witness Jesus standing alongside Moses and Elijah, shrouded in some form of ethereal white light – "his face did shine like the sun, and his raiment was as white as the light", we are told – presents scholars with a problem. If this happened to those disciples, the speculation goes, it would have provided such irrefutable proof that Jesus was indeed 'God in a bod' that they would have never deserted him at the time of his arrest, trial and execution. There would not be a shred of doubt in their minds that he was indeed a messenger from the father, who, in some kind of alternative light-suffused dimension, lived with the 'greats'. As a result, it is considered that this episode is misplaced, and might have occurred after the crucifixion, as one of the resurrection apparitions. But why should the evangelists make such an elementary error? If it were a post-crucifixion vision, it would lose none of its power for being placed in that department of the gospels, and would if anything add dramatically to the rather meager number and quality of actual resurrection sightings.

But if we accept the possibility of Jesus showing his disciples how to have an inner experience, it makes sense. The first clue that this is the most likely interpretation of the event is that we are told that Jesus took his close disciples up a mountain, a regular metaphor throughout the Bible – and in other scriptures also – for rising up to enter the realm of the divine, as is the lifting up of eyes, possibly mud covered eyes, and as always we find the little ever-present element of physical contact – "Jesus touched them". The second clue is that it was not of course the real Jesus who was standing in a shining aura alongside a real Moses, now dead for several centuries, and Elijah, only slightly more recently deceased. It is only internally that such an experience can take place, as it did with Paul and also at the time of the baptism of Jesus by John.

What we have here instead is probably the nearest description of the effect of an actual revealing of the mystery of the Kingdom of Heaven by Jesus to be found in the accounts of his life. This might have been a first initiation for the three but since they were already apostles, it was more likely a special occasion when they had an inner experience together, probably with Jesus himself actually performing a further initiation on them, leading to a vision of light in which they believed they had encountered the three great men of their pantheon. The vision turned into a cloud – another frequent metaphor for the inner light – and when they opened their eyes, only Jesus was still with them, exhorting them, as he did in all the cases of his 'healings', to tell no-one of their experience. At some point in the future one of them obviously felt no longer bound by this promise, or the story – maybe like several others where the vow of silence was maintained – would never have come out.

We can accept that under the direct tuition of this powerful and charismatic Jesus, the three disciples had a profound experience of inner light, but why should this have materialized for them – or more likely just one of them, which in the re-telling grew to include all three – in the form of Jesus himself alongside the two great Jewish prophets? Let us revisit for a moment the phenomena of NDE's – near death experiences – and the tunnel of kindly light the clinically dead person feels drawn along. In many such cases there is a vision in the light of a revered figure one has associated with God, which varies according to the religious tradition of the patient. Christians will report they sensed or even saw a Christ-like figure in white robes with arms outstretched in welcome. But Buddhists have reported feeling the presence of the Buddha, Indians seeing their own Hindu gods, and so on.

Several typical examples tell how patients during an NDE sometimes seem to encounter their own loving relatives, before entering the presence of God himself, and before, of course, returning to tell the tale. If these examples are credible, it means the near death experience, while containing the universal element of a tunnel of light, also has the possibility of allowing the clinically dead person to impose their own vision of people, including revered or divine personages, they hold dear. And this might be what happened to the three astonished disciples.

Accounts of such internal phenomena might not be surprising to scholars studying Indian teachers of recent centuries where, with no inference that the master in question has any Christ-like powers, the inner light experience is sometimes alluded to. Mark Juergensmeyer, Professor of Sociology at the University of California, in his book *Radhasoami Reality*, quotes one as saying: "When the spirit is withdrawn from the body you will see a steady light," in which, adds Juergensmeyer, "the master's physical form takes on a luminous, radiant appearance". Returning to the time of Jesus, or at least soon after, we have as evidence of a similar phenomenon the experience of the first martyr, Stephen, who shortly before being stoned to death, enraged his accusers, who included Paul, by claiming to have entered an inner heaven where he witnessed "the Son of Man standing at the right hand of God". And if we can suspend momentarily our rational sense of disbelief at such considerations, we might have alighted on a possible explanation for the post-crucifixion visions of Jesus: they might have been internal manifestations of 'the master's physical form', later transformed into stories of actual physical appearances.

About the Transfiguration, we are invited to make up our own minds, but the interpretation we should resist is one which has the two major Jewish figures from centuries past actually meeting a radiant Jesus on top of a high mountain, for Jesus himself tells his disciples, as he did at all his 'initiations', to tell no-one of their 'vision', using an unusual Greek word – *arama* – for something that was clearly not physical. He was probably just as surprised as they were at what they had seen, but at least understood what had happened, and why. In any event, it did not do the cause of the post-crucifixion church any harm in its attempts to win over Jewish converts to have Jesus so clearly associated with the founding fathers of the Jewish faith. And this might well have been the reason the story was allowed to leak out.

The point to be made here, however, is that see-ing the inner light, if that is what happened when Jesus bestowed his initiation in the Holy Spirit, did not neces-sarily confer on him divine status. To his disciples, he was still a messenger from God, a servant of God, even a son of God, but was not necessarily one with God. At the same time, he was also not necessarily *not* one with God. What he was, one or the other, was up to the recipients' own judgment, formed from a mixture of the inner experi-ence and the outer interaction with, and observation of, the man himself. This is the real reason why, in the three early gospels, the synoptics, Jesus seldom says who he is, but bounces the question, "Who are you?" back on the inquirer, most famously when Pontius Pilate asks if he is the king of the Jews and Jesus says, "You have said so". Why didn't Pilate persist in face of this obfuscation, say-ing, "Don't play with me. I am asking *you* what you think you are?" But we sense that whatever Pilate threw at him, Jesus would get the better of the exchanges.

In the fourth gospel, that of John, Jesus cannot have sufficient opportunities to provide his divine credentials, for which feature it is often called the "I am" gospel: "I am the light", "I am the way", "I am the bread", "I am the life", "I am the gate", "I am the vine", "I am the shepherd", and of course, many times, "I am the Son of God". And when the woman by the well says to him, "The Messiah is coming," Jesus replies, "I who speak to you am he". We know that John had his reasons for embellishing his account, but Jesus himself was subtler. He is not quoted making similar claims in the synoptic gospels, not out of inherent modesty – he had a strong sense of his own identity – but because he did not want to put ideas in peoples' minds. It was for each of his disciples to develop their own sense of who he was. It was *their* journey. He could not take the steps for them, and, as suggested in an earlier chapter, the connection they felt with him in all probability precluded the need for verbal definitions. For different reasons, Professor Robert Price, the author of *Deconstructing Jesus*, comes to the same conclusion, suggesting none of these "I am" claims was a "genuine utterance of the historical Jesus", but were later additions.

* * *

What happens after the initiation has taken place? Is that it, or is more required? It is possible that Jesus expected his privileged followers – those who had received the inner teaching – to let it imbue them in their everyday lives, so that it became an ongoing, regular experience of 'inner connection', perhaps in the form of a daily period of inner communion.

Some of the parables of Jesus indicate that the path of 'the way' is one of growth. In one of them, the experience starts, like a seed, very small, but gradually expands until a tree has emerged which has birds lodging in its branches. This parable is generally taken to refer to a future 'church' which will start small but one day spread its branches over the whole world. It is a far-fetched interpretation. Nowhere does Jesus talk about future growth of a 'church' let alone one that encompasses the world, when he only worked within the confines of Jewish society. As Geza Vermes points out: "It is remarkable to note that the concept of the church as an institution intended to continue the mission of Jesus, and the ceremony of baptism as a gateway into that community, are completely absent from the gospels of Mark and Luke, and only mentioned three times in Matthew", and on those occasions there is strong suspicion, says Vermes, that the references were added with the benefit of hindsight. Rather than talking of the greatness of a future church, one thing modern scholars, Christian or otherwise, have agreed upon is that Jesus is all about personal experience in the present, whatever that experience may be, and not at all about a future time of redemption, life after *physical* death, and the long-term growth of a church in his name.

An alternative explanation is that the parable refers to a process of personal growth. But how would this personal growth be achieved? Apart from his teaching of *The Lord's Prayer*, there are no references in the Bible to the apostles themselves praying to the 'father', either singly or in groups: for them it is Jesus, not God, who is their focus. But he himself is described as taking himself to a remote place to have his own communication with his father. Luke gives one such reference which probably indicates a regular morning practice: "Very early in the morning, when it was still dark, Jesus got up, left the house, and went to a solitary place where he prayed". Something similar was possibly the mainstay of the apostles' devotions, for Jesus also tells his disciples to pray in secret, "where others cannot see". Why should this be? Possibly just for the quiet ambience privacy would generate, or it might be that certain practices and techniques are involved which require a degree of secrecy, maybe under the linen cloth of Lazarus, or in the 'tent' mentioned in the story of the Transfiguration.

We must avoid assuming that this 'prayer' would have taken the form of a verbal conversation. If Jesus had shown them how to focus internally during their initiation, then we are probably right to conclude this communion with God also took the form of the same wordless internal experience of union with the divine.

There is, of course, the solemn occasion of Jesus praying verbally to his *abba* before his arrest in the Garden of Gethsemane. Sadly, for it is a beautiful story, most scholars conclude that this moving prayer – "Father take this cup from me" – was added after the event, not least because as he was praying 'a stone's throw' from his disciples there would be no-one near to catch his words, and in any case, the disciples had fallen asleep, earning his reprimand. After a scuffle, and the implied attempt to defend Jesus by the naked youth, Jesus was led away, presumably without an opportunity even to say anything comforting to his disciples. Now, in any event, we have the persuasively argued theory of Morton Smith, that Jesus was not delivering a last prayer to his Lord on this occasion, but was conducting one of his nocturnal initiations, without any sense that his arrest was imminent.

More likely, when Jesus did pray, he went deeply and privately into the recesses of his own inner being, to spend a period of union with the divine, of non-verbal communication, undergoing a reconnection, a blending of identities, with his beloved one, his *abba*. And the disciples, in their own way, would do something similar.

Chapter Fifteen

Jesus has left the Building

While he was alive, it is clear that Jesus regarded himself to be as much 'the story' as the great works themselves. Without him, the 'magic' would not manifest. Maybe the experience of God, the access to heaven, the visualization of the inner light, and the immortality they in some way conferred, were the final destination, but Jesus controlled the access. And who would know this, who would recognize his indispensible role, more than he himself? Many of his sayings refer obliquely to this, his own central importance in the drama. He is the bridegroom, he is the provider of the feast. "I am here", he seemed to be saying, "take advantage of it while it is available". Nowhere is this made clearer than in the story of Mary and Martha, the washing of his feet with expensive oil, and his meaningful – although some might think, along with Judas, a trifle callous – declaration that the poor will always be with us.

But after his death the apostles were still able to conduct initiations, and it appears this is what happened. References to an initiation continue to appear.

We are told in *Acts* that "many signs and wonders were regularly done amongst the people by the hands of the apostles". Paul was clearly so initiated within a few years of the crucifixion on the way to Damascus. He had such a powerful experience, together with what he interpreted to be an inner message from Jesus, that he was blinded for some time afterwards. It was a strong enough detonation to make him turn his life around and use his dynamic talents to begin building the organization of Christians into a smooth running group of communities. Obviously a light did not come out of the sky like a spotlight, nor a heavenly voice boom forth. Someone initiated Paul, and clearly not in the open air, on the busy highway with its carts, mules, camels and pedestrian traffic. Maybe he came across a group of followers of 'the way' – as Jesus' movement was called – in a hostelry on the route, and was strongly impressed. Perhaps one of them had been empowered by Jesus himself to initiate, or he received the initiation when he finally arrived in Damascus. We are told in *Acts* the person who performed the initiation was called Ananias, who "laid hands on him". Like Jesus at the time of his baptism by John, Paul was "filled with the Holy Spirit. And immediately something like scales fell from his eyes and he regained his sight". In keeping with other initiations, maybe it was hardened mud that fell from his eyes, allowing him now to see everything. Who Ananias might have been was evidently of no concern to Paul, who clearly felt this was a straight gift of enlightenment, and with it divine power and instruction, from Jesus to himself – the actual initiator being no more than a conduit.

Professor Sanders suggests that to Paul, seeing Jesus in a vision was just as good as seeing him in real life, but he also made much of the actual sightings of the resurrected Jesus in the days after the crucifixion. From the start these resurrection appearances, on which Paul built the beginnings of his 'church', were highly suspect. We have seen how dubious the early sightings were, but how they grew in strength as time passed. In Mark, the first gospel, they are absent altogether, though a young man in a 'white robe' – in Luke this man has become two men 'in dazzling apparel' while Matthew calls him an angel whose clothing was 'white as snow' – by the tomb does tell the women Jesus has gone to Galilee. This could be an indication that Jesus survived crucifixion but more likely the incident refers to the probability that, as was the custom, the family of the deceased – most likely two of his brothers, since the carrying of corpses was men's work – had claimed his body at first light after the Sabbath to carry it away for burial in his family location. Tombs were seldom the final resting place for the deceased at the time, and the man or men in white could have been either local workers – maybe cemetery workers if the 'garden' where the tomb was located was, as is likely, a cemetery – who had seen the removal of the body, or, more likely as he is identified as a young man in a white robe, the youth Jesus had been 'baptizing' at

215

the moment of his arrest, and out of loving loyalty had remained in vigil by the tomb until his family claimed the body.

The last verses of Mark, missing at first but which suddenly started appearing in copies of the Bible from around the fourth century, providing a strong hint that they were a 'later addition', contain posthumous phrases and predictions from Jesus – "they", those who believe, "will speak in new tongues: they will pick up serpents with their hands, and if they drink any deadly poison, it will not hurt them" – which even to the layman today do not resemble the genuine words of the man we came to know during his lifetime. Matthew and Luke add more appearances, but by the final gospel, that of John, written thirty years later, we have a veritable catalog, almost a book in itself, of conversations and meetings – including a fishing trip and a breakfast picnic – between the deceased master and his apostles. It would be difficult to disagree with most scholars that this growth in resurrection appearances, together with other increasing references to Jesus' divinity as the gospels emerged one after the other, indicate a deliberate effort to increase Jesus' divine credentials in the struggle to keep his memory alive as the decades after his crucifixion passed.

What, then, are we to make of Paul's claim that Jesus appeared to five hundred people at one time? It is quite possible that a burst of proselytizing fervor after Jesus' death led to a mass initiation, maybe all at one time, but more probably in a series of smaller groups, where people who had already been preparing to undergo the process had been brought together to teach them Jesus' secret method for entering the inner kingdom, and as a result having various internal experiences which Paul at least understood, when he heard about them a few years later, to be encounters with the living Christ, similar in nature though possibly not in intensity to the one he had undergone. They would have needed a facility, a large room, for this activity which might well have been the upper room where the last supper allegedly took place, a room it has been convincingly suggested had been 'borrowed' from the Essene community in Jerusalem. This was a sect which, as we shall discover, had many beliefs and practices in common with the first Christians, and from whom the 'many priests' who became Christians, according to the *Acts of the Apostles*, would have originated, as the only other Jewish spiritual clan with a priesthood, the Scribes, was fundamentally opposed to Jesus' teachings.

The where and when details of the post-crucifixion activity are less important than that such activity was taking place at all. The entire religion which was to grow up in Jesus' name has placed its roots on what happened *after* Jesus had lived, a period when he was no longer present. In the absence of the cat, the mice can construct a fine city of systems and belief. The one thing we can be sure of is that it would bear no relation to how the cat would have done it if he were present, for of course, they are both coming from diametrically opposed premises: one – Jesus – from being a living channel of divine understanding, the other – Paul – from a mental construct of what this might be like.

Early Christianity tempts us towards a tantalizing series of 'what-ifs'. What if Jesus had explained just a little to Judas what he was really about, thereby removing from the story Iscariot's betrayal? What if he had not been so confrontational with Pontius Pilate in their head-to-head, giving the governor a let-out clause? What if John had not been executed on the whim of Salome and had continued his work? What if Paul had been successful in spreading his new religion in the deserts of the Middle East – to the south and east – instead of finding them not ready for benevolent monotheism and choosing to move north and west, to Greece then Rome itself? What if Jerusalem had not been destroyed in 70 A.D. and the church there had taken ascendancy over the new religion, keeping it within Jewish confines? What if Paul had not been executed, as is commonly believed, during the reign of Nero and had instead lived a long life, becoming the undisputed father figure of the church? What if the crumbling Roman Empire under Constantine had not accepted this Jewish cult as the state religion? What if the Gnostics had prevailed in the internecine warfare with those who wanted to subvert the path of inner *gnosis* and create instead an organized religion?

The projections are idle speculations. But one more, idle maybe but in itself fascinating, gives us pause for thought. What would have happened if Paul had actually come across Jesus some two or three years earlier than his 'Road to Damascus' epiphany? Would he have become one of the twelve apostles? Would he have been able to subjugate his immense will and intelligence into obedience to this difficult and challenging master? Would he, after the crucifixion, have proselytized the religion of the risen Christ with as much passion and fervor as he did?

In the absence of Jesus himself, certain strands of activity were left: the group in Jerusalem, possibly meeting regularly, maybe even living together, remembering and honoring the presence of Jesus amongst them, the little similar communes in other towns and cities, and, later, Paul's own activities, going forward to spread the news of Jesus, with some success, further afield – the desolation of one group and the optimism of the other, in silent counterpoise. And without the electrifying presence of the master, the central focal point was taken away, leaving a hollow space. No longer could the gossip be, "What is he doing, where has he been, where is he going next, did you hear he did this, did you hear he said that?" Instead, it could only fluctuate between reminiscence on the one hand – which turned eventually into the gospels – and attempting to keep his work alive on the other.

Here we detect a little feature of this scenario – the more frequent mention of the 'Light', either referring to Jesus himself or to the experience initiates had had within themselves at the hands of either Jesus or his appointed helpers. The more Jesus' physical presence recedes, the more 'Light' is bought in as a substitute topic. By the time John wrote his gospel the trend is pronounced. Matthew stated: "The people who sat in darkness saw great light, and to them that sat in the region and shadow of death light is sprung up". And Luke quotes directly from Jesus about how fortunate were those people he had thus far initiated: "Blessed are the eyes that see what you see! For I tell you that many prophets and kings desired to see what you see, but did not see it, and to hear what you hear, but did not hear it". It was left to John, however, the most philosophical of the four, to make it the central part of his gospel: "In God was life and the life was the light of men that shines in the darkness. John the Baptist came to bear witness about the light. The true light was coming".

But we have to assume there was great dilution in the power of the initiation if Jesus himself were not performing it. In her work of fiction, *The Liar's Gospel*, Naomi Alderman speculates that after Jesus gave his apostles permission to go out and perform miracles in his name, Judas found he couldn't, he didn't have the gift, and this made him dubious about his master. We now know Jesus did not tell his apostles to do miracles, but to perform initiations, involving not just practical teachings of how to 'go within' but an empowerment, a transmission of his authority that made the experience come alive for the recipient. But Ms. Alderman's point holds some value – at second-hand it was not the same thing as the original.

What first struck people about his teachings? Time and again the word 'authority' is used. He knew who he was; he knew the power he had. He *was* one with his 'father', his *abba*. It might be, of course, that we all are, the all-important difference being that he *knew* it. Jesus had no intrinsic difference in his DNA that marked him out as 'God'. This is the topic about which the great synod of Nicaea in 325, C.E. where the Roman Empire formally adopted Christianity, became so excited, in the end deciding that he was some kind of celestial hologram, not made of flesh and blood at all, for how otherwise would he have been able to walk on water, or, more importantly, share an identity with the father? It was the culmination of the process begun by Paul and John to deify Christ. But 'being one with the father' did not necessarily mean he was of 'one substance with the father', the formula of words arrived at by the synod: the oneness was presumably an internal union, not a physical one.

Jesus' acolytes, baptizing, or rather initiating, on his behalf, had no such conflict, neither about Jesus nor about their relationship with him. They took their strength from him. Their reality was that he was indeed God's representative, he did indeed have the power to show people the light, and *their* power came from their loyalty and unshakable devotion to him. It worked, but possibly not as much as if the initiation came from him himself, for now it was second-hand.

And this would have been the case after Jesus' death, with the process becoming even more diluted if the 'power' to initiate was passed down even further, until it became not just second-hand but third or fourth-hand. This goes some way to explaining why the Gnostics, so powerful in the early years of 'Christianity', faded out as generations passed, the personal connection with Christ, as he was now beginning to be called, lost and with it the intense devotion and loyalty that was at its heart.

* * *

We have already looked at the idea that a civilization needs belief in spiritual or hidden powers to explain the inexplicable, and early civilizations invested these powers in natural phenomena – the sun, moon, and stars, trees and rivers, storms and earthquakes, seasons, birth and death. There comes a time in the evolution of such societies when the growing collective intelligence outstrips these elementary belief systems and looks for something more mature, a more grown-up religion, which sees the divinity not as separate forces occupying the phenomena of nature but as a single, unified creative power, one god, behind the entire stage of human endeavor, with greater or lesser powers of involvement in human affairs.

A society cannot just invent a religion. Instead, it usually comes about when a catalyst of the kind that Jesus appears to have been gathers a small but committed following who have received from him an inner experience of the creative energy, the primordial consciousness, but also emerges at a time when society is ready to change over from multiple deities to a one-god religion. Jesus arrived on the scene just as the ancient, pagan, Mediterranean world was beginning subconsciously to examine and find lacking its traditional belief system and was searching for something that more accurately reflected its desire for a more mature, a more believable, 'god'. People, individuals, need a personal inner communication with their god, an on-going connection, not in terms of a conversation but of a sense, an experience, of the divine's presence. Society, on the other hand, does *not* require an internal experience. It desires a structured system whereby the one god can be worshipped, prayed to and whose help can be invoked, together with a moral framework of the rules of behavior that the society sees as necessary for its own well-being. Some of these would be universal and timeless, some peculiar to a particular society's predilections. In the main they are a variation on the golden rule: do unto others as you would like them to do unto yourself. If 'successful', the religion becomes a stanchion of society, but without the inner experience, an imbalance inevitably develops which over time leads to decline.

When did these big turnarounds in a society's view of the divine take place? We can say that for the Jewish people it happened around 1,200 B.C.E. possibly under the guidance of Moses. He gave out the same basic teachings with great personal authority: there is one God, abandon your graven images and false gods, and behave in a good way without killing, stealing, committing adultery and so on. It is possible he was a 'revealer', like Jesus, leading people who followed him towards a promised land, not a physical territory but the inner world of light, of eternal life, of 'milk and honey'. Moses would first of all have had to have achieved this inner oneness with that power for himself, as would Jesus over a thousand years later, and climbed up the mountain, an inner mountain of course, where he witnessed the inner light in the form of a burning bush.

Moses' communion with God gave him the authority to endow the people he belonged to with rules and guidance, and the belief in one unique deity who accepted them as his chosen people. In this interpretation, the parting of the sea to lead them to their promised land was not a physical phenomenon but an inner one – using a metaphor often found in literature about such cataclysmic events around a representative of the divinity, the ability to walk through or upon water as a symbol of the journey across the impassable obstacle that leads to salvation or reunion with the divine. It explains why, to the chagrin of some Jewish historians, no archaeological evidence has been found relating to the crossing of the sea pursued by the Pharaoh's army.

By the time of Jesus the religion had become a dry fossil, relying on book learning, ritual and the authority of a priesthood rather than real experience, and the time was ripe for a new Moses, or Elijah, a clear master in his own right, to appear to set matters aright. Jesus himself, in a quotation from the *Gospel of Thomas*, shows his understanding of this scenario: "The Pharisees and the scholars have taken the keys of knowledge and have hidden them. They have not entered, nor have they allowed those who want to enter to do so". He uses the same word, knowledge – *gnosis* – as the Gnostics later do, meaning inner knowing. Already one breakaway group, the Essenes, had washed its hands of this charade and sought inner peace within its own private commune, and we will look at this interesting phenomenon in a later chapter.

A similar process had taken place in India where an original religion based on inner experience, and described in the most ancient of scriptures, the *Upanishads*, had degenerated into a multiplicity of deities, reached or communicated with in the time-honored way of ritual, pilgrimage, penance, offerings and charity, but gradually losing any sense of direct connection with the inner divine. Buddha was the catalyst who put things back on track – for a time. He lived far longer than Jesus and was able, with the help of wealthy followers, to establish a system of centers spread widely over the Indian subcontinent and beyond. But once the inspiration of the personal touchstone was gone, it was hard to maintain the standard he had set, and a gradual reversion towards multiple gods took place. Now Buddhism is a very small sect in the land of its birth. Buddha had also claimed not to be the first, or the only, teacher of 'the way'. According to one of his biographers, Karen Armstrong, "He always insisted that he had simply discovered a path of great antiquity...which has been traveled by human beings in a far-off distant era. The other Buddhas, his predecessors, had taught this path...but this ancient knowledge had faded over the years and had been entirely forgotten". These sentiments are very close to those of Jesus in the *Gospel of Thomas*.

We know Buddha lived. We are not so sure about the semi-mythological figure of Krishna, but he also expressed the same philosophy in his own way: "In the revolutions of time immemorial, this doctrine was forgotten by men" – and gave words to the process of revival in a simple sentence from the *Bhagavad Gita*, which said: "Whenever there is a decline in the true religion, I will reappear to establish once again the true path". Such 're-establishers of the true religion', are only, said Buddha, showing things 'as they really are'. 'The way' was written into 'the structure of existence', to quote Armstrong, and like a subterranean river, it would inevitably have to surface time and again. Neither he nor Krishna were predicting the future, but stating a primeval law that to them was clearly understandable; a teacher of 'the way' appears, but after a time his message is again forgotten.

Amongst almost all ancient civilizations, there comes this point when a revival of similar teachings takes place. In the desert world of Arabia, the writ of Abraham, Moses and Jesus had also gained influence until a new prophet, Muhammad, adjudicated that the way had been lost and his conveying of a new teaching from the one true God, Allah, would gain ascendency, recommending seekers to return to him by entering the 'sanctuary', the home of God. It is still being debated whether, when he undertook his famous 'night journey' from his home in Arabia to Jerusalem, encountered various masters, including Moses, and then ascended to heaven where he met with God himself, he had under-gone some form of inner experience or had literally made an actual journey. Less ambiguously, Jesus was bold enough to suggest that the home of God might be 'within', and it appears that Buddha agreed with his Galilean counterpart in saying that *nirvana* is found in the human heart.

If we feel that a thousand years B.C.E. is reaching too far into the distant past for clues about the origins of notions about God, we are indebted to Karen Armstrong for introducing us, in her majestically detailed book, *A History of God*, to the theory that the very earliest human communities, around some 14,000 years ago, had acknowledged one God only in a form of primitive monotheism. This 'Sky God' gradually gave way, as man became more 'civilized', to the multiple gods of nature. People thought this early 'Sky God' had faded away, had even died, leaving a 'god-shaped hole', a condition Ms. Armstrong feels is akin to the human situation of the present day.

The 'god-shaped hole' might have described the situation in the period following Jesus, when his message came just in time to catch the beginnings of a new wave, a wave of wishing to reject the multiple gods of ancient Greece and Rome and find something more substantial and real. This accounts for the successful spread of Christianity, but it is not how Jesus himself saw his role. It was not his intention to start a new religion. He had appeared to show people how to connect with God in a visceral, personal way. He would do this only for as long as he lived. After that, maybe another 'comforter' would appear. *His* task, as Jesus of Nazareth, would be over.

On his death, the band of brothers and sisters who followed 'the way' were distraught. Should they continue teaching his message although he was no longer alive to do it himself? Their instincts might have told them, "Probably not". He was unique. Moreover, the essence of his initiation was that to be fully effective, it required devotion to the messenger.

But to keep his memory alive – that *was* worth doing. And after all, some of the disciples had been given the power by Jesus to conduct the initiation themselves. If people sincerely wanted it, why not give it to them, as long as it was made clear this gift was being made in the name of Jesus? This is what they had been doing anyway while he *had* been alive. But would it be as good as the original product? As Richard Bauckham in his authoritative little volume, *Jesus: A Very Short Introduction*, pointed out: "In the case of his exorcisms, it is remarkable that Jesus uses no techniques or incantations, utters no prayer to God, and evokes no name of a powerful being beside himself. He does not tell demons to depart in the name of God, where his disciples do so in the name of Jesus in order to expel demons by its power. Jesus seems simply to exercise God's authority over demons". Only Jesus had the special key: "To have faith in Jesus was to have faith in God. To obey Jesus was to obey God…Jesus opened up his own special and intimate relationship with the one he called Father for others to share".

Thus, initiations which took place after Jesus' death could only be by their nature second-hand. While Jesus could deliver in the name of God, the disciples could only do so in the name of Jesus – a divine experience at one step removed. It does not necessarily mean the initiation had to be less effective; it seems that the one undergone by Paul was immensely powerful, changing his life at a stroke. The indication is that the efficacy depended more on the openness of the subject rather than the power of the initiator.

It is quite likely, then, that after the shock had abated, a reaction to the execution of their leader would set the disciples on a renewed surge of proselytizing, of teaching Jesus' message and initiating in the spirit, or the light. In the earliest writings of the apostles after the crucifixion, the light seems to take over as the main preaching point. The theory of Jesus having died for our sins had not yet developed. It was still all about the showing of the light. Peter, possibly the apostle Peter, in his New Testament letter, was able to address the followers of 'the way' by saying:

> "Ye are a chosen generation, a royal priesthood, a holy nation, a peculiar people that you should show forth the praises of him who hath taken you out of the darkness into his marvelous light."

The death of Jesus had been sudden and unexpected. There had been no time for him to speak with his apostles and his other close disciples about how he would like things to happen after he was gone. They were left, suddenly, alone and rudderless. He had relied on Peter as his staunch right-hand man, a practical person who seems to have acted much as a personal manager during Jesus' life, so much that Jesus had called him his rock. But the quote which says, "On this rock I will build my church" was, scholars agree, probably added later to justify Peter's role at the helm of the developing religion. Peter was around the same age as Jesus, so there was no assumption that he would outlive him, and the word 'church' had no meaning comparable to our understanding of the term today. *Ecclesias*, the word used in the gospels, meant a gathering of people, not a building nor a religious organization.

And so the tradition of giving out the secret teaching continued, and in many cases the secret teaching, and the right to initiate, was passed on to ever new generations, gradually dissipating, until, after two or three hundred years, it had run its course and had been superseded by a new 'dry' religion, the authoritarian structure of the universal Catholic church. It is time now to take a look at the most fascinating Christian discovery since Helena, the Roman empress herself, and mother of the first Christian emperor, Constantine, claimed to have found the original cross – the cache of books that have become known as the Gnostic gospels.

Chapter Sixteen

A Non-Stick Religion

Contrary to some opinions, Gnostics were not the people who invented *Teflon*. It is widely known that the word means people with 'knowledge', not in the normal sense of book learning but referring to an experience of the divine, of the mystery of the Kingdom of Heaven.

It goes without saying that every disciple of Jesus who had received the initiation was a Gnostic, and so mainstream was it that no special name was needed to describe them. If they had wanted a title, it would have been 'followers of the way', or possibly 'disciples of Jesus'. But after a hundred years or so, when a new form of Christianity, the church, saw the followers of *gnosis* as a threat, they found 'Gnostic' an easily identifiable tag; they certainly could not be called true followers of Jesus, for that is what they, gradually becoming the major group, considered themselves. Groups are often named and defined by their opponents. People who followed Christ were not called Christians until they began to be noticed by Roman chroniclers as a troublesome sect, and were given the name so common now.

In the same way, Gnostics were named not by enemies from Roman or Jewish society but by Christians who were organizing themselves into a prototype 'church' and saw the theories and beliefs of people who followed the initiation teachings of Jesus as a heretical deviation. So from a time when all the apostles, all the surviving disciples such as Mary Magdalene, Jesus' brother James, and the very new converts such as Paul, were to a man or woman, Gnostics – a word which, being Greek, would have meant little to them in any event – by the second and third centuries a point had been reached when the Gnostic element had been weakened and a more 'orthodox' system of belief was gaining ascendency. These people were fast becoming the acceptable face of Christianity within the Roman Empire, but were dismissed as misguided by surviving Gnostics, such as the author of one of their tracts who called newly self-appointed bishops 'waterless canals'. These waterless canals proved adept at facing this challenge, going as far as to call Gnostics 'agents of Satan'. When they finally became the official religion of Rome, their first act was to declare Gnosticism a heresy and order that all Gnostic books and scriptures were to be destroyed.

This destruction meant that until the last century we have only known about Gnosticism through the writings of its sworn enemy, the official church, and why the discovery of a large cache of Gnostic writings in 1945 was so significant.

The find was made by Muhammad Ali, a simple farmer in northern Egypt who, whilst digging for fertilizer near his village, Nag Hammadi, struck his spade against a huge sealed vase. In a story reminiscent of Aladdin and his magic lamp, fear of an evil spirit possibly hiding within and awaiting release was overcome by the hope of finding gold. He was so disappointed that it contained only an assortment of ancient leather-bound papyrus codices – forerunners of books – that he dumped them in the corner of his simple home where his mother allegedly used some of them to kindle the morning fire, while others were, in Muhammad Ali's words, 'thrown away'. But he gave one or two to a local Muslim priest, who in turn showed one to a local history teacher, who recognized its potential importance and sent it to a friend in Cairo to be appraised.

From then on, it is a convoluted story of haggling, changed ownership, illegal sales, and separation of pages from even the same manuscript, as intermediaries thought they would get more for them if sold by the page, until finally a still extensive amount – some fifty-two texts of what we would now call Gnostic writings – has been retrieved, translated and studied. It turned out that the books were copies made in the fourth century C.E. of earlier manuscripts written in Greek, the language of the New Testament, before 140 C.E., as from that date some of them are referred to in the writings of the more orthodox Christians whose leaders viewed Gnosticism as an enemy. The most interesting of the many texts found at Nag Hammadi is considered to be the *Gospel of Thomas,* not, like the canonical gospels, an account of Jesus' life, but a list of many of his sayings, the majority of which were already known from the gospels, leaving others as probably authentic but previously unknown.

Although wildly diverse, and often containing previously unknown ideas about creation, God and Satan, the main thrust of these hastily hidden writings is that a separate strand of the Christian faith was in existence from around 80 C.E. to 400 C.E. which stressed an inner path to the truth, and that this was a secret teaching of Jesus. Although vehemently denounced by its detractors, its adherents considered themselves to be the true followers of 'the way' of Jesus, and a battle for hearts and minds ensued until, with the acceptance of Christianity as the official religion of the Roman Empire, the Gnostics were finally defeated. But if it were true that Jesus was teaching *gnosis,* and was performing initiations, it means that Gnosticism was the first form of Christianity, and the later church, worshipping the person of Jesus, an offshoot from it, rather than the other way round.

Why were the Gnostics so victimized by the early church? It was not just for their assertion that Jesus actually initiated people into an experience of the divine within themselves, and rejected the belief that he was resurrected after three days as childish nonsense. Nor for the Gnostic belief that men and women were equal, there was no seniority of one over the other.

Nor were they derided for relatively minor revelations such as the insinuation that Jesus and Mary Magdalene were closer than previously thought. The reason lay, instead, in the Gnostic refusal to accept any form of authority, for as they all had the inner experience of the divine within themselves, there was no need for an intermediary in the form of a priest or bishop. Similarly, no structure was required, except an informal one to keep various communities of Gnostics in touch with each other. Irenaeus, the bishop of Lyons in the south of France at the end of the second century, became their most vehement opponent, and it is from his book denouncing them, *Against Heresies*, that, until the Nag Hammadi find, we knew anything about them. Irenaeus complained that they met in each other's homes and drew lots to see who would be the chairperson for that evening's meetings, where people would speak extempore from their own inner experience. This would not do at all. The newly formed 'church', with its hierarchy of bishops, deacons and priests had no place in their system. This was a challenge to the Church's very existence.

Regarding the question of sexual equality, it was a fundamental tenet of Gnosticism, not because of any modern view of equality but because in the state of grace in which these Gnostics believed they were living, such differences as gender did not come into play – something Paul had made clear with his "We are all equal now" (now we are in the Kingdom of Heaven) speech: "There is neither Jew nor Greek, slave nor freeman, male nor female, for you are one in Messiah Jesus". One of the best-known Nag Hammadi manuscripts contains a profound poetic expression in praise of the female essence that has become famous in its own right, even being appropriated, malodorously one might say, for a perfume commercial:

> "For I am the first and the last.
> I am the honored one and the scorned one.
> I am the whore and the holy one.
> I am the wife and the virgin…
> I am the mother and the daughter.
> I am the barren one,
> And many are her sons.
> I am the silence that is incomprehensible…
> I am the utterance of my name."

But if the new church was to thrive, was to capitalize on its recently-gained position as the official religion of Rome, it required orthodoxy, and an acceptance of its power structure. It could tolerate to an extent different views and opinions, as long as those holding them accepted the central point that the church was in charge, and its hierarchy possessed inviolable authority. Within this constraint, theologians were free to work out their interpretations and resolve their differences, with the resulting winners and losers.

The Council of Nicaea in 325, where the Roman Empire adopted Christianity, provided a cauldron for such a dispute, around the divinity or otherwise of Jesus. Another major example arose at the beginning of the fifth century, when the relatively enlightened British monk, Pelagius, who had become enormously influential in Rome, clashed with Augustine of Hippo, the famous North African bishop, considered the greatest catholic theologian, on the question of free will and sin. Augustine had developed the doctrine that all human beings bear equally the original sin of Adam and Eve, and can only be released from it by baptism, which by this time was invariably understood to be a water baptism. The idea of sin, in its meaning of an offence against God, being created when Adam – not a historical individual from the beginning of time but every man – turned his back on the Garden of Eden, and Jesus having the ability to turn men – and women – back again to re-enter the garden within them, was a pure Gnostic understanding. But as Gnosticism receded, Adam's original sin was being increasingly reinterpreted as a historical incident, requiring salvation by a church baptism. Augustine's great step forward was to assert that not only adults but infants who die before baptism are unfortunately denied entry into heaven.

Pelagius took issue with this. Not only did he reject the concept of original sin and suggest that men and women had the free will to decide their own spiritual destinies, but he held that Jesus had pointed in particular to infants as being the first who would enter the Kingdom of Heaven because of their innocence; it did not matter if they had not been baptized. Pelagius did not think this was such an important sacrament in any case; he was probably well aware that it dated from the post-Jesus period rather than from the man himself. Augustine won the day. In this instance, in spite of the notion that the church could include many different opinions, Pelagius had overstepped the mark and was finally expelled from the church for his heresy. He was not heard from again, and the year and place of his death are unknown.

Meanwhile, it is from Augustine's obsession with original sin that the strongly misogynistic streak seen even today in the Catholic church first arose, for he declared that Eve was the real culprit in that seduction in the Garden of Eden and every woman would forever carry this stain of bringing sin into the world. Men could not be blamed, he astonishingly asserted, because they could not control their libido. "It is Eve the temptress," he claimed, "that we must beware of in any woman," agreeing with another Christian leader and vehement opponent of the Gnostics, Tertullian, whose language was even stronger: "You (women) are the devil's gateway, you are the first deserter of the divine law. Man was made in God's image, and you destroyed him...Because of you, even the Son of God had to die".

Augustine, this greatest of Catholic thinkers, even wondered why God had created woman, since two men would have made a much better job of running the world they had been placed in, rather overlooking the obvious missing ingredient in this line of speculation. It is not a surprise to learn that sexuality had been, for Augustine, something of a problem before his conversion to Christianity, and even then prayed, "Lord give me chastity, but not yet." It would be hard to disagree with Karen Armstrong's conclusion: "Western Christianity never fully recovered from this neurotic misogyny".

This is what is at risk of happening in a new religion when the original archetype has left the building, and his unique message is watered down or disappears: before long, debate and theories start filling the void. The creation of dogma was to become an on-going passion of Catholic theologians. A key stage in the transition from an experience-based Christianity as followed by the Gnostics to the path being unfolded by the hierarchical structure of the new Catholic church was the development of ritual as a substitute for inner experience, and the investing of the rituals with mysterious powers of their own. So we have the sprinkling of 'divine' water, the use of incense and the laying on of hands by the bishop, to convey God's acceptance. These were not just symbolic acts but were now considered actual steps towards a divine experience.

* * *

But away from the theological battlefields, both Gnostic and orthodox Christians shared a sense of well-being, a feeling that they had been redeemed and were already in a safe place, the arms of God. Accounts of their happiness, their willingness to share, to help the less fortunate in those early centuries before guilt and sin took their place, are many. The non-Gnostics may well have accepted the accessibility of an 'inner knowledge' teaching to those advanced enough to have the 'mystery' revealed, but were happy with their own condition. The Gnostics, for their part, seemed to decry not their fellow Christians but those anxious to turn it all into a rather rigid organization with its powerful intermediaries, the priests.

Their writings make frequent reference to the inner light that presumably was still available to them via initiation from people who had been endowed, or at least authorized, by their own teachers to hold the initiation ceremonies, or sessions, since we do not have reference to any ceremonial content to these occasions, besides a solemn oath of secrecy.

One of the Nag Hammadi manuscripts, called the *Teachings of Silvanus*, asks: "Why do you pursue the darkness, although the light is available for you?" and in the same piece, "Light the lamp within you". Another text, titled the *Gospel of Trust*, states: "Within you dwells the light that does not fail". In another, named *Dialogue of the Savior*, a person called Matthew asks to be shown "the place of life, which is the pure light", while in the *Gospel of Thomas* Jesus' disciples ask him to "show us the place where thou art, for it is necessary for us to seek it", both of which remind us of the request made in St. John's gospel by the first disciples that Jesus show them 'his home'. The *Gospel of Thomas* quotes Jesus as replying, "There is a light within a man..." claiming, "The darkness vanishes when light appears", whilst also saying he grieved for mankind because they are 'blind in the heart'. The document known as *The Great Seth* refers to Gnostics as the 'sons of light'.

The writings seem not to harp on the past, or on the actual life of Jesus. It seems the details of his life described in Matthew, Mark, Luke and John, are not of primary importance. Only his role as the giver of *gnosis* is of real interest to the Gnostics. It could be of course that the gospels which would later be included in the official Bible were not easily available. It was only after the Roman acceptance of the Christian faith in the fourth century that Bibles began to be produced. Before then, Christians of either persuasion would have little knowledge of the events of Jesus' life and his 'miracles'. To one group, the only important thing was that he had been resurrected as they believed they would also be, and to the other, that he enabled people to discover 'God' within themselves by providing special teachings, a spiritual resurrection. They were not worshipping the man but the 'God' he revealed.

One text, the *Apocalypse of Peter*, which might refer to the apostle Peter, comes close to accounts of Jesus' bestowing sight in the Bible: "[The savior] said to me…'put your hands upon your eyes, and say what you see'. But when I had done it, I did not see anything. I said, 'No-one sees this way'. Again he told me, 'Do it again'. And there came into me fear with joy, for I saw a new light, greater than the light of day…and I told him about the things which I saw".

If this were a description of the actual initiation of Peter, it is typical that he should complain that, at first, he was not getting the experience; he was not seeing the light. Little wonder that Jesus marked out this bold and fearless personality as someone to hold close to him. This incident also sounds familiar to us because it is comparable to the blind man into whose eyes Jesus rubbed mud made from his spit, and at first saw something indistinct that looked like 'trees walking', but on trying again, 'saw everything clearly'.

We should mention at this stage another Gnostic gospel *not* found at Nag Hammadi but more than three decades later, in 1978, in the same region of northern Egypt: the *Gospel of Judas*. Previously only known about from Irenaeus' second century polemic, *Against Heresies*, it was discovered along with some Gnostic texts which *were* also amongst the Nag Hammadi find, but suffered worse than most in the haggling and changed ownership of subsequent years, so that much is lost, and what remains contains many lacunas – missing words. Nevertheless, the gospel is considered one of the most important of all the Gnostic documents, for, while containing, like other Gnostic writings, various theories about creation and the role and nature of the divine, it also reports excerpts from what appear to be conversations between Jesus and Judas. "Your God is within you," Jesus tells him, in an 'eternal realm' where "neither the sun nor moon rule". And in a passage which the editors take to be some form of Transfiguration event, Jesus tells Judas to "Lift up your eyes and look at the cloud and the light within it," whereupon a "luminous cloud appeared there".

From various texts and letters, not all found at Nag Hammadi, we gain an insight into how the Gnostic system worked in the two hundred years or so after Jesus' death. We learn that Paul himself was a Gnostic teacher who passed on his secret teaching to Theudas, who passed it – now called *gnosis*, knowledge – to Valentinus, an influential Gnostic poet who travelled to Rome, referred to in the letter of our friend Clement of Alexandria. He lived around 140 C.E., and claimed Jesus had shared 'certain mysteries' with his disciples, that were kept secret from outsiders. He in turn passed the flame on to Marcellus, whom we are told 'initiates into *gnosis*'. He in turn teaches Heracleon who was a prominent Gnostic around the year 160 C.E.

There is much also that is fascinating, of interest, or simply controversial in the writing of Gnostics, suggesting that without the clear insight and example of the living master among them, people who might experience the light but are not really one with it as Jesus seems to have been can stray into associated beliefs and theological theories, much as the orthodox Christians of the same period were doing. Some of the writings for example seem very concerned to portray the old God of the Hebrews as a malevolent minor deity, who introduced pain and suffering to the world. Jesus on the other hand taught that there was a higher god, a God of love and compassion.

It is commonly accepted today that the Old Testament God can be fearsome, judgmental and jealous, while Jesus' *abba* is indeed the 'God of Love', to such an extent that he is defined *as* love. But Jesus himself does not mark down the old God of Israel; this is the work of the later Gnostics. There is also the controversial Gnostic theory, expressed in the *Gospel of Judas*, that Jesus did not really suffer on the cross, for only the clothing he wore – meaning his body – was being crucified, while he was as it were in another body, a body of spirit or light, away from the suffering of the mortal frame. This clearly relates to the view that the human being is a 'hinge', with a physical and spiritual dimension, the spiritual one being the 'real' one, which lives in a timeless reality. It was this notion, adopted by some Gnostics, that only the spiritual body was important and we can therefore give our physical bodies over to carnal pleasures, that caused the letter to Clement of Alexandria, and he answered by saying, as you would expect, that they had completely misunderstood Jesus' teachings. Even Buddha said that suffering couldn't be overcome, but paradoxically, while suffering, peace can still be experienced.

We then have the much-discussed role of Mary Magdalene. Had she been a prostitute, as the church is still debating, based on her wonton behavior in anointing Jesus' feet with expensive oils and drying them with her long, loose hair? The evidence is thin indeed. As in any society harboring a disproportionate number of foreign soldiers, and given the loose sexual morals we now know abounded in Roman society, a living from prostitution was probably easily available. But another view of Mary from an apocryphal source claims that she was a wealthy woman in her own right. The truth is, more likely, that she fell between such social extremes. As most of his close disciples appeared to be, and like Jesus himself, we are probably safe to assume she also came from the middle range of society. What is more relevant is that, until she came across Jesus, she was in a bad way *spiritually*, forlorn, without hope, and desperate to know the answer to the fundamental questions, who am I and why am I here? When he 'saved' her, her attachment to him was consequently profound, accounting for their mutual love and loyalty.

Even fifty years before the Nag Hammadi finds, which included the gospel carrying her name, the *Gospel of Mary Magdalene* had been in circulation, a copy having been discovered in the late nineteenth century. But the Nag Hammadi documents suggest a far more central place in Jesus' close circle than had previously been thought the case. From the *Gospel of Philip* we have the famous mention of the kissing we have referred to in an earlier chapter, and can now look at again in context: "The companion of the savior is Mary Magdalene. He loved her more than all the other disciples and used to kiss her often on her mouth. 'Why do you love her more than us?' " his disciples asked, to which, in his own unmistakable style, he replied, "Ask yourself why she loves me more than you". The church has suggested the kiss possibly refers to the kiss of peace, or the kiss of friendship, that sometimes take place in Christian ceremonials, such as the consecration of a new bishop, and maybe Jesus kissed other disciples in the same way. We are left to form our own judgment.

After the crucifixion the other disciples, according to the *Gospel of Mary Magdalene*, asked her to teach them, since she had been so close to the master, which the chauvinist Peter resented since she was only 'a feeble-minded woman', but he was contradicted by the apostle Levi, who asked, "If the savior made her worthy, who are you to reject her? The Lord knew her very well. That is why he loved her more than us".

Mary might well have been a confident, outspoken woman, for in another text, called *Faith Wisdom*, Peter asks Jesus to tell Mary not to talk to him so much, in answer to which Jesus tells him, in effect, to mind his own business. The picture of a woman unafraid to chat to Jesus without inhibition reminds us of the attitude of the sisters Mary and Martha, who also exhibit an easy-going relationship with their master, and the intimate conversation he holds with the Samarian woman by the well. Quite apart from dry investigations about age and authenticity, such eavesdropping into the personal exchanges between Jesus and his disciples, over a distance of two thousand years, gives us a priceless sense of being there when it happened, amongst real people dealing with real issues. No doubt Peter was the natural choice to lead the disciples after Jesus' death, but the claim that he held this right because he was the first one to whom the resurrected Jesus had revealed himself leaves a big question unanswered. What of Mary's claim to this distinction, since all accounts agree that it was she, not Peter, who had the first sighting of a resurrected Christ, although according to John she did not at first recognize him? It is this strange feature of all the disciples who saw the resurrected Jesus not immediately recognizing him that allows the author Philip Pullman, in his fictionalized biography, *The Good Man Jesus and the Scoundrel Christ*, to hypothesize that Jesus had a twin brother who looked almost, but not quite, identical to him, and whom the disciples had come across and mistook for their Lord.

It seems clear that Mary and Peter are the main characters in the close group around Jesus, along with the unnamed person, possibly Lazarus, possibly John, or even Mary herself, for whom Jesus had special love. There is a feeling that, while much is covered of Jesus' life in the gospels, a richer and more satisfying picture of the living Jesus and his companions has been denied to posterity. If not Jesus' wife, it is clear that Mary supersedes Jesus' mother as the most important female in the New Testament and appears to have been, at the very least, Jesus' closest companion.

There is a legend that says Salome was a rival to Mary in holding Jesus' affections. With no evidence other than a faint aroma of tittle-tattle from twenty centuries ago, we will not linger in this area. But a warm and vibrant picture begins to build up of a real group of people, living and traveling with their charismatic master. Within a few years, a new leader, Paul, would have seized the reins, driving the Christian movement to wider fields. But somehow we cannot imagine this fiery, intelligent man fitting comfortably into this close-knit group whose whole ethos was support for, love of, and undying loyalty to their living master.

And this gives us the occasion to take a look at the dynamic and controversial man who is usually regarded as the founder of the Christian religion.

Chapter Seventeen

The Gall of Paul

The great advantage of having the words and experiences of Jesus' disciples during the decades after the crucifixion expressed in writing by Paul and others is that we can hear what people felt about Jesus' message and role in a way not previously possible when the focus was unerringly on the main attraction, the hero of the story. The four gospels, the *Acts* and the *Epistles* do not altogether take us, *Rosencrantz and Guildenstern* style, into the wings and changing rooms of the theater where the play is being enacted, but they do provide us with an insight into what became of the company after the leading character unexpectedly expired mid-performance.

What we find from the post-Jesus records is a conviction, shared by the earliest followers of the preacher from Nazareth, those who had been baptized by Jesus himself or, after he had gone, by those he had empowered to do the same, that they are very different from other people. They have been given access to a new and far more profound reality, one that was truly life-changing. It is as if they had been shown a hidden door-way to an inner room of enormous dimensions – a room full of a richer feeling of life's presence – and saw the rest of humanity as still crowded in the vestibule with its noise and chatter, unaware, either blissfully or painfully, of the treasure within.

This was a transformation of a completely different character than the simple 'belief in Jesus' of future ages. They had no doubt that they had passed from darkness to light, from ignorance to knowledge, from 'death' to life, from bondage to liberation – all of these in some inner way. It was not a physical transformation, neither was it a metaphorical or allegorical one; for them it was real. However we explain it – Morton Smith's hypnotic experience supported by magical incantations, Elaine Pagel's Jungian self-searching combined with trance-like meditation, or the theory expressed in this book that it was indeed a real entering of an inner 'heaven' – they were utterly convinced it had really happened to them.

After he had gone, while acknowledging Jesus as their father figure who had brought about this new reality, he was no longer their living inspiration. Instead it was a new form of Jesus, a new incarnation, which they called the 'Holy Spirit' – the spirit of God – that inspired and energized them. In some way they were in touch with, if not actually embraced by, an inner source of life re-generation. Paul was clear that this is what he understood by the notion of a resurrected Jesus, a more real, more present Jesus even than the physical one who had so recently walked the earth.

For these followers the possible arrival of a returned Jesus was not the central plank of their joy; it was the absolute conviction that in the present moment they were inexorably tied to the life-giving power that they had been shown how to connect with. This was their new reality. Their teacher was still with them, but in a different way. As Luke Johnson puts it in his *New Testament: a Very Short Introduction*, "The first Christians claimed that they had been seized by a divine energy field and that the power they experienced came to them from the man who had been crucified under Pontius Pilate". Through the power of this 'Holy Spirit', "a man who in the recent past had died violently in Palestine was now in the present even more powerfully alive among his followers".

Presumably after a suitable period of shell-shocked mourning and re-evaluation, the renewed fervor seized the remaining disciples like a troop of soldiers whose heroic captain had been killed in action. They would make amends; they would do him proud. The work a cruel fate had prevented him from carrying out himself, they would now complete on his behalf. They would charge and take the hill. Possibly they felt some self-recrimination. The accounts of Jesus' last days are replete with the cowardice of his male – but not female – disciples, who slunk away rather than step forward in his defense. But for whatever reason, they now stood up with conviction and determination. Paul says five hundred saw the risen Christ at one time – a probable reference to an induction into the inner light of a large number of aspirants, either at one time or possibly over a few crowded days or weeks. And we have the courageous example of Stephen, the disciple who, so imbued with the joy of what he had experienced, threw caution to the wind in proclaiming it until he pushed his luck too far, becoming the first Christian martyr.

But the most influential of all these new Christians who came to Jesus in the aftermath of his execution was, of course, Paul, the Christian persecutor-in-chief, active on two fronts: as an organizer of some of the first Christian communities in areas outside of the Jewish homeland, and, mainly, as the first person to attempt to create a theological framework around his essential understanding that Jesus showed his disciples how, by 'dying', they could be reborn.

Paul's letters, particularly the ones to the new followers of 'the way' in Rome and Corinth, throw light on a feature that must have been prevalent, without necessarily causing any difficulties, in any small Christian community, be it Corinth or Capernaum, Thessalonica or Jerusalem; the presence within it of those who had been shown the inner experience and those who had not – who were presumably either waiting for the opportunity or quite content to accept the new faith at its face value, as a way of life pleasing to God and his recently deceased messenger.

The later endorsement of Paul as a founding father by the early Catholic church, as it began to gain an increasing degree of influence with the Roman authorities, is paradoxically at variance with the antagonism in the first generation of post-Jesus Christianity between Peter, head of the original disciples, based in Jerusalem, and Paul, controversially keeping away from them and instead preaching amongst the gentiles.

The late Michael Goulder argues persuasively that the dispute between them, the ferocity of which is only thinly disguised in the New Testament, is all about the Jerusalem-based followers feeling they must operate within the rules and parameters of the Jewish faith, and Paul's insistence that for the new non-Jewish – gentile – followers of Jesus, rules about kosher food and circumcision simply did not apply. At the same time – 1992 – that Goulder was writing his book on the subject in England, Elaine Pagels in America was producing her detailed analysis of Paul as seen by the Gnostics which gave a very different interpretation: that this was all about those who had been initiated and those who had not.

In the very first attempt by Paul to visit his new-found co-religionists, barely three years after the crucifixion and before he had enjoyed any real success in 'converting' the gentiles – his first trip, to the desert area to the east of Jordan, was an abysmal failure; the people there were not ready for the new religion – such topics would not be prominent. At the same time, neither man would have cause to dispute what was clear and obvious to both of them, that there were those with the gift and those without. Peter had actually walked with Jesus and was the addressee of many of those sayings referring to a mystery seen by only a few, while Paul had also received a baptism in light 'from Jesus', this time posthumously.

Their antagonism might have been a genuine difference about the future direction of the movement, Paul as a more sophisticated and educated man than the simple Galilean fisherman, and notwithstanding his early failure, seeing the opportunity for spreading the new faith amongst neighboring countries. Or it might well have been a case of pure alpha-male rivalry between these two giants of the early church. By the time Paul visited and spent time with the Jerusalem faction, Peter was the acknowledged leader. Paul would have had to submit to his authority or go his own way as something of a Christian maverick, which is, of course, what he did, with such far-reaching consequences.

We know much of Paul's work from his letters to Christian groupings around the Eastern Mediterranean and, eventually, in Rome itself. Had Peter been in charge of, and therefore needing to communicate with, far-flung communities, as did Paul, he also might have written letters to encourage them, to solve their problems and mediate in their disputes with his superior wisdom and experience. But in the Jerusalem-centric early church with its many Christian communities within a short traveling journey, letters would not be needed. These 'homeland communities' also had the immeasurable advantage over the more distant ones shepherded by Paul of having enjoyed a personal connection with Jesus, hearing his teachings from his own mouth and savoring his charismatic, even divine, presence, giving them a calmer, less unruly profile than Paul's. It is quite possible in any case, that Peter did not know how to write.

It has been speculated by some scholars that Jesus also wrote letters to his followers, which are lost to history. One can imagine what a sensation such a discovery would cause. They quote his knowledge of the scriptures, which would, one would think, have required reading skills, his middle-class upbringing as the son of a master-carpenter, and the one time Jesus appears to have written – when "he wrote with his finger on the ground" before proclaiming that he who is without sin should cast the first stone – as clues to the idea that he might have been a literate man who wrote letters. However, it is unlikely he would have done so, firstly for the same reason Peter would not – with such short distances correspondence was not required – and secondly because we cannot imagine Jesus needing to express his teachings by the written word. The immediacy of his message, his sense of urgency, his passion, his inner strength, all depict a character living in the moment, experiencing the inner presence of his father swirling around his mind, his soul and his consciousness. He was not a thinker, even though his intelligence is beyond doubt. He was a man of the living experience, the immediate present, and quite different from this busy-minded organizer Paul who, well after Jesus had left the playing field, picked up the ball and ran with it, calling for people to join him.

There is, of course, another good reason why Peter would have viewed the visiting Paul with great suspicion. He had, till recently, by his own admission, been the most implacable enemy of the followers of Jesus, persecuting them wherever he found them with a vicious dedication, "dragging off men and women and committing them to prison". He was on this very business when he was 'converted' on the road to Damascus – "breathing threats and murder against the disciples of the Lord". Not only this, but he had encouraged the mob in the stoning to death of the first Christian martyr, Stephen, who would undoubtedly have been dear to Peter and the Jerusalem Christians for his fearless avowing of Jesus' credentials. We do not know Stephen's age, but his combination of intense fervor and fearless promotion of the message of salvation leads to an inference that he was a young man, who was himself performing the initiation – "Stephen, full of grace and power, was doing great wonders and signs amongst the people" – and was able to enter into the heavenly experience even while being confronted by the angry crowd: "He was full of the Holy Spirit, and gazed into the kingdom". Luke, the author of the *Acts of the Apostles*, knew this because Stephen had called out moments before his death, presumably with eyes closed and a smile on his face, "Behold, I see the heavens opened". What emotions this terrible day must have roused in the hearts of Peter and the early Christian group we can easily imagine, for besides Stephen obviously being a much-loved, if hot-headed, younger brother, what happened to him demonstrated the fate that could well be in store for many of them.

Now one of the instigators of the mob that killed him had turned up with beaming loyalty to the cause, asking to be admitted to the inner circle, putting forth grandiose plans for taking the message further afield. It is not hard to imagine, even at a two thousand year distance, the kind of looks the apostles exchanged with each other as Paul made his case.

There is also to consider the far-fetched but persuasively argued theory of A.N. Wilson that Paul had been part of the group who came to arrest Jesus in the Garden of Gethsemane, and could well have been a witness to the crucifixion. Wilson bases his argument mainly on questioning what Paul actually meant when he later said he had seen Jesus while he was still alive, but if his theory were true we would expect such an important fact to have been mentioned in the detailed stories in the New Testament about Paul and his life. Wilson goes even further, suggesting that Paul was Malchus, the assistant of the High Priest who has his ear cut off by Peter and restored by Jesus. This explains to Wilson why Paul cryptically stated, in his letter to the Galatians, "I bear on my body the mark of Jesus". "If I had the chance to return in time and meet Paul," Wilson says darkly, "I should take a close look at his ears". This most outlandish of all Wilson's theories might, indeed, be true, but it would make the subsequent meeting between Paul and Peter even more dramatic and the disciples even less willing to accept into their bosom someone who must have been second only to Judas on their list of least desirable people. It is hard to believe such a fact would not have been mentioned in the *Acts of the Apostles* or in the highly autobiographical letters of Paul. Nevertheless, even without this spurious speculation, there was more than enough reason for the surviving apostles to treat the newcomer warily.

* * *

According to the Pauline (not a female name in this instance) specialist, Professor Jerome Murphy-O'Connor, the greatest service Paul did for the early church was to recognize that the death of Jesus was not a tragic accident, but part of a great plan. Unlike the early Jerusalem church led by Peter, which, embarrassed by the ignoble death of their master, "remained resolutely silent on how Jesus had died", Paul concluded that Jesus must have chosen to self-sacrifice himself for his cause, and although he had never hinted that his death would be required for the benefit of humanity, Paul, looking for a reason why he should have chosen death, alights on this, to him, obvious solution. To sacrifice himself was, in Paul's view, the ultimate act of altruism, a veritable manifestation of divine love in action. "It now becomes understandable why his death is the only event in Jesus' life to which Paul returns again and again", says Murphy-O'Connor. Jesus' death "became the key to the meaning of his life".

This dilemma goes, even today, to the very heart of Christian faith. We might ask, if Jesus' purpose was to reunite individuals with God, what would be achieved by actively seeking death in what could only be interpreted as a suicide, since the scenario implies he deliberately brought an avoidable situation upon himself? By what sequence of logic could it be demonstrated that Jesus's execution would cause the sins of every future generation to be 'forgiven', if, of course, they are first confessed to the representatives of the church? When Professor Sanders protests that to Jesus sin was not such a big issue, why would he want to die for this relatively unimportant cause? And did Paul really go through this process of deduction in making the crucifixion the centerpiece of his teachings, enabling a new religion to be created based on the salvation of humanity through Christ's death?

Of course, Jesus' demise was only one part of this equation, the other being his reappearance, proving that by believing in him death could be overcome. But we have already seen how vague and weak are the accounts of Jesus reappearing to his disciples after his crucifixion, and the examination that has gone into the Nag Hammadi library of Gnostic texts has revealed a new understanding of the letters of Paul which paints a very different picture and shows that he had a more sophisticated understanding of the situation than Professor Murphy-O'Connor would have us believe.

In the opinion of those scholars who agree that Jesus had two layers of followers – those who had received his initiation into the Kingdom of God and those who had not – these letters were coded in a simple way so that they could be easily understood by both levels at once. In the first sentence of his two main letters, to the Romans and the Corinthians, he introduces himself as Paul, who is 'called', and identifies himself as somebody talking to the 'many'. Additionally, he says that he is also writing to the group who are 'sanctified in Christ Jesus', the inner group who have been shown 'the mystery' – these are 'the chosen'.

This differentiation did not, of course, begin with Paul but with Jesus himself, who, as we have seen, makes no secret of the notion that some of his followers are parties to hidden teachings, the way to 'enter' the Kingdom of God, while others, a much larger proportion, it seems, have not yet had this privilege, if, indeed, they ever will: a key phrase here is Jesus' well-known aphorism, "Many are called but few are chosen". As Elaine Pagels says, the later Gnostic followers of Paul "perceive that this problem has characterized Christian communities from the first – from the time when the savior chose to initiate only a few into the secret meaning of his parables, and deliberately let them remain obscure to 'those outside' ".

By examining the writings of prominent Gnostics, Pagels has uncovered evidence that not only did Paul acknowledge and skillfully handle the twofold division within the Christian ranks, but that by the time the church-Gnostic battle was in full swing some two centuries later, an important element of it was a struggle for the soul of Paul. In this battle the Gnostics claimed him as one of their own, while the church, led by Irenaeus, attempted to show that the apostle had really taken their side of the argument and was favoring an organized church built on belief, liturgy and a priesthood, rather than the anarchic Christianity of the Gnostics.

The truth, we can now see, embraces both of these positions. The new Christian communities *did* comprise both kinds of members. But this was not the cause of their questions to Paul about matters of 'contention' which had arisen within the community; these were mainly moral issues such as whether rules about eating food that had been offered in sacrifice to pagan gods could now be ignored by the new Christians (it wasn't important, said the apostle), or whether a man could

sleep with his stepmother (not kosher, opined Paul).
He did not really want to have to give such rulings, but
was more concerned about what lay beneath these questions and disputes – the pride and sense of superiority
being shown by those who had been initiated over those
who had not. If they could live with a greater sense of
Christian love, then such attitudes would be left behind.
He extolled this virtue of love as the bedrock of the
faith, and in doing so gave expression to a passage that
has become one of the most quoted in the entire Bible.
Although full of references to the secret knowledge, he
makes it clear that one thing is above all:

> "Although I speak with the tongues of men and
> of angels, but have not love, I have become like
> a sounding brass or a clanging cymbal. And
> although I have the gift of prophesy, and under-
> stand the mystery and all knowledge, and have
> all faith, so that I could remove mountains, but
> have not love, I am nothing."

It is actually quite remarkable that Paul apparently
knew so little about the life of Jesus: everything to him
was about his crucifixion – he had an obsession about it,
says A.N. Wilson – and the possibility of 'dying in Christ'
to rise again into a new life. He was working of course
long before the gospels were written, but even if they
had been disseminated during his lifetime you get the
feeling they would not mean very much to Paul. Like the
later Gnostics he was not very interested in the actual

physical actions of Jesus, but only in the possibility of a baptism in the spirit he originated, enabling people to be 'saved' by having access to 'eternal life'. When he met the Jerusalem followers, the very people who had lived with the master, he did not insist on being told the stories they remembered, but on asking the central question, "Where do we go from here?"

We know Paul spent between six and nine months in Corinth, presumably teaching every day or night and gradually gathering a large but unruly group of dedicated converts. But what would he be teaching? We could imagine that were he to attend a church service from a future time he would sit bemused and bored by readings from 'lives of Jesus' and affirmations of faith. We have to assume that he taught the message of new life with the same passion and persuasiveness that we find in his letters, and capped it off by baptizing those who were ready – 'mature' was the phrase he used – for the life-changing moment of rebirth.

Paul does indeed provide some practical guidance, and acknowledges that in the widespread communities there were leaders in a loose sense, reliable, dedicated people who could keep the new Christian groupings together. They were either men or women, and were not in any way intermediaries between humans and God. The first letter to the Corinthians, who claim they belong to this or that intermediary, makes it quite clear that the relationship that matters is between the individual and God. Who had passed on the secret teachings – in many cases Paul himself – was of no importance. The rudimentary foundation of communal living Paul recommended would apply very well to the later Gnostic communities with their egalitarianism and lack of authority, which Iranaeus complained so much about. While Paul had an unparalleled zeal to proselytize the message of Jesus, and at the time of his probable execution in Rome was planning to strike out even further afield, this time to Spain, his letters show no sign that he intended a 'church' to grow up with a hierarchy of bishops, deacons and priests. It is easy to see how the later church organizers felt they were only building on Paul's preparatory work, but in the process waged a war on any talk of baptism in light or spirit, and the ridiculous notion that an intermediary was not needed to have a genuine connection with God.

By re-reading Paul's letters through the prism of the Nag Hammadi texts which refer to them, Elaine Pagels concludes: "We discover two conflicting images of Paul: on the one hand, the anti-gnostic Paul familiar from church tradition, and, on the other, the Gnostic Paul, teacher of wisdom to Gnostic initiates".

There has always been some question about Paul's division of his readers into two groups. He speaks at length about people who have been baptized in the spirit, or, in his original Greek, *pneuma* – some translations of his letters retain this terminology and call such people *pneumatics* – and those not so blessed, the physical followers, alternatively called 'naturals', 'psychics' or simply 'earthly'. Just as frequently, Paul divides his readers into the 'strong' and the 'weak', and less prevalently but still frequently, the 'wise' and the 'foolish' – foolish not being the insulting word it is today but indicating in a non-judgmental way those without inner wisdom, or *gnosis.*

Until the re-interpretation in the light of the new understanding about *gnosis* and inner baptism, these terms were thought to refer just to followers who were extremely dedicated – the strong – and those, the weak, who were looser in their attachment to the new teachings. Some Christian scholars still hold to the old tradition – Murphy-O'Connor himself called the wise 'Spirit People' and assumed this referred to those new Christians with greater wealth and education, who seemed to think they had a closer link with God than those who were not in their own social class. Their denial of the idea of a physical resurrection, he suggested, gave Paul a headache, for he appeared to be teaching such a doctrine to those who were not 'of the spirit'. We learn from the letters of Paul that some communities of followers of 'the way' did not even know of Jesus' arrest and execution, so to them the idea of a teaching with the death on the cross as a starting point was strange indeed.

Much of this new interpretation of Paul – new only in the sense of recently discovered, for it predates the attempts by orthodox Catholics to retrieve Paul for themselves – comes from the Gnostic writings of Valentinius, who lived around 140 C.E., or his followers, the Valentinians. Valentinius claimed to have received the secret knowledge, the *gnosis*, from Theudas who had received it from Paul, and called this lineage the true 'apostolic succession' from Jesus' teachings, not the one instituted in Rome by the Catholic church some three centuries later. It is from Valentinius that we learn about the two-fold teachings to be found in Paul's letters, which also include the information that Paul's frequent division of the early Christians into Jews and gentiles, or sometimes Jews and Greeks, was also a coded way of depicting those who had received the initiation into the spirit and those who had not, or had just been accepted into the fold by means of the symbolic baptism in water. It is a line of conjecture that explains Paul's otherwise mysterious quote about circumcision, which, he seems to imply, is not connected with the separation of a man from his foreskin:

> "He is not a Jew who is one outwardly, nor is circumcision what is outward in the flesh: he is a Jew who is one *inwardly*, and circumcision is of the heart, pneumatic, not literal."

In other words, Paul is using the word Jews to refer clandestinely to 'the chosen'. It is not the only New Testament account of this unusual comparison, for the first martyr Stephen had incensed his persecutors, led by Paul, with similar words: "You stiff-necked people, uncircumcised in heart and ears, you always resist the Holy Spirit".

Referring to those 'called' who are ready to be 'chosen', Paul says, "Among the mature we impart wisdom, although it is not a wisdom of this age or of the rulers of this age, which are doomed to pass away, but a secret and hidden wisdom of God". Paul's promise of what lies in store for those chosen for initiation is made quite clear, in terms similar to those used by Jesus: "What no eye has seen, nor ear heard, nor the heart of man imagines, God has prepared for those who love him". The *Gospel of Thomas*, the one book found at Nag Hammadi which is universally accepted as being of equal validity to the New Testament, quotes Jesus as saying, "I will give you what eye has not seen, what ear has not heard". During the initiation of people into the inner experience, this quotation from Jesus is used as part of the Gnostic oath of secrecy: "If you wish to know what eye has not seen and ear has not heard, and what has not entered the heart…swear that you will keep the secrets of the discipline as those that are to be kept in silence". From Jesus himself, to Paul, and through to the Gnostic teachers of the second and third century, and no doubt beyond, this simple phrase has a continuance which gives it great validity, but only in terms of its association with the revealing of the inner experience. At the same time, Jesus did not use it as a kind of oath from his converts; we know from the canonical gospels that he did not require any solemn vows when he was initiating, but just gave an instruction to 'tell no-one'. Unlike his later would-be successors, he did not need to rely on formulaic promises.

It was this distinction between the haves and the have-nots which became the crux of the great divide in the centuries ahead, defined by Gnostics as a battle between 'stagnant water' and 'living water'. By that time, however, the 'living water' was drying up, and would soon evaporate completely. It would be wrong to put the blame for this at the door of the church, no matter how hard it pursued those heretical Gnostics and confiscated or destroyed their writings. It was already disappearing of its own volition. The immediacy, the fire, the passion of Jesus' whirlwind assault around the Sea of Galilee, could not be sustained. His surviving disciples did spread the inner gift widely but in a Faustian pact it seems to have lost the depth and power of the original transmission, until, like a flood plain after years of drought, just a few shallow ponds remained. When long periods – years in many cases – of austerity and preparation were required, and solemn oaths intoned, before initiation, when the teachers themselves were becoming fewer and fewer as the generations passed, the world of living water, of 'pneumatic' experience, finally disappeared into dormancy.

Chapter Eighteen

The End of the Gnostics

It would be interesting to know how, over a period of three or four hundred years, Christianity moved from a situation where a great number, if not all, followers of 'the way' either had experienced or at least knew about the light and the initiation of Jesus, to one where this inner experience had been replaced almost completely by a religion based on doctrine, ritual, liturgy and ceremony. This is not to say the new Christianity was not underpinned by sincerity and deep commitment. The people who suffered dreadful torture and death rather than renounce their commitment to Jesus were absolutely convinced that the prize of eternal life would be theirs. They might not have had the experience, but they certainly had the faith.

If we set aside the often cruel and intolerant side of Christian authoritarianism over the next fifteen hundred years, the worship of Jesus and acceptance of his simple message of love, forgiveness, humility and charity, have provided comfort for countless millions of people, as the basic tenets of other religions have done for the people who came into *their* orbits. As Elaine Pagels said, if Gnosticism had won the day, Christianity might have died out altogether, for it needed the structure of the church and the backing of the civil authority to settle and prosper. It is almost impossible to imagine the history of Western Europe had Christianity not existed. What, if anything, would its religion today be? But if the Christianity that emerged from the developments of the first two or three centuries was one that even Christ himself would not recognize, would the alternatives be preferable?

The beginning of the decline of Jesus' teachings can be said to have started at the moment of his death, or, paradoxically, on the resurgence of proselytizing fervor once the shock of the crucifixion had worn off. One great and fundamental difference immediately became evident between what Jesus taught and what his disciples subsequently taught in his name. He was all about 'saving' individuals by showing them how to have the internal experience. As A.N. Wilson says, "Jesus... promised that the way to the Father was through individual rebirth, not by church membership". It was a very personal path. It was one-to-one. He was not dealing in communities. He wanted to save people; he did not want to save the world.

But his disciples did. Maybe there was some discussion about it – we cannot imagine Mary Magdalene being enthusiastic about the idea – but they quickly came to the conclusion that since his teachings opened up a new life for individuals, it was incumbent on them to make sure this message was widely spread. Once they felt they had the authority of Jesus by means of a rush of what they believed was the Holy Spirit they were on their way, proselytizing with great enthusiasm, not only bringing into the fold those who had been hoping for it before Jesus died – they were already 'in the pipeline' – but as many new people as wanted to join the evident fervor, including three thousand assorted bystanders who had apparently been attracted to where they were meeting by the sound of the 'mighty wind' of the Holy Spirit. Goodness knows what they told their spouses when they finally returned home. Paul was no better, moved by the power of his experience on the way to Damascus to pursue his own insanely energetic quest to start up Christian communities wherever it was possible, where the group was more important than the individual, requiring guidance and, where necessary, rules for living.

Jesus, we know, was not in the business of providing such guidelines. Moral instruction where necessary, yes, but again, mainly founded on the simple principle of' 'love one another', not a series of rules for communal living. How somebody who had received the inner experience got on with his or her friends, family or other social contacts was up to them, as long as Jesus and his teachings were their priority. But for Paul, the new Christians in a city had to stick together as if in an association, with rules, leaders, courts to settle disputes, punishment and even exclusion for misdemeanors. It was not what Jesus would have wanted. But, of course, alone amongst the very early apostles – and he only had this title because he gave it to himself – Paul had never been a disciple of the living Jesus, he never had that special loving closeness and loyalty to the real man. To him, no matter how dedicated he was to the work of spreading the news of Jesus' apparent resurrection, devotion was an ideal, a concept. He knew all about the sudden revealing of inner light and the sense of being enveloped in the presence of God – he had had such a powerful experience of it himself that it changed his life. But he did not go on from there to have the shared devotion to a living human being which we suggested in an earlier chapter was the real 'secret behind the secret', and why, in its absence, with nowhere to channel his newly-gained feelings of divine love, he had to pursue what he thought was his God-given role. That inner secret involved keeping the secret teaching secret, but when Paul received his transformation there was no Jesus there, perhaps wiping the mud from his hands, to look him in the eye and say, "Now make sure you tell no-one what has happened".

Without this restraint, of course, community coordinators would become, in time, spiritual leaders of their particular flock, with a new title – *episcoli*, or bishop – unashamedly comparing themselves to Christ and *their* flock to his, endowing themselves with the same powers and authority he had. By the second century, some were already claiming that their authority rested on 'apostolic succession', although the earliest examples were voted in democratically, or were the owners of the houses used for gatherings of the faithful, and there is no evidence of a direct hand-me-down link between the genuine apostles and the new bishops. Paul was the creator of many of the new Christian communities and while alive he either confirmed or appointed the community elders, the precursors of the *episcoli*. But he, unlike the eleven, had not been a Jesus-appointed apostle. It was important therefore for the later church to make sure Peter was portrayed as not only the senior disciple but also that he, not Paul, was the first bishop of Rome, although there is dubious evidence of the first – it appears from the gospels that the unnamed 'beloved disciple' (possibly Mary Magdalene) held that honor – and even less that he had even been in Rome, let alone held the leadership of the Christian community there. Ironically, it is the letter from Clement of Alexandria about the secret teaching of Jesus – anathema to the new church – that gives the clearest evidence that Peter had lived for a time, and then been put to death, in the imperial capital.

It was the literate, articulate Paul who, while a Gnostic himself, created the foundation of the future church, and, without the presence of the master as a touchstone and reference point, needed to support his work with a theoretical framework. In this he had no recourse other than his own powerful intellect, active mind and, as a former Pharisee, deep knowledge of Jewish beliefs and conventions. Fearlessly squeezing new wine into old bottles, Paul dredged up the great story of Adam and Eve and their exclusion from the Garden of Eden. In the kernel of the full philosophy later set out by a similar active-minded Christian theologian, Augustine, he set up a hypothesis that, since that sin, disobedience of God, was what had driven humanity from the Garden, the new baptism would remove it and draw one once again into God's loving bosom. In this interpretation Jesus was a 'second Adam', cancelling out the misdeed of the first.

It was in this resorting to the story of creation, and the first man's great sin, that Paul showed his true genius for straddling the two horses of the 'called' and the 'chosen'. To the uninitiated, his analogy appears to refer to the historical Adam of Jewish scripture, and the sin of eating from the tree of knowledge. But to the initiated he was clearly referring to the inner Garden of Eden, the paradise, that did not exist in historical time but intrinsically within each human heart – each 'Adam' and 'Eve' – at no matter what point in history they are alive. The 'sin' committed, in this interpretation, is not about sexual misdemeanor, but is the even more original one of losing the inner connection with the inner heaven, the 'garden' where God communes with humanity. It is *this* breakage that Jesus was able to repair by re-establishing the link with the place of eternal life within. The original sin was indeed referring to a loss of innocence but one more fundamental than being embarrassed about nakedness or libido. In this interpretation, when Jesus talked about the blind leading the blind he was not just conjuring up another interesting metaphor; he meant there really was a journey to be taken which required a 'seeing' guide: himself. And in this understanding, we can see why he so loved children; they were still close to the 'garden', they had no need for initiation, or 'baptism'. But gradually and inevitably, this umbilical cord becomes untethered, and the reconnection required.

This understanding of Paul's message about Adam and original sin would very easily be comprehended by the followers with *gnosis*, while those without would interpret it as a literal analogy, requiring a series of external procedures, including baptism, rituals and the mediation of a priest, to bring about reconciliation with the divine.

The double meaning of the Genesis story goes right to the heart of the divergence between the Gnostics and the later church. If the Kingdom of God is the same as the Garden of Eden and can be *returned* to, then we were there in the first place, which is not generally considered the church's teachings. Yet it is a returning that Jesus is offering, a true 'repentance' in its original meaning of going back, of returning to the source. This example of Paul cleverly addressing both constituencies of the early Christian following is in alignment with his separation of strong and weak, pneumatics and psychics, Jews and gentiles, wise and foolish, those who have had the inner path shown and those who can only depend on outward forms, to whom Paul says he speaks 'as a fool'.

But this re-reading of the story of creation does not equal the even greater two-horse feat Paul managed to pull off with his parallel interpretations of the story of the resurrection; a real physical miracle for the uninitiated, and a much more meaningful coming back to true life for those who had been gifted. On the one hand those who because they had received the baptism knew what resurrection really meant, and on the other the simple believers, granted membership of the fraternity on the understanding that for them resurrection will happen when Jesus himself returns and calls all his followers to join him in heaven.

One of the anomalies Paul had to address was that although he appeared to affirm that Jesus had risen again shortly after his crucifixion, he could not use this resurrection as the key to his theology, for Jesus had not come back in glory 'through the clouds' to lead his people to freedom and to raise all his loyal followers, dead or alive, into heavenly glory. So there was to be a second resurrection – a third coming – which would be taking place in the very near future, and which of course, neither Paul not any of the original apostles lived to witness. What happens, Paul was asked, to those who have died before the day of reckoning arrives? No problem, he replies, they will also be raised up out of their graves.

But surely their bodies will not be in a fit state? No, it will be alright, for they will be given 'celestial' bodies to begin their new life in heaven. Why, one might ask, were the old bodies preserved to be raised again if they were to be immediately abandoned? It is, by anyone's stretch of the imagination, very far from the simple and straightforward message of Jesus, and provides the lurid inspiration for multiple portrayals of bodies emerging at midnight from their graves, from the legend of Dracula to tales of zombies.

Jesus has acquired many personae. According to Geza Vermes, he is a charismatic Jewish teacher; to Morton Smith, he is a magician-hypnotist. The synoptic gospels portray him as the 'Son of God' who performed miraculous cures and talked mysteriously about the Kingdom of Heaven, while the Gnostic interpretation depicts a master who could lead people into an inner union with the father. John's gospel sees him as a full-blown Messiah who had existed from the beginning of time, while Paul defines him as a crucified icon whose earlier life on Earth had little value. But in none of these portrayals does Jesus speak of a mission to convert the world to his teachings after his death except in cases, usually on the occasions of his post-mortem visitations, which are widely accepted as later additions, created to justify these new directions. The heavy-handed quotes about future church development put into Jesus' mouth at the last supper in the fourth gospel are, says Wilson, 'obviously a literary creation', nothing like the more human Jesus with whom we are familiar from the earlier, synoptic gospels. "It is...inconceivably unlikely", he concludes, "that Jesus founded a church, or felt himself to have any mission to neighboring gentiles in Palestine, let alone to Italians or...ancient Britons." Such assertions, says the respected expert, Robert Price, dismissively, are 'post-game stuff'. Other pronouncements about the basic beliefs and practices of the early churches, which were not part of Jesus' teachings while alive but were given by him during his resurrected appearances, were also, concludes Maurice Casey, "written with the current needs of the Christian communities in mind".

To help hold these Christian communities together, Paul made much of the communal meal to which he gave the name the 'Lord's Supper', where followers of Jesus could come together and break bread as a 'eucharist', a Greek word meaning 'giving thanks', which later became the Christian mass, although Paul's account of the one that happened in Corinth sounds like it was something of a free-for-all, far away from the solemnly decorous ceremony of today's churches. The blessing of bread and wine at meals by a priest was already a tradition both in Judaism and at the ceremonial meals of the Essene sect, whose teachings are increasingly being accepted as having a close affinity with those of Jesus. This mass was gradually absorbed by the church as not only the senior Christian ritual but as the very mainstay of the faith, able to be withheld as a punishment for people the church wished to discipline or exclude.

Did the gospel writers build on this tradition by turning the 'Lord's Supper' into the 'Last Supper', and having Jesus speak those strange words about the bread being his body and the wine his blood, which allowed so much criticism of cannibalism to be thrown at the early Christians, words that John chose to omit from his account? More adventurous scholars have come to the conclusion that this concept of transubstantiation was the property of pre-existent pagan Middle Eastern sects such as the cult of Mithras, from which Christianity appears to have borrowed much of its symbology, and would have been very much out of character and at odds with the rest of his teachings for it to have come from Jesus himself. The words do form the essence of the assumption that although the disciples knew nothing of the terrible events that were to happen over the next few days, Jesus, with his unquestioned knowledge of the future, knew full well what was in store for him, and so needed to institute this little ceremony of remembrance for himself before departing to perform a nocturnal initiation in the Garden of Gethsemane.

But Jesus did not have powers of prediction. He did not know what was going to happen to him. The dinner drama was laden with symbolism – something Jesus had little truck with – and it is a case where Paul's own interpretation was probably influential on the gospel writers, who composed their accounts twenty years or so after his. Price also considers that this ritual with its pagan antecedents was "not initiated by Jesus," pointing out that the menu of early 'last supper' commemorations often varied from the bread and wine of the gospel accounts. Once again, he has an ally in the British historian Maurice Casey, who claims Paul needed the celebratory meal to help hold together his new troubled church in Corinth. "The notion that the Eucharist was instituted on this occasion (the last supper) was invented by St. Paul", he says, pointing out it was not Jesus' intention to leave his disciples "celebrating memorial meals".

Of much greater influence, since it promised access to God's Kingdom without having to have the baptism in the spirit, we find from the late first century instruction manual called the *Didache* that water baptism itself was again making an appearance as a Christian sacrament. Whether Paul or other apostles or apostolic successors reinstated this practice, not known since the time of John the Baptist, we cannot tell, but it is in line with the growth on the one hand of prototype Christian congregations with their developing liturgy and lines of authority, and the decline on the other of the availability of 'baptism in the spirit'.

The problem was already built into the decision to carry on Jesus' work without him, which would in time require an organization with leaders, powers to cement their authority, and sacraments and acts of worship to substitute for what the original master alone could do. Little wonder that the Gnostics mocked this parallel religion as a waterless canal. But mock as they may, it was the one that would, in due course, win the day.

However the passage of early Christian history unfolded, we are left with these two powerful positions, often intermingling and overlapping, with one eventually ready to take over from the Roman Empire itself as the dominant authority in both Western and Eastern Europe, and the other left, like the Cheshire cat, to fade away, with only the smile remaining, till that too becomes lost in the mists of time.

* * *

As the generations passed, the link to *gnosis* was weakening. Fewer candidates were presenting themselves as bearers of the flame in proportion to the large numbers around the Mediterranean world who were content to 'believe without seeing'. Elaine Pagels also points out that by the second century an inordinately long time, several years of preparation, together with stringent lifestyle requirements, were being stipulated before initiation took place, whereas with Jesus, initiations were often rapid affairs, reflecting the supreme power and 'authority' he carried compared to later generations of less certain revealers. A simple declaration of faith, and the symbolism of a water baptism as offered by the new Catholic church, with its promise of eternal life in the hereafter, was becoming a far more attractive option to people who very much liked what they were hearing about a God of love, compassion and forgiveness, and his messenger who visited earth relatively recently. It must have been revolutionary indeed compared to having to worship a plethora of deities including the emperor himself.

And so, alongside the informal gatherings in private homes of Gnostics, a growing organization was gradually coming into existence, with its own leaders and hierarchy. As early as twenty years after the crucifixion, Paul was appointing 'elders' to co-ordinate the activities of Christian communities, and within a hundred years these had become 'bishops', with spiritual as well as organizational authority. The biggest step came when one of the earliest of those bishops, Ignatius of Antioch, the Syrian city which was the home of the largest Christian community at the time, announced in a letter that he and his fellow-elders had the power to act on behalf of Christ in forgiving people's sins, as the gospel of John had the resurrected Jesus empowering his disciples to do during one of his last 'appearances' before rising into the clouds. In time, this 'power' had the potential to degenerate into an asking for forgiveness not for the major sin of detachment from the inner divine – not that this would require 'forgiveness' in any case – but for moral 'crimes', which has blanketed the later Catholic church in an atmosphere of trepidation in case one finally dies without having first confessed and been absolved.

The two branches of early Christian faith were not always mutually incompatible. Many of the new church leaders were themselves Gnostics – Paul himself is the outstanding example of someone who straddled both horses – and it seems certain that Clement of Alexandria, the keeper of Mark's secret gospel, was also one. Alexandria could be said to have become the home of Gnosticism, a fact acknowledged by the great Argentinian writer Luis Borges when he said if Alexandria rather than Rome had won the power struggle of those early centuries, we would have seen the emergence of a very different kind of church.

It could be said that that the purge of Gnostics and Gnosticism which was immediately embarked upon once the Emperor had finally agreed to adopt Christianity as the official religion of the Empire, as he believed the Christian god had given him victory in a crucial battle, was not the new church's finest hour. The groundwork had already been laid by the late second century bishop of Lyon, Irenaeus, and a close-knit group of fellow bishops – including the first bishop of Rome, Victor – who pursued a vigorous campaign against Gnostic teachings. He promoted the gospels of Matthew, Mark, Luke and John as the only ones to be included in the official collection, the 'book', or Bible, and waged a kind of 'dirty tricks' campaign such as withholding communion bread and wine from people who belonged to Gnostic groups. The Gnostics fought back, saying that the orthodox leaders "call themselves bishops and deacons as if they had received their authority from God". They…"want to command one another, outrivaling each other in their empty ambition and…lust for power". The highly regarded orthodox theologian, Tertullian – the one who held women in contempt – hit back, claiming the Gnostics are "frivolous, worldly, without seriousness, without authority, without discipline… they all participate equally, they listen equally, they pray equally – even pagans, if any happen to come. They also share the kiss of peace with all who come…all of them are arrogant, all offer you *gnosis*". He especially complains that the Gnostics see no distinction between men and women, who can teach, discuss and possibly even 'baptize' on an equal footing with men. This comment provides a clue about the role of women. While Jesus was alive it would have been foolish and dangerous to send women out to teach and 'baptize' on his behalf, as he did with the male apostles. But as the new beginnings developed into a 'movement' with some degree of organization, women could step forward and play a key role. Paul mentions women whom he trusts to represent him as community leaders – communities which would contain both initiated and uninitiated members – and under the protection of a group activity, they would also have been equally capable of teaching and baptizing – initiating – in the inner *gnosis*.

Elaine Pagels suggests that Tertullian's comments show what he considered to be essential in the Christian religion – distinctions between newcomers and experienced people, between women and men, between clergy and laity. It would come as no surprise to see that Tertullian also provided the missing link between Paul's portrayal of Jesus as the redeemer of Adam's original sin, and Augustine's development of this theory to exclude anyone not baptized from 'salvation', by dreaming up the pernicious thought that a child's soul is *inherited* from its parents, hence locking the new-born from its first moment into Adam's original transgression. The child is born sinful – something Diarmaid MacCulloch interprets with his customary restraint as a "pessimistic view of the human condition".

Irenaeus in turn complained that the Gnostics not only ignored the bishop's authority but employed powerful *theological* arguments to justify their position. He believed, states Pagels, that, "If God is one, then there can only be one true church, and only one representative of God in the community – the bishop". Irenaeus was particularly challenged by the insidious pervasiveness of the Gnostics. He wrote to Victor to warn him that there might even be secret Gnostics amongst his own priests and bishops, and he should root them out, his zeal setting a template for future purges.

We know from all the surviving documentation that the battle had been intense and the outcome by no means certain. Once over, it would have needed a leader of Churchill's – or maybe Jesus' – caliber to say 'in victory, magnanimity'. The surge of newly-empowered orthodoxy was the final cataclysmic destroyer of the Gnostic tradition – the meteor that eliminated the dinosaurs, the earthquake that ended the civilization of Atlantis. Throughout history, book burning has been considered a sign of a society fearful and unsure of itself. We can be grateful that the four evangelical gospels *were* selected to be included in the New Testament, for they at least tell us the story of Jesus, and put flesh and blood into an otherwise shadowy figure. Never mind that the reasoning at the time for this choice – that as there are four corners of the earth, and four points of the compass, so there can only be four gospels – does not seem to hold much validity today. But some other candidate texts from the *Apocrypha* – writings from the time which were excluded from the authorized Bible – or the Gnostic gospels, especially the highly regarded *Gospel of Thomas*, had at least as good a claim to be included as the ones selected, and more so in cases where, as with some of the letters attributed to Paul and others, true authorship is anonymous.

The bishop of Alexandria at the time of the Roman adoption of the Christian faith – and ironically since he was the successor of the tolerant 'big tent' rule of Clement – was the dogged dogmatist Athanasius, who sent a letter to his 'flock' instructing them to "cleanse the church of every defilement", with especial reference to Gnostic gospels, which were "filled with myths, empty and polluted". As Elaine Pagels surmises, "It is likely that one or more of the monks who heard his letter read at their monastery near the town of Nag Hammadi decided to defy Athanasius's order and removed more than fifty books from the monastery library, hid them in a jar to preserve them, and buried them near the cliff where Muhammad Ali would find them sixteen hundred years later".

There is hope, although not expectation, that one day a similar discovery might be made, for it is estimated that so much was written by both orthodox and Gnostic Christians in the first two hundred years after Jesus that only ten per cent has survived, or has been discovered. Most of the remainder, especially of the Gnostic variety, was either destroyed, lost, or in many cases thought too heretical to deserve copying once the original papyrus began to tear and crumble.

There is just one central piece that is missing – what is the *gnosis* itself? Again, as with the gospels, little is given away in the Gnostic texts, and again, the experts in the field have done their best to decipher the clues. Elaine Pagels concludes that at the heart of *gnosis* is an inner experience, but feels that this process is akin to the modern day self-searching of psychology, possibly backed by meditation practices leading to trance-like visions, or the kind of group ecstasy experienced sometimes today by charismatic Christian congregations. The Gnostic writings which talk about the process seem to suggest it incorporates a 'silent sound' leading to an 'out of the body' experience of a 'divine vision', creating a sense of ecstasy. The sound appears to be 'spoken in silence' but seems very much like a modern day mantra. Its purpose, like a mantra, is to eliminate the 'chaos in the mind' before the initiate eventually receives 'knowledge of the eternal light'.

Mantra meditation is well known for its ability to bring calmness to the mind by the repetition of a sound, whether it is the sacred Hindu word, *Om*, the name of a deity such as Rama or Krishna, or a specially chosen sentence or word. Scientific testing has demonstrated that the meaning of the word or sound is not important. It is the silent or spoken repetition that brings calmness to the mind. But we can be reasonably certain that this is not the experience Jesus was imparting in his baptism of the spirit, except as a possible starting point for something much more powerful. He stated clearly and repeatedly that he could show people the Kingdom of Heaven, the light within, something that is already there, awaiting a breakthrough that enables it to be seen. The initiation might have begun by a calming technique before the serious business of revelation unfolds, but this is not indicated in the way Jesus is reported to have baptized people.

Later, when the authority of the master was no longer available, the initiation process seemed more regulated, taking the candidate in stages to various levels of experience. One of the Nag Hammadi texts, the *Discourse on the Eighth and Ninth,* appears to describe something of a Gnostic initiation. Again, it involves silencing the mind by repeating a 'silent' mantra, possibly using a *zza zza* sound as described in a previous chapter – a sound which may well be associated with breathing – before a 'divine vision' arises which brings ecstatic feelings of happiness and self-knowledge. In this example the initiator and the initiate are going through their experience in unison. The description of this awareness gives an indication of the sheer power of the successful initiation. First of all, the teacher has the experience: "I see! I see indescribable depths. I see the mind that moves the soul! I see myself. I have found the power that is above all powers, the one that has no beginning. I have seen! Language is not able to reveal this. And I understand".

The initiate then goes into a similar ecstatic trance: "Father, what shall I say! We have received the light, and I myself see the same vision (as) you...I pray to the object of man's quest, this immortal discovery. I see myself. I have received power from thee, for thy love has reached us". The teacher, possibly because his pupil possessed the unusual gift of literacy, then tells the initiate to write down what had transpired, a rare occurrence which now, nearly two millennia later, has given us this unique insight.

If this is similar to the initiation Jesus himself gave while alive, then we can begin to understand much of what he said about the mystery, as well as the devotion and loyalty it seemed to kindle amongst his following. But what is noticeable from this and other accounts is the absence of acknowledgement of Jesus, the original master. The student says, "I have received power from thee", appearing to refer either to the teacher or to God himself. It is possible that a dedication to Jesus and 'the way' may well have formed part of the preliminary preparation for the initiation, but while he was alive, when he delegated power to his apostles to initiate on his behalf, they knew very well that any ability they had came from him, and they baptized 'in the name of Jesus'. He was given full credit. The intermediary had no importance other than as a channel for the flow of instruction and grace.

But now, a hundred or more years after the death of Jesus, it is possible this sense of ownership was becoming weaker. It was to counter this trend, suggests Pagels, that the newly forming church increasingly portrays Jesus as a divine being, part of the Holy Trinity itself, to be worshipped as equal to God, rather than a teacher for his own generation alone. It is easy to see how this parallel system, based on deification and worship of Jesus, together with the Pauline notion that by his death one's 'sin' had been expunged and entry to heaven guaranteed, could take the lead in the battle for hearts and minds over the more laid-back, intensely personal, form of Christianity practiced by the Gnostics.

We have seen how the experience can appear to those having it as being breathtakingly beautiful, but something else must be at play that triggered an emotional response of ecstasy, a sense that one is really in the holy place. We have not examined the possibility of sound, of a sense of music, accompanying the vision, but it seems possible that such an effect also forms part of the experience. An indescribable sense of the presence of an ethereal music certainly plays a part in some of the 'near death experiences' we alluded to in an earlier chapter. Otherwise we have something like a dance sequence in a silent movie, or a Christmas tableau without the accompaniment of festive music. In risking the criticism that an important, if not sacred, topic is being trivialized, we could say that in the Kingdom of Heaven quite a party is going on.

The difference between the Gnostics and the Catholic church could be said to be that while they both believe that access to this 'heaven' is the goal of human life, for the former it is available while still alive if only one learns how to 'die to the self', whilst the latter believes it will be waiting after death – and not immediately after death but at a future day of judgment. It is understandable that so many 'foolish' Christians would think there could be no better way of dying to the self than by being executed for one's faith, and this is why it is recorded that so many of them welcomed or even sought their own martyrdom. At the time of Irenaeus, at the end of the second century, this was happening to many of his fellow Christians, including his own predecessor and mentor, Pothinus. Little wonder he despised the Gnostics who appeared to follow Christ with all of the gain and none of the pain. To him the highest act of devotion, as it is today for many millions of Catholics, was to participate in the Eucharist, the mystical ritual that promised union with God. The Gnostics had the same aim, but were sure that such communion could only take place through an internal effort of self-discovery.

But if we could transport ourselves into a typical Christian group, meeting secretly in a Roman churchhouse, or in the catacombs, in the century or two after the death of Jesus, we might not have found the division between 'orthodox' and 'gnostic' so pronounced. That fragment of early Christian chanting which asked for a boy to be wrapped in linen and turned towards the sun, or light, seems to carry an uncanny echo of the mysterious light baptisms of the New Testament and the 'secret gospel', while obviously being part of a prototype Christian gathering, with its rituals and chanting. The two strands of belief in Jesus would still require quite some separating before one emerged triumphant.

Chapter Nineteen

Deciphering the Signs

For many of his 'patients', Jesus' 'cure' was a life-changing experience which bound them closely in devotion to their unique and charismatic master. Jesus was performing his 'great works' on a regular basis. Just a few are mentioned in the gospels, for, as John's gospel says: "Were every one to be written, the world itself could not contain the books that could be written". Yet it was not enough to guarantee undying loyalty. There was something compelling about the man himself that drew people to him – the recognition that here was a veritable touchstone of inner truth.

We do not expect Jesus to be the saintly image of a certain brand of religious iconography, a calm and serene person, blessing all and smiling benignly on them as he graciously glided past. But he did possess remarkable qualities. The great Biblical scholar and expert on St. Paul whom we have already quoted, Jerome Murphy-O'Connor, distils from a detailed study of the writings of Paul what the apostle had learned of the character of Jesus, presumably from his interaction with those, particularly Peter, who had lived with and knew him. He said that Jesus had two main characteristics. The first was his 'steadfastness': his 'total dedication to his mission'. We are told, "Jesus never wavered; his life was an enduring 'Yes' ". The second was a personality suffused with 'gentleness': "He did not please himself, but gave himself totally in love, kindness, and tenderness in his dealings with others". This equanimity and one-pointedness did not prevent him showing his emotions. Mark says of one confrontation with the Pharisees, "He looked round at them with anger, grieving at their hardness of heart", and several times in the gospels we come across Jesus' temper and no-nonsense language. By contrast, we also find him capable of being moved to tears, and the word 'love' is frequently on his lips. These indications give the impression of a warm and richly human personality.

We have clues that his initiation, either of individual people such as Lazarus, or the 'blind' men, or in groups of three, six, or even more – enough, maybe, to fill a room, a roof top or a piece of rough ground in the corner of a vineyard or olive orchard – involved more than just the revealing of an inner vision. It seems the people being 'baptized' were having their very consciousness turned inwards, leading to an awareness of a new dimension, an inner location of which they had previously been unaware, illuminated by a 'self-effulgent' light, but possibly also possessing other attributes. There are references in Hindu, Buddhist and Taoist scriptures to mystics going deeply within themselves, where besides seeing 'light', they might hear sounds resembling ethereal music. There is also the mystery of the many references by Jesus to an inner well where water is always available. To the Samaritan woman he promises to show her this well, after drinking from which she will "never thirst again", and at the last supper, he promises that, "whoever believes in me...out of his heart will flow rivers of living water". We need to observe, however, that apart from these pronouncements by Jesus himself, and as opposed to the seeing of inner light, we do not find further references to anyone actually experiencing 'living water'.

Nevertheless, a poem from one of the Hindu *sants* – holy men – named Brahmanand, proclaims:

> "Without earth, there stands a palace in which shines a brilliant light.
> A blind man sees it again and again, and is filled with bliss.
> In the midst of heaven is the well of divine nectar
> A lame man climbs up without a ladder and drinks.
> The living man dies and then lives again.
> Without food, he is vital and strong."

Brahmanand, although living later than the medieval *sants*, presumably had little knowledge of the existence of the teacher from Nazareth, but his eloquent verse bears comparison with the promises of Jesus, and makes it clear that the physical deficiencies he, and presumably Jesus, were talking about were metaphors for spiritual blocks.

We can now look again at what Jesus said to the disciples of the imprisoned John asking on his behalf if he really was the one 'who is to come'. Jesus didn't answer directly but said, "Go and tell John what you hear and see: the blind receive their sight and the lame walk, lepers are cleansed and the deaf hear, and the dead are raised up". Jesus speaks so frequently of the inner light, which enables the recipient to 'see everything' or to know the mystery of the Kingdom of Heaven, that there is little room to doubt this is what he was doing in giving sight to the blind men in the examples provided in the gospels. But this new understanding also applies to his claim that he was able to 'cure the lame'; he was enabling the spiritually lame to have spiritual legs, to journey to the heart of life within themselves. And from here it is an easy leap to see that all his curing miracles were in fact metaphors for the initiation that was his central work.

At the heart of the answer Jesus wanted to be delivered back to the imprisoned John was the most significant of miracles, so important that the whole Christian faith depends on it – the resurrection of the dead. It is surprising that in the thousands of words written, the hundreds of books authored, the many hours of thought, research and contemplation spent on the resurrection miracles, the connection between them and Jesus' frequent assertions that he is in the business of bringing the spiritually dead back to spiritual life has not gained wider acceptance. Most Buddhist scholars, for example, looking over their garden fence at the world of Christianity, would automatically take this to be the case.

Although Jesus performs, according to John, countless 'great works', and gives sight to 'many', he only 'resurrects' three dead people. Two of these are included in only one gospel, raising the question of why the others did not record such important occurrences; after all, healing is one thing, reviving the dead is an altogether different level of 'miracle'. Only one of the stories is clear that a raising of the dead took place: Luke's account of Jesus bringing back to life the deceased son of the widow of Nain. But this is the one resurrection miracle which is regarded as least genuine, since it is based closely on a similar miracle performed by the prophet Elijah in the Book of Kings. It appears that Luke replicated it in his gospel to demonstrate the equality of the two men. In the other two cases, there is a question concerning whether the people resurrected are really dead. "She is not dead, she is sleeping," Jesus said of the ruler of the synagogue's daughter. "Lazarus has fallen asleep, but I go to waken him," he said of the brother of his close friends, Mary and Martha.

Far from being an invention to prove Jesus' divinity, as Professor Casey and others assert, we can now see that the raising up to new life simply referred to the reconnection to the inner source Jesus was offering. By claiming to raise the dead, he evidently is not meaning people are actually physically deceased, but detached from the inner experience; they are suffering from a form of spiritual death. This is serious enough: someone without the connection, says Jesus, a 'foolish man', meaning one without the inner wisdom, will find his house in danger of being washed away in a storm as opposed to the 'wise' who build their home on a foundation of rock. It is a theme that reappears in various scriptures, and in the Dead Sea Scrolls we find a similar analogy: for someone whose eyes "have gazed on that which is eternal... the way of (their) steps is over stout rock which nothing can shake". This appears to be the true meaning of the resurrection miracle. Jesus is indicating that there is a source of life within, a heaven, which can be seen or even 'entered'. It is this 'heaven-entering', with its possible equivalence to Buddha's 'stream-entering', that is at the heart of both Jesus' teachings and his miraculous healings.

We know that 'heaven' is not just a vague reference to a divine location one might gain access to after death, but a present reality within ourselves, from the story of Jesus' 'curing' of the 'deaf' man described in Mark. As was his usual practice, he took him "aside from the crowd privately, he put his fingers into his ears...and looking up to heaven...said 'Be opened' ". The implication is that it was the ears themselves which Jesus commanded to be opened, and the man could suddenly hear again. But in line with the theory that the curing of physical disabilities is an analogy for the process of inner revival, we sense that here, behind the camouflage, is yet another baptism of the spirit, and a closing of the outer senses is a prerequisite to the inner experience. The subject is taken to a private place, and the 'curing' ends with Jesus' usual admonition, 'Tell no one'. We also have this command from Jesus, 'Be opened'. The question of how the writer knows this, as the 'cure' is being performed privately, is not addressed. But we do know that elsewhere in the New Testament the verb 'open' is generally reserved for heaven itself; at his baptism by John, Jesus 'saw the heavens opening', and before his death by stoning, Stephen called out, "I see the heavens opened". The term 'heaven' in these cases evidently refers to an inner vision, not in a metaphorical sense but as a tangible reality. In this particular healing, when Jesus 'looked up', it is unlikely he was looking to the sky for inspiration. The 'cure' could just as easily have taken place indoors, or under a tent. It is far more credible that some kind of inner 'looking up' was at play as Jesus taught the 'deaf' man how to access the inner experience.

The evidence is therefore in place to suggest that the people Jesus initiated, 'cured', baptized, or 'awakened' – the deaf, the blind, the mute, the lame, the deceased, the possessed – were shown the secret of how to enter the inner location. But it was not something that just anybody could receive. It would only work if you had faith, the word that originally meant trust. You had to trust that Jesus could do it. If you did, if you really had the trust, you were ready for it. Jesus many times used his key word, faith. Have faith and you will be healed. Have faith and you will be made whole. To the woman hemorrhaging who touched his cloak, he said, simply, "Your faith has made you well". And what brings the faith out, what raises the trust to such a level that it is complete, is what is found on the other side of the scales – the *authority* that Jesus personifies.

What struck people was the sense of divine power, the authority that he exuded: "They were astonished at his teaching, for he taught them as one having authority…". "They were all amazed, saying, 'What is this? A new teaching with authority!' " He clearly possessed a sense of inner power, of personal charisma, that people found astounding. In Jesus a master had arrived on the scene with the authority to represent the divine, someone with the ability to connect people to the life-source within themselves. His teachings soared above relatively petty concerns such as the forgiveness of sins. They were about life, about feeling the embrace of the inner divine, about the opening of the inner door: "I came that they may have life and have it abundantly", he stated. Without undertaking this quest, people are in some way wasting a golden opportunity. The parable of the talents was obviously not about making productive financial investments. Jesus makes it quite clear that the accumulation of possessions and wealth – and by extension status and reputation – is not remotely in the equation. It was about investing in the opportunity life provides for clearing the debris blocking the wellspring within, letting that new surge of life flow freely around the rooms of one's existence, creating an exhilarating sense of being alive, and, in Jesus' words, 'entering the joy of the master'. As Luke Johnson in his memorable phrase expressed it, Jesus' disciples were experiencing a 'divine energy field', not as a 'hope for the future but…a present reality'. Rather than awaiting a future return of Jesus to complete an unfinished task, they were instead filled with an immense joy at what he had brought into their lives. A lid had been removed from a resplendent source of inner power.

It seems as if the barrier that might stop someone experiencing that abundance of life, however sincere they might be, is the sense of self, or, to use the psychological term, the ego. Humility is a quality Jesus regards highly. The more the sense of self diminishes, it appears, the more room is made available for the inner experience to manifest itself. It was the Christian mystic Meister Eckhart in the thirteenth century who coined the aphorism, "Where God is, I am not. Where I am, God is not". It is a question Buddhists wrangle with – if the self has to disappear in order to enter *nirvana*, what is it that is left to experience the joy of merging? Isn't this tantamount to death? Or, in the Hindu tradition, what happens to the drop when it remerges with its source, the ocean? And if one comes to accept that, in fact, nothing is lost but something much greater is gained, how does one overcome 'self' in order to have the promise of life eternal? It seems it has to be by a process of genuine and heartfelt surrender. But this is hard to achieve on one's own. Like jumping in an attempt to defy gravity, it may be that it cannot be accomplished unless someone is actually assisting, someone who has already, metaphorically speaking, conquered gravity.

Could it instead be just an ideal to which one can direct one's devotion? History is littered with examples of the most courageous people who have given their lives for something they believed in – including, or course, countless Christians. But if that were possible, then there would be no need for the appearance of someone like Jesus. It seems that when we are talking of the opening of the inner door, the human catalyst needed to be present to make it happen, to drive the process. Without him, as we have seen in our survey of Gnosticism, the experience gradually weakens and fades, eventually disappearing altogether.

* * *

What are we to make of this phrase, the Kingdom of Heaven, so common that it has become part of everyday language, and its wider context, "Repent, for the Kingdom of Heaven is at hand" – 'repent' now usually being understood to mean 'turn within' and 'at hand' an archaic term meaning 'immediately available'? This could be said to be the one phrase that sums up Jesus' entire teachings, rather than Karen Armstrong's belief that the golden rule – do unto others as you would like to be done unto yourself – is the foundation of all religions. This was Jesus' reply to being asked, "How should we behave with each other?" not, "What is the great message you have for humanity?"

Some at the time appeared to think it referred to an earthly kingdom, ruled by Jesus, or more precisely a returned Jesus, at some time in the near future. Alternatively, the belief grew after the crucifixion that Jesus would return for the purpose of bringing about the 'Day of Judgment', fulfilling John's prediction that he would allow the 'chosen' to accompany him back to heaven, something this book argues he accomplished very effectively during his own lifetime. Michael Goulder says: "Jesus' return was expected in the lifetime of some of his hearers, or in rough terms before (the year) 90: that would be when the Kingdom of God would begin". Casey's opinion is that it would have been expected within a year or two of his first ascension, certainly before Paul's sudden conversion. When it did not happen within the lifetime of Jesus' surviving disciples, its imminence has become the mainstay of Christian belief over the centuries. Most recently, the re-establishment of Israel as a Jewish state in 1948 is believed by many evangelical Christians to be the precursor of Jesus' return. It might, however, be speculated that if Jesus had told his disciples that his promised return would not actually take place as early as they might be hoping, but would happen two thousand years or more into the future, he would have met with some degree of mystified consternation.

Whatever its meaning, the Kingdom of Heaven is possibly the most familiar term in the entire world of Christianity. It is a most striking phrase, strong, powerful, calling to mind high city walls and an imperious gate, held in place by great military might. It was translated in the sixteenth century during the great age of kingdoms, when such was indeed the normal state of government, unlike the time of Jesus, when many Greek city states were republics, Rome had recently moved from being a republic to an empire, and the Kingdom of Judea, ruled by Herod, was under Roman authority. Commentators have pointed out that the original word used in the Bible is not as strident or well-defined as the later 'kingdoms' of medieval Europe. Like the equivalent phrase found in the ancient Vedic scripture, the *Upanishads* – the 'region of heaven' – it was more nebulous, with a softer meaning, not ruled by a king on a throne but a benign presence: God. If Jesus had called it something else, such as land of immortality, home of the divine, or source of life, these terms would possibly carry more of a flavor of what he meant. But they would not have the powerful impact 'Kingdom of Heaven' brings to the table. Westerners prefer Jesus' strong, direct language to the softer, more ethereal tones of Eastern scriptures.

In the final gospel, that of John, Jesus had been transformed from a personable, practical teacher, striding around the Galilee area with his band of cohorts, into a messianic figure, the 'Logos', the living 'word', who was already in heaven before his birth and was sent down by God to save humanity. But his repeated use of the phrase 'eternal life' tells us something about the Kingdom of Heaven which is not revealed in the other gospels: that heaven is eternal, it lasts forever, an idea feeding into the concept that life will continue in future time, even after death. The phrase might, alternatively, mean no more than that in heaven there is a complete absence of time, no future, no past, just an eternal present, a concept impossible for the human mind to comprehend.

But the phrase again brings us across this central part of Jesus' teachings; that there is more to life than we imagine – there is an inner 'home' from where life springs. Jesus was offering to show people the bridge and lead them across while they have the capacity to take advantage of his offer. That was why he seemed to have such a sense of urgency: seeking the kingdom needed to be treated as a life priority. And quite possibly it was not a case of all or nothing, as implied by the city wall image evoked by the phrase Kingdom of Heaven. The inner journey might not have a fixed destination but might be a gradual process, a merging with something which by its nature is never-ending: the infinity of the *abba*. Either way, an immediate 'entry' or a gradual moving towards 'perfection', taking people there appears to have been Jesus' view of his role.

A final observation on the cures of Jesus might cover the question of their purpose in his mission. Some scholars, such as Graham Stanton, the author of *The Gospels and Jesus*, grapple with the strangeness of Jesus' cures, and raise the question of why he even performed them. What had this to do with his work of teaching people how to approach the Kingdom of Heaven? They were not in themselves acts of God. The ability to instantaneously cure serious illnesses, blindness and so forth would have Jesus accepted, as other miracle-cure workers were around that time, as just that, a miraculous cure worker, not as the 'Son of God', messenger of God, or Messianic Christ-figure. Why should he be doing this kind of relatively minor work? In the absence of any clear answer it has been postulated that it was to draw attention to himself, to gather the crowds to whom he could then begin to teach. This belies his frequent admonition to those he has cured not to tell anyone about it. The answer to which this line of inquiry has to revert is that they were there simply as a sign that God's kingdom was about to arrive. If this were the case, Jesus would again be relying on miracles to prove the truth of his message, as if the message alone were not enough. If, however, these cures were themselves initiations – admission procedures to the inner realm – the conundrum of their purpose is solved. They were themselves a turning within to the path of engagement with the inner divine.

Chapter Twenty

Other Sightings

We have so far established certain factual reference points about Jesus of Nazareth. He lived. He had specific teachings which attracted undying loyalty and at the same time hateful enmity. Included in his teachings was a promise to show people the Kingdom of God, or Kingdom of Heaven – names that are not used in the fourth gospel, that of John, which used the term 'eternal life'. And he possibly initiated those who 'had faith' into an experience of this place 'within themselves'. They in turn appeared to witness some form of inner illumination in which they claimed to 'see everything', or have a vision of 'heaven', together with a sense of a divine presence and a degree of joyful euphoria.

We should not be too surprised at this because such 'inner light' experiences can also be found in the writings of other spiritual or religious traditions. They are not usually associated with a named master, but one who is clearly given credit for such an initiation is Krishna, the ancient 'living god' of the Hindus, whose exploits were written about in the 5th century B.C.E. Legends about him abound, that he was blue-skinned as a result of a near drowning as a child at the hands of a Herod-like mortal enemy, and that in early life he was a playful youth who had a following of milkmaids – *gopis* – whose relationship with him is one of intense personal love. When he leaves them they pine for his return. Their lives revolve entirely around him, far more so, it seems than those of Jesus' disciples, and one of them, Radha, became his consort. Westerners will be familiar with the temples in many major cities sometimes called Radha Krishna temples with statues of the couple, Krishna of course carrying his ubiquitous flute, together on an altar. If indeed, as has been indicated by the discovery of the Gnostic gospels, Jesus was in a similar relationship with Mary Magdalene, and if the evidence of it had not been omitted from the canonical gospels, we could speculate that, as with Krishna and Radha, churches today might have comparable images and statuary, and Mary would take the place of Jesus' mother as his female counterpart.

That speculation aside, the most famous tale about Krishna concerns the time he was a chariot driver for his master, Prince Arjuna, in a great battle, where, about to commence fighting, Arjuna has doubts about the impending contest, as it would pit him against many of his own relatives. Krishna gives him a long lecture about the nature of the divine, defining it, in a similar way to the New Testament references, as immortal light, and then proceeds to reveal to him a vision of this manifestation of God. Afterwards, he says: "By my grace and my wondrous power I have shown to you this form supreme made of light, which is the infinite, the all".

It is clearly not the same language as Jesus would use, but if it were paraphrased into the style of speech of Jesus, it would be exactly the same kind of claim he was making to those privileged to know the mystery of the Kingdom of Heaven. He goes on to say, again, as Jesus could have done: "Thou hast seen now face to face my form divine so hard to see".

He also adds that austerities and other practices cannot bring this enlightenment, but only belief, faith and love: "Only by love can men see me and know me. He who loves me in truth comes unto me". Like Jesus, he claims to personify an inner vision of the glory of the supreme being, warning, "Thou can never see me with these mortal eyes but I will give thee divine sight". In turn Arjuna, in envisioning the inner light, comments that he sees 'countless visions'. "If the light of a thousand suns suddenly arose in the sky," he says, "that splendor might be compared to the radiance of the supreme spirit".

Much like the description already quoted of a Gnostic initiation, Arjuna speaks excitedly about what he can see: "the splendor of an infinite beauty which illumines the whole universe". "I see thee as fire, as the sun, blinding, incomprehensible." He also finds it at some point during the procedure quite frightening, and Krishna has to reassure him that all is well. At the end of the initiation, Arjuna expresses sentiments that we have already seen were used in various forms by the colleagues of Jesus and the companions of Buddha. The one they thought was their friend, their equal, they are now ready to call their master, their teacher, their 'Lord': "If in careless presumption, or even in friendliness, I called you 'my friend', this I did unconscious of thy greatness".

Unlike Jesus, nothing is really verifiable about his Hindu near namesake. No rich, real, living personality shines through the accounts of his life as emerges from the stories of Jesus. It is not surprising given the distant time in which he lived, and it is quite possible that his whole life was allegorical. But this vivid vignette of his revealing of a divine vision to Arjuna is worth recounting for its similarity to what was happening five hundred years later a thousand miles to the west.

Many sacred writings of various religious traditions, and usually from the mystical end of such traditions, refer to this phenomenon of inner light. Elsewhere we have quoted a fragment from the Taoist scripture (*Tao* coincidentally meaning 'the way'), *The Secret of the Golden Flower*, which is replete with references to the inner light which it variously describes as shining like a golden flower, a city of jade, or a "silver moon standing in the middle of heaven". And in its reference to a lover with a white eye waiting in paradise for those who have 'died' for their faith, we can see a similar theme in the *Koran.*

The idea of an inner experience as the essence of Jesus' teachings has formed a central belief of Christian mystics down the centuries. The thirteenth century book, *The Cloud of Unknowing*, speaks of the need to break through that inner barrier if one wants to encounter the divine. The sixteenth century Spanish mystic, St Teresa of Avila, had a clear sense of the value of internal experience: "The magnificent refuge is within. Shatter the darkness that shrouds the doorway. Put away your incense and forget your incantations. Close your eyes and follow your breath to the still place that leads you home". George Fox, the founder of the Quaker movement, also had an understanding of the 'Inner Light', his Society of Friends garnering admiration and respect for its attempt to follow Jesus' inner meaning.

Going back to ancient religions, we again find powerful references to a light within, shown by a 'master'. Without revealing the name of the teacher it refers to, the morbidly titled *Tibetan Book of the Dead* is in no doubt about what he is able to give:

> "The master puts you face to face with the clear light within which you then experience as reality...everywhere is eternal, unlimited light,

315

> unobstructed light, matchless light, the king of blazing light, the light of all purity, the light of joy, the light of insight, a light surpassing sun and moon...the light of the heart of heaven."

We are advised to ask the deity not to "withhold your compassion but to lead us on the path of radiant light", where we will encounter a light "vibrant, resplendent and naturally beautiful...a radiant and vast mandala".

This obscure book became famous when it was adopted by the 'psychedelic' professor, Timothy Leary, as a talisman, and was then adapted for the well-known Beatles' song, *Tomorrow Never Knows*, with its urging to "turn off your mind, relax and float downstream". Leary and Lennon were not misguided in thinking the book, while representing instructions and words of calming guidance to the spirit of a deceased person as it journeyed from one life to another, was in fact describing an inner journey into an inner world undertaken by someone still very much alive. If you could arrive at "true awareness while still alive", the book advises, your later journey would become so much easier. Again, the "path of the clear light" will lead one who has "intense faith" towards the "light of the pure lands", which "are not anywhere else but abide within your own heart". To encounter this "mandala of clear brilliance" is like "meeting an old friend".

Many mystical Buddhist sutras mention an inner luminosity. A typical one, apparently addressing someone about to undergo initiation, says: "There will appear to you, swifter than lightning, the luminous splendor of the colorless light...recognize that the boundless light of this true reality is your own true self, and you shall be saved". Muslim scriptures also refer to the light: "Allah guides to his light whom he will", and, "The light of Allah may be compared to a niche that enshrines a lamp, a lamp within a crystal of star-like brilliance".

The ancient Indian scripture, the *Upanishads*, carries similar references: "There is a bridge between time and eternity. Neither day nor night cross that bridge, nor old age nor death, nor sorrow...to one who goes over that bridge, the night becomes unto day, because in the world of the spirit there is an everlasting light". And: "Behold the light eternal...behold the eternal one who is radiance beyond space, the everlasting soul never born".

In surprisingly modern language, the *Upanishads* says that God "is known in the ecstasy of an awakening that opens the door to life eternal. The sacred knowledge is not attained by reasoning, but it can be given by a true teacher". In a further reference to an inner light, we read, "Always dwelling within all beings is the *atman*, a little flame in the heart. Know this pure immortal light". And in a passage which might cast some light on the central theme of this book – that Jesus' 'cures'

were metaphors for his teaching of the mysteries of the
Kingdom of Heaven – it tells us: "When the bridge has
been crossed, the eyes of the blind can see, the wounds
of the wounded are healed, and the sick man becomes
whole from his sickness". The equally ancient *Vedas*,
written several centuries before Jesus, advise: "Let our
silent meditation be on the glorious light of God".

We have alluded to Moses and his confrontation
with God in the form of a burning bush. The Jewish
mystical work, the *Book of Splendor*, takes this reference
further, saying, "Moses stood in the white supernatural
light which does not consume and does not diminish".
Staying for a moment with the Old Testament prophets,
it should not be a surprise to find Isaiah telling us that
when the Lord comes to reveal the "Way of Holiness",
the lame shall leap like deer, the deaf will hear, a stream
will break forth in the desert, and, of course, "the eyes of
the blind shall be opened".

It cannot be a coincidence that so many references
to this inner experience occur with such similarity of
terminology in the scriptures and sacred writings of so
many religious traditions, with the often anonymous
writer clearly being unaware of the others. Even in
translation we have to acknowledge the sincerity of the
language used. The notion of Jesus having performed
initiations is without doubt the major breakthrough of
the past forty years or so in Christian investigation, but
even those most convinced by the evidence speak in

terms of Jesus being a magician or hypnotist, concepts that undermine or even deny the unfathomable devotion he instilled in his disciples, and their conviction that he was genuinely a representative of God.

It is only when we step back from our obsession with the Christian phenomenon, and maybe the underlying discomfort some may feel in relinquishing the idea that Jesus was unique, and take account of these other traditions, these other 'sightings' of the divine vision, that we are forced to recognize that they stand alongside Christian writings in both the experience they describe and the sincerity and quiet authority with which they do so. We are forced to consider the strong possibility that others taught the same ability to experience the 'eternal life' as Jesus. Either that, or there have been an awful lot of magicians and hypnotists walking the planet at various times.

We dip into these other examples of an inner light experience to draw comparisons with the references in the New Testament to a similar phenomenon, and to acknowledge the thought that Jesus' teachings might have parallels in other traditions. They indicate that in revealing the light Jesus was not unique. But Jesus' message is not just about revealing the light; it covers a depth and wealth of insight and teachings on behalf of his *abba* that give enormous joy and comfort to people who might have no interest in taking an inner journey to a place of light. As Jesus said, only a few privileged ones need to have access to that experience. For the rest, the love, the forgiveness, the tenderness, the comfort and the grace of that father is enough. It is in giving out these two arms of divine instruction that the greatness, not to say uniqueness, of Jesus can be said to lie.

Chapter Twenty-One

The Game of the Name

One unexplained aspect of the Jesus story as recounted in the New Testament is the multiplicity of references to the 'Word of God'. We are told by John that Jesus was 'the Word made flesh'. Luke says that the original disciples were 'eye-witnesses of the Word'. Yet, when asked by his disciples what the parable of the sower meant, Jesus said, the 'seed' is the 'word', which the sower – himself – is planting, thus providing another definition of the 'word'; that which Jesus is disseminating.

A further common interpretation, which is widely promoted by evangelical Christians, is the idea that the Word of God refers to the Bible itself. This is the least plausible explanation. Not only was there no comprehension at the time that a book called the Bible – *the book* – might some two centuries hence be compiled from various accounts of Jesus and his disciples, but the different definitions of the 'Word', not least that it is indestructible and will last forever, clearly cannot apply to a book, however sacred it might be.

Geza Vermes points out that in the early Christian writings there was some interchanging of the two terms, 'word' and 'spirit', but separation between them gradually became the adopted position of the Catholic church, the 'word' being either Jesus or the Bible and the 'Holy Spirit' a disembodied force that can visit people and change their lives. For a further thought on the subject we can return to our controversial friend, Professor Morton Smith, who suggests that the powerful experience of the 'spirit' amongst Jesus' disciples in the aftermath of the crucifixion was taken unquestionably by them as the power, the presence of Jesus, returning to them in another form. But gradually, as the decades passed and the strength of his memory became less intense, a separation took place, and the 'Holy Spirit' assumed an identity of its own, away from Jesus: "He (Jesus) was the cause of the spirit seizing people, but...as time went on and personal memories of Jesus faded, the spirit became an independent personality...it pushed Jesus aside".

It is an area of Biblical research where history has to give way to theology. Neither discipline is completely comfortable with this mystery of the third member of the Holy Trinity, and we are left with an intriguing but unexplained symbiosis between these indefinable words – *pneuma, spirit, logos, ruah* (the Hebrew word for wind or spirit) and *word* itself – which in various ways are used to mean a vibrant essence of life. We have already suggested that if modern English had been the native language of the Mediterranean countries in Jesus' time, we would find all these various names for 'spirit', including 'spirit' itself, uniformly translated by the word, 'breath'. 'Holy Spirit' would simply have become 'the breath of God'.

Was John to blame for promoting this confusion when he began his gospel, "In the beginning was the Word, and the Word was with God and the Word was God," going on to say, "All things were made through him"? Looking at a literal translation of the phrase, "The Word was God", in the original Greek text, we see that this is not quite what was said. The Word was not God but was '*in his essence* God'. No discernable difference maybe, but it allows for the possibility of a separate force joined at the hip, or in essence, with something called God. As the next sentence says, "He was in the beginning with God," not presumably at a point in the distant past, but at the commencement of existence. If God does exist, of course, then he, she or it, or a word not yet invented that covers all three, had no commencement; time – beginnings, endings, past or future – presumably have no meaning in the Kingdom of Heaven. Dimensions of time and space are qualities of the physical world. But again, 'with God' is not quite the same as 'God'.

If we try to look at this through a modern mind-set, we might come to the conclusion that the term 'word' referred to what we might call 'God in action'. If there *is* a God, a divine being, living in, and inseparable from,

his 'heaven' and possessing the kind of ineffable qualities he (she or it) has been accredited with, and on the
other hand there is the material world we ourselves live
in and with which we are so familiar, it follows that there
should be an interface between them. Such terms are
impossible to imagine of course and we can only deal
with them by means of metaphor. The author of *Genesis*
did this very effectively, by suggesting the 'Word' was a
movement on the surface of God, the first stirring of
action by the divine. The movement is referred to in all
scriptures, including the Bible, as God 'breathing' life
into his creation.

By extraordinary coincidence, the latest scientific
research is exploring a similar theory, which postulates
that, far from there being 'nothing' before the 'Big
Bang', there was a form of undetectable, 'latent', energy
which burst into life at the moment of 'creation'. It is
a theory which, for all its newness to the physicists and
mathematicians, fits in with the Biblical metaphors, and
which is not at all alien to Hindu and Taoist ideas on
the subject, where an 'unmanifest' universe is constantly
interacting in an eternal dance with the 'manifest'. A
tidy explanation of this view can be found in the autobiography of the scion of a wealthy Californian family
who became an Indian sadhu, Ram Peri: "Before the
world comes into existence," he says, "there is only
consciousness. Matter exists in potential, and is indis-
tinguishable from consciousness...I visualized this as a
calm, mirror-like lake, reflecting only itself...the cosmic

mind. A single drop, the primordial desire for identity, and therefore separation, hits the mirror lake, causing ripples, and in this way identity, or ego, appears as movement, distinguishing it from its background stillness". The 'other' is therefore born, "is excited into manifestation", and the world comes into being.

It is strange language to the western mind, and does not mention the divine qualities we most admire, the love, the compassion – possibly the central reason for this eternal dance – for every part of 'his' creation, but in its own way it tells the same story as *Genesis*, with the caveat that it is happening in a timeless present. We might ask why God should possess a 'primordial desire for separation' in the first place, and might conclude that, if his nature *is* an ineffable and incomprehensibly profound 'love', built into 'his' nature must be the urge to manifest this, to give it form and definition by 'creating' an entity which 'he' can love and which can love 'him' in return.

Whichever description is most palatable to us, there appears to be an axis, a portal, a junction between 'God' and 'his' creation, and this joining is, possibly, the very point at which a meeting of minds, 'his' and 'ours', takes place, perhaps the *pivot* of Buddhist terminology or the *hinge* of some Christian thinking. Contemplation and prayer are well-tried attempts to approach this point within our own souls. But when we look at the words used in the Bible for this point of fusion, of which 'word' is one, they seem to indicate that this primordial connection point between human and divine is in some way associated not with our psyche but with our breath. It is as if the breath is a mid-point, a channel, linking the inner and the outer – the silent inner permanent and the noisy outer temporary.

Jesus, in his altercation on rebirth with the Pharisee Nicodemus, reported in John's gospel, comes close to explaining this notion of a bridge:

> "What is born of flesh is flesh, and what is born of spirit is spirit. It is necessary for you to be born again. The breath blows where it wishes and you hear its sound, (alternatively translated as 'The spirit breathes where he desires and you hear his voice'), but you do not know from where it comes and where it goes."

When Jesus claims that he has revealed the 'word', it is possible he means that as part of his teaching of the mystery of the Kingdom of Heaven the recipient of his initiation is shown this interface, this doorway. In some way not explained Jesus brings it to life, or maybe guides the recipient in an unknown manner into the very heart of the breath so that it is experienced as the bellows of existence, a rich flow of energy that gives us the life with which we are familiar, and in which the presence of the 'father' can be felt.

This is not a theory unique to Jesus. Statues of Krishna, the Hindu 'Christ', invariably show him holding a flute, which is considered a metaphor for the human body, into which he breathes life so that it can come alive and make music. The reference is reminiscent of Jesus lamenting that "We played the flute for you, and you did not dance". From this doorway of breath, looking inward rather than outward, it might be possible that the initiate begins to see, dimly at first but gradually coming into focus, the inner light we have seen mentioned so often, and garners a sense of the presence of the 'divine within'.

* * *

When we hear of the disciples, in the period of disorientation and uncertainty after the crucifixion, being comforted by the 'Holy Spirit' which surrounded them like a 'mighty wind', it could not have been an external wind that swirled around them, for our *sine qua non* thesis is that no such unexplained or miraculous events actually took place during, or after, the life of Jesus. But it might have been some powerful experience of this internal 'Holy Spirit', literally the *pneuma* or 'breath of God'. Maybe they had already received this baptism in the spirit or breath while Jesus was still alive, but it is hardly ever mentioned, possibly because it was not clearly understood or experienced by the recipients. It could, however, be that once he had died this experience really came into its own – not a miraculous visitation by Jesus but, as Luke Johnson suggested, a powerful inner surge of energy and recognition.

Yet we are still left with a mystifying conundrum. What is it about the *pneuma*, the breath, which makes it the elephant in the living room, the most frequently mentioned entity in the entire New Testament, yet one we gloss over or wrap in a miraculous 'this is not to be explained' cloak? If we accept that this is where the enigma lies, we can perceive what Jesus was alluding to when, in the *Gospel of Thomas*, he tells his disciples, "If they ask you, 'What is the sign of the father in you?' say to them, 'It is a movement and a rest' " – a phrase that seems clearly to refer to that simple continuum of life, the breath.

Ruach, the Hebrew word used in the Old Testament for 'spirit', means literally a wind, a movement of air. Winds, movements of air, we can say we understand. Like every movement in the universe, it can be traced to simple causes. The 'Big Bang' is usually considered the only action to have taken place that does not appear to have a cause – hence its focus as the center of the current debate about the existence of God. At the opposite end of the spectrum, however, is an equally mysterious movement that likewise has no apparent explanation: the continuous transportation of a few cubic inches of a gaseous compound from one location to another. Medicine will have its explanation for the phenomenon of breath which suffices, just as in their way, theories are being developed that 'before' the 'Big Bang' there was not nothing but some kind of pre-existent energy. But we can nevertheless be intrigued by the Hindu theory of *prana*, not breath but the power that draws it in and out, and the possibility that this is indeed the interaction between stillness and action, latent and potent, 'God' and the created world.

It is a theory expounded in the ancient, 6th century B.C.E., Chinese scripture, the *Tao Tze Ching*, written by the endearing master Lao Tzu who, legend has it, wishing to spend his final days in the wilderness outside the city, was only given permission to pass though the city gate if he first wrote down his teachings. Claiming that the entity which is the 'originator of heaven' has no name, but when named becomes the 'mother of all things' – a concept that makes some sense of the mysterious line in the Gnostic scripture about the 'female' essence, "I am the utterance of my name" – the author then suggests, "May not the space between heaven and earth be compared to a bellows? It empties, yet loses not its power; it is moved again, and sends forth the air once more". The title of the book famously means the *Way to Heaven* and suggests that this path is indeed an internal one. Its advice to 'close the doors' in order to 'understand everything', and to 'close the windows' if one wants to witness the light of heaven, is understood to refer to the senses and a process of meditation. "Whoever uses well his light, reverting to its source so bright, will from his body ward all blight", as a Victorian translation by James Legge expresses it in the style of his time. Again such language brings to mind Jesus closing the eyes – presumably 'windows' – of the blind so they can 'see everything'.

Many modern teachers of meditation, yoga, or inner calm, advise a period of focusing on the breath to induce a sense of inner serenity. Could Jesus, in his 'baptism in the spirit', in some way be placing the initiate's focus, his or her profoundly guided attention, into an inner place where he or she felt primordially wrapped into this powerful movement of breath, so that it did indeed manifest to them as a 'mighty wind' carrying with it an aroma of the inner divine, the 'I am' of the creator, the *abba* of Jesus?

It might indeed be that during some intensely moving and grief-filled gathering, or gatherings, after the death of Jesus, the apostles, after addressing each other in emotional terms of loyalty, love and mutual encouragement, together entered a profound state of inner experience, calling for the master to give them some sign of his living presence. And even given the tendency for a story to grow over decades of re-telling into something far greater than the original event, something happened – possibly the "amazing event...of equal force" to the resurrection identified by Shusaku Endo. It might be that they went into their individual 'wind tunnels', experiencing this 'mighty wind' but more importantly having a clear revelation of the inner source from which the wind was emanating, and identifying it as the master who so recently left them, now conjoined with the father he once claimed to be one with. "There he is," they might have concurred in the depth of this experience, "there is our living master. He has transcended death; he is here, pouring his love, pouring his life, into us".

Whatever happened to the disciples on these occasions explains their new optimism, their determination to complete Jesus' work on his behalf. They find themselves able to speak in a new language, the language of prophecy, not in the more usual meaning of predicting the future, but the language in which only Jesus had previously been able to communicate. Not the superficiality of a different physical language, for the arrangement of vowels and consonants into the myriad languages of the earth is of little importance in this context; those early apostles had translators when needed, just as modern international communicators have. The new language would have meant being able to speak on behalf of God, or of their recently transformed master Jesus, from direct understanding of their message.

* * *

This time and landscape, the unknown years after Jesus' death, is explored by the scholar we have already quoted in this book, the former Benedictine monk and professor, Luke Johnson, who says that to the disciples in this post-crucifixion period, "Jesus is not less alive, but *more* alive". They had "claims that were out of all proportion to their position in the world". As a small defeated band, he asks, what right had they to "claim cosmic significance", and that "the world belonged to them"? But instead of despairing, they seemed to rejoice.

And in a reversion of the usual Christian position which has them desperately waiting for a returned Messiah to usher in the Kingdom of Heaven on earth, "the terms used for this transition – salvation, redemption and reconciliation – all point not to hope for the future but to a present reality. Believers existed now in a state of peace, reconciliation and joy. They had a disposition of faith and hope and love, and such dispositions had behavioral expression".

Johnson continues, "Most spectacularly some could speak in tongues, others could prophesy, reveal or heal" – all metaphors, as we have seen, for speaking of and passing on the inner revelation, the initiation, taught to them by Jesus. "The basis of all these specific claims is the general one of having received a power from God that enabled everything else", says Johnson, "The central symbol for this power is the Holy Spirit...In short the first Christians claimed that they had been seized by a divine energy field ...The first believers saw themselves, as a result of their divine empowerment, to be in a new creation and part of a new humanity". And finally, "A man who in the recent past had died violently was now in the present even more powerfully alive among his followers".

If this was the case, they would not have had an expectation of Jesus returning, the non-fulfillment of which hope led to their successors writing down their stories for future generations. To them the truth was not so complicated. Jesus had lived amongst them, showing how to know God and live a life of joy and love one would expect such *gnosis* to bring. Modern scholars have expressed amazement at the speed at which the new faith spread, to the point where it took over the entire known world. This could not have occurred if it were merely a matter of ideas, a new set of concepts about the divine. It could only have happened in such a contagious way by a spread of fervor, an emotional communication underpinned by the reality of an actual experience, and the certainty of being raised up into God's loving embrace.

As a postscript, there is room for considering that the idea of the 'name' of God could also be an alternative phrase for *word, spirit* or *logos*: not *God, Dios, Dieu,* or *Gott,* but rather an 'unpronounceable' subtle movement of energy from the source to its perimeter; from the heart of one side of the membrane to suffuse the entirety of the other. The Old Testament joins all the other scriptures of the world's religions in praising the 'name of God'. In the New Testament, only Jesus seems to acknowledge the sanctity of this name, making it the key statement in *The Lord's Prayer* – "Hallowed be thy name" – but he was clearly not referring to the familiar word for papa, *abba*. As the *Tao Tze Ching* says: "The name that can be spoken is not the true name. The word that can be pronounced is not the true word". When we read the countless references in the Old Testament and other scriptures such as the Sikh holy book, the *Guru Granth Sahib*, to the inordinate holiness of the 'name of God', there has to be a suspicion that these do not refer to an arrangement of letters which varies in every language, but something silent yet spoken in stillness, 'a vibration of energy at the heart of one's being', as one expert on Sikhism has expressed it. The Jewish name for God is known as the *Tetragrammaton*, the four consonant sound too sacred in its original state for it to be spoken, but which is represented by the syllables, *Yah* and *Weh*, forming the word Yahweh, themselves sounds which resemble a silent prayer of the breath.

Moses, of course, standing before the burning bush, had the temerity to ask God his name, and received the reply, "Tell them that *I Am*". In spite of this message from the horse's mouth, 'I Am' is not used as the name of God, which is rather a pity given that Jesus' name in Aramaic – Yeshuah – provides a highly appropriate response to the divine self-naming. But the 'I am' interpretation has a rival, which says the origin of *Yahweh* is the word *Hawah*, which means 'the one who blows, then falls', giving rise to the theory that this ancient Hebrew god was in some way associated with storms. It could equally convincingly be suggested that, like the *pneuma*, the 'Holy Spirit', of the New Testament, the word is again referring to the life-giving process of breathing – the "movement and a rest" of Thomas' gospel. Likewise, the bush that burned but was not consumed has given rise to many explanations, not least the tradition that comes down from the Eastern orthodox Christian church, which understands Moses was witnessing God's "uncreated energy, manifested as light".

All this is informed speculation. Nevertheless, the suspicion remains that there is more to this question of the 'Word of God' and the 'Holy Name' than first seems to be the case, and far more to the works of Jesus than a brief period of preaching and a litany of seemingly miraculous cures.

Chapter Twenty-Two

Essene Essentials

No new look at the life of Jesus is complete without visiting that sensational find of the mid-twentieth century, the Dead Sea Scrolls. After all, here was a community of people – a Jewish sect which had rejected orthodox Judaism in favor of a more 'Christian'-like approach to God – previously completely unknown, yet living not only at the time of Jesus but right on his doorstep, with enough similarities in outlook and beliefs to justify strong suspicions of some connection between the two.

Almost by an uncanny coincidence, the two greatest discoveries of ancient texts ever made – the Gnostic Gospels and the Dead Sea Scrolls – came at an almost identical moment and in a spookily similar fashion. Just as the Nag Hammadi Library – as the cache of books found in Northern Egypt in 1945 is called – was discovered by a peasant digging for fertilizer and striking with his spade a large buried urn which he at first feared might contain a genie, an evil spirit, the Dead Sea Scrolls, discovered only two years later close by the Dead Sea in Israel, were found by a Bedouin goatherd idly tossing stones into a cave and hearing a 'clink' sound which led to him scrambling into the cavity to see if anything of value might be hidden there.

In one way, the Dead Sea discovery was vastly more significant than that of the Gnostic texts of Nag Hammadi; they were several hundred years older. Whereas the Nag Hammadi codices – pages of papyrus joined together to form a primitive precursor to a book – were, scholars now agree, fourth century C.E. copies of second century C.E. manuscripts, the Dead Sea Scrolls are not only original in their own right but have been carbon-dated to up to 200 B.C.E. – *before* the common era: around five hundred years earlier than the Nag Hammadi find. And while the Nag Hammadi documents were no more than revealing references to various contemporaries of Jesus, most famously Mary Magdalene, Gnostic initiations, and a series of previously unknown quotations from Jesus, mainly found in the *Gospel of Thomas*, the Dead Sea Scrolls contain copies of Old Testament books a thousand years older than any previously discovered – together with records of a sect that might have played a part in the very origins of Christianity.

Beside this claim to pre-eminence on the part of the scrolls, copious as the Nag Hammadi find was, the discoveries from not one but many caves near the Dead Sea contain vastly more material: large numbers of scrolls alongside thousands of fragments, plus shards of inscribed pottery, and a couple of scrolls of copper, so tightly rolled and rusted that they could not at first be opened.

There was also a great divergence in their post-discovery history. While the Gnostic texts of Nag Hammadi had a horrendous birth passage into the light of day, with haggling, losses and countless apparent cases of 'Murphy's Law' delaying their recognition and the opportunity to study them properly, the discovery of the Dead Sea Scrolls was immediately hailed as the archaeological find of the century, with newspaper headlines around the world.

But then the positions reversed. Once in the hands of scholars, the 'Gnostic gospels', as the Nag Hammadi find came to be known, were pored over and studied with relatively great speed, translations and commentaries beginning to appear within a few years. On the other hand, the course of the interpretation of the Dead Sea Scrolls, after a lively start, soon fell into a morass of scholarly jealousy, political interference, Arab-Israeli wars, and strong suspicions that the experts in charge, Catholic priests, were being inordinately possessive and secretive in case anything damaging to their church became public, so that their contents have only come to light little by little, and only fully in the first decade of the twenty-first century – some sixty years after their discovery.

The ruined settlement, named Qumran, which is so close to the caves where the scrolls were stored that the nearest is just a few yards away, was originally thought to have no connection with them, until as an afterthought on the part of the manager of the project, a French monk called Roland de Vaux, excavations were begun which produced strong but not conclusive evidence that the two were related. De Vaux pronounced that the settlement had been the chief 'monastery' of the Jewish sect called the Essenes, and the scrolls had been its library, hastily hidden in the nearby caves when imminent destruction by advancing Roman troops threatened.

It appeared the Essenes had been a Jewish sect from up to two centuries before Jesus, who retreated from society into their monastic base around the year 150 B.C.E. to pursue a more personal and internal communion with God than practiced by society at large, and to escape from a degree of persecution which might have claimed the life of their leader, a mysterious character called the Teacher of Righteousness. In 66 C.E. the famous Jewish rebellion against the Romans, which was to lead to their Diaspora around the Mediterranean world, began, inviting the inevitable response, culminating in the destruction of the Great Temple in Jerusalem where Jesus is said to have turned over the tables of the moneylenders and observed the widow putting her 'mite' into the collection box. Archaeological evidence shows that the sect's buildings were destroyed by burning and its inhabitants killed around this time, and the fact that the contemporary historian Josephus, whom we rely on for the only believable references to the life of Jesus outside the Bible, tells us the Romans destroyed the area in 68 C.E., enables us to be fairly certain that this was the actual year of the community's demise.

The cherished hope of Christian scholars, that the Dead Sea Scrolls would cast important new light on Jesus of Nazareth and early Christianity, turned out, after a false start, to be a mirage. They contain no apparent references to Jesus, early Christianity, or John the Baptist. But if Christian scholars have been disappointed that no connection has been made between their man and the Essene sect, Jewish historians have been well-rewarded, for almost half the documents found were copies of books of the Old Testament over a thousand years older than what was already available, which dated from the eleventh century C.E. They offered a fascinating insight into how the existing texts differed from the earlier versions, and on occasion provided fuller accounts of Biblical incidents.

A version of *Genesis* found amongst the scrolls, which has the first sixteen pages – including the stories of the Creation, the Garden of Eden and the Great Flood – missing, provides an extraordinary example, covering the account of the great Jewish forefather, Abraham, and his wife Sarah, journeying to Egypt at a time of famine in their own land. Abraham tells her that because of her great beauty she will be taken from him and he will be killed, so she should pose as his sister, and he might be spared. According to the *Genesis* we are familiar with, Abraham said to Sarah: "You are a woman beautiful in appearance. When the Egyptians see you they will say, 'She is his wife', and they will kill me and let you live... (so) say you are my sister...so that my life might be spared for your sake", a judgment which proved astute, as this is exactly what happened. But where *Genesis* says only that, "When the princes of the Pharaoh saw her, they praised her to the Pharaoh", the version found amongst the Dead Sea Scrolls has Pharaoh's men waxing lyrical about her to him in a passage of poetic quality:

> "...how beautiful her face.
> How... fine is the hair of her head and how lovely are her eyes.
> How desirable is her nose and all the radiance of her countenance...
> How fair are her breasts and how beautiful all their whiteness.
> How pleasing are her arms and how perfect her hands.
> ...how fair are her palms and how long and slender are her fingers.
> How comely are her feet and how perfect her thighs.
> No virginal bride led into the marriage chamber is prettier than she.

She is fairer than all other women – truly her beauty is greater than theirs.
Yet together with all this grace goes abundant wisdom
So that whatever she does is perfect."

Although recounting words allegedly spoken two thousand years *before* the Common Era, the text sounds like a poem comparable to Antony's paean to Cleopatra, and certainly would not be helpful to initiates of the Essene cult trying to practice their compulsory celibacy, who might find their quiet meditations disturbed by such sensual images. We can agree with Geza Vermes, who translated many of the Scrolls, when he laments that the missing pages at the start of this early version of *Genesis* leave "ample space for a detailed retelling of the account of the creation...Adam and Eve...etc.," which, of course, is lost to us.

But the remainder of the discovered texts is not so fascinating, dealing for the most part with the daily routine and rituals of a large community of maybe two or three hundred people residing at this headquarters by the Dead Sea. If indeed they *were* the Essenes, we know from Josephus's description that up to two or three thousand lived in surrounding cities and towns – a gate in Old Jerusalem was called the Essene Gate, indicating that one of these groups lived in this neighborhood, which was adjacent to the early Christian community.

Amongst the thousand or so neatly buried skeletons in the Qumran cemetery, less than five were of women or children, suggesting the community there was for males only, following rules of celibacy as specified in the scrolls. But these rules also cover married life, giving prescribed times when intercourse was permitted and dictating that it should only take place for purposes of procreation.

It appears then that family members of the sect lived not in the confines of the main settlement but in communities within cities and towns at large. The nearest we would be able to find to this arrangement might be in the Hindu and Buddhist traditions, where celibate monks would live together in an ashram, with 'householder' members of the group living in the community at large, supporting the monks with money, food and *seva* – service – and turning up on holy days to feast, dance, worship and celebrate.

Various archaeologists have formed different opinions about the site. Some thought it might have been a fort, for it contains a stone tower, which could have been for defensive purposes. Others have suggested it might have been a summer seaside retreat for wealthy Jewish people – amongst the massive finds of simple crockery is some expensive and beautiful ware. Or a staging post for travelers and merchants, who would use its many baths for relaxation rather then ritual purification, a theory that has given the settlement the nickname, the 'Qumran Hilton'.

The most unusual scrolls found in the caves of Qumran were made not like the others, of parchment, papyrus or animal hide – vellum – but of copper, and which proved impossible to open. Enter one of the most colorful characters in the long drawn-out saga of the Dead Sea Scrolls and Biblical research, John Allegro of Manchester University, England, who was one of the original team of experts deciphering the cache and had already expressed frustration at the inordinate delays of the overall directors of the project.

Allegro prevailed with colleagues at the Manchester College of Science and Technology to invent a tool that would carefully cut the scrolls in slices which could then be worked upon. It was found that the writing in them was inscribed, not written – a painstaking process – and that their contents were no less than a series of detailed instructions on where the sect had buried or hidden its treasure. It was time for our friend to change professions and become a treasure hunter in the mold of Indiana Jones, a hunt that yielded, in the end, nothing. Although the veracity of the information contained in the scrolls was widely accepted – for why else should such an exotic and expensively made object have been created if it were no more than a hoax? – the instructions given were, after two thousand years, impossible to follow.

Not to be daunted, Allegro then suggested that the elder of the settlement, the 'Teacher of Righteousness', had been crucified and could consequently be identified as Jesus, which his colleagues were very quick to point out did not match the evidence, as this particular text appeared, although not with complete certainty, to date from a century or more *before* Jesus. But the scrolls also talk of someone, 'The Wicked Priest', who deviated from the master's teachings, causing much confusion. Some experts have nodded towards the possibility of these two characters being Jesus on the one hand, and Paul on the other. This would fit well with the thesis of *this* book, that the inner truth that Jesus taught was at variance with the tenets of the religion started and developed by Paul. But we cannot call it as supporting evidence, firstly because the master, if he *is* the Teacher of Righteousness, appears to have lived well before Jesus, and secondly because the 'Wicked Priest' is described in the scrolls as someone who, although starting out as a personage 'called by the name of truth', then 'ruled over Israel', became proud in his heart and 'took the wealth of the peoples'. This was clearly not our cheerful, ascetic and slightly crazed proselytizer, Paul. Nobody has yet considered the equally implausible theory that the Teacher of Righteousness might have been John the Baptist himself, who certainly possessed the qualities and self-confidence to be the leader of a sect, and Jesus the renegade who, without the authority of the Essene superiors, began disseminating his teachings after John's execution.

It was not, of course, the last the academic world, or indeed the world at large, was to hear of this mercurial and unorthodox scholar, John Allegro. He was shortly, as his contemporaries unkindly expressed it, to 'commit academic suicide' by publishing his controversial book, *The Sacred Mushroom and the Cross*, which attempted to demonstrate that Christianity was a new version of an ancient fertility cult which relied on the hallucinatory experience of the 'psychedelic fungus' – claiming, no less, that 'Jesus' was a code word for the plant, and the symbol of the cross was based on the shape of a mushroom. The theory caused a sensation when the book was published in 1970 but was roundly condemned by his fellow experts, not because of its intrinsic improbability but because his conclusions, based on much surmise and mistranslation, did not fit the linguistic evidence upon which he was relying.

Nowhere in the scrolls can the name 'Essenes', which means holy ones, or healers – a title which should cause people interested in Jesus to prick up their ears – be found. This is not surprising as it was outsiders who called them by this title; they called themselves *Sons of God*, or *Sons of Light*, a discovery which caused some interest, for these names were until now associated only with Christianity. The Essenes also called their particular path 'the way', as did the early followers of Jesus. The scrolls tell us that the sect appears to have rejected conventional Judaism as being too reliant on ritual and dogma in favor of a much more personal relationship with God based on 'divine revelation' and 'inner

experience'. They were required to share their possessions and treat people with kindness and love.

New recruits would progress gradually, over a three-
year period, to a point where they were initiated into
full membership, a kind of priestly class. And it is in this
section of the manuscripts that we come across items
of possible relevance to those looking for connections
with the teachings of Jesus of Nazareth. In particular, we
find references to an internal experience reminiscent
of that which appears to be given by Jesus, imparting in
some way the mystery of the Kingdom of Heaven. For
example, the aim of the sect – its 'mission statement' – is
given as to "seek God with a whole heart and soul, and
do what is good and right before him". This is clearly
Gnostic – neither the Jewish faith nor the later church
was in the business of 'seeking God'. We learn further
that "the Lord will impart true knowledge to those who
have chosen 'the way' ". From here we find many apparent references to the inner light and secret *gnosis*.

In the initiation, the novitiate says:

> "In his hand is the perfection of my way and
> the uprightness of my heart. He will wipe out
> my transgressions through his righteousness.
> For my light has sprung from the source of his
> knowledge…the light of my eye has beheld the
> mystery to come. He that is everlasting is the
> support of my hand. The way of my steps is over

stout rock which nothing can shake….from his marvelous mysteries is the light of my heart".

"My eyes have gazed on that which is eternal, on wisdom concealed from men, on knowledge and wise design (hidden) from the sons of men. On a fountain of righteousness and a storehouse of power, on a spring of glory (hidden) from the assembly of flesh, God has given to his chosen ones an everlasting possession, and has caused them to inherit the lot of the Holy Ones."

"I thank you Lord, for you have enlightened me through your truth. In your loving kindness and your marvelous mysteries…you have granted me knowledge."

These formulae, these statements, apparently written long before Jesus, are in fact very 'Christian' in content, referring to a God of great love and kindness, a 'Christian' God no less. The prayers, poems and incantations are characterized, says Geza Vermes, by "profound humility and limitless gratitude towards a benevolent God".

From the sayings of the novitiates being initiated, we are reminded of many gospel passages which refer to Jesus teaching the mysteries of the Kingdom of Heaven, or leading his chosen ones into 'everlasting life'. It is possible the initiates are given the responsibility of initiating others, for they promise, "I will impart knowledge with discretion", if we assume 'knowledge' is a reference to an inner knowing of God rather than the conveying of information.

These words would not be out of place in the New Testament gospels. And neither would another prayer which has been compared to the Beatitudes, while not being by any means in the same class. But uncannily similar to the words of Jesus, which we have seen have resonances in other traditions, is another passage: "He...liberates the captives, restores sight to the blind, straightens the bent. He will heal the wounded, revive the dead and bring good news to the poor (in spirit)". Each of these claims replicates those of Jesus except one. He never promised to "liberate the captives". In this passage, the scrolls are not advocating violent action to free prisoners from their shackles. Evidently this is a metaphor for enlightenment of people enchained in spiritual ignorance, or darkness. And if *this* is a metaphor, then the other claims in the passage – restoring sight to the blind, reviving the dead, etc – must also be metaphors. It does not require a great jumping of the tracks to see that if they are metaphors here, then they must also be metaphors when described in the gospels as similar cures and resurrections. Once again, it is a line of highly probable reasoning that has eluded the experts, though Professor Vermes concludes, "At the very least the inclusion of the miracle of reviving the dead in both the gospels and the Dead Sea Scrolls text emphasizes the common milieu in which they were written". If John and Jesus had both emerged from an Essene background, these phrases, almost identical to Jesus' famous reply to the imprisoned Baptist, would explain why Jesus used the terms he did: they, and their meaning, would have been indelibly etched in the spiritual DNA of both men.

There was also, in passing, another scroll which has proved impossible to decipher, with strange and apparently meaningless lettering. We can rely on the discoverer of the 'secret gospel', Morton Smith, to jump to his own conclusion about these 'outlandish alphabets', suggesting "one of the secrets thus concealed was probably the technique of self-hypnosis that was believed to enable the magician to ascend into heaven". While deploring his references to magic and hypnosis, with their implication of deception, for we are clearly dealing with something full of sincerity, his point about the unintelligible writings might not be too wide of the mark.

One of the commands is of particular interest; the members of the sect had to devote four hours a night to 'prayer, study and discussion'. We must not assume this took the form of a Christian monastery with its early morning vigils and chanting, or a Jewish gathering where novices ponder and learn by heart scriptural texts, while nodding their heads fervently up and down. These hours were more likely spent in an effort to attain an experience of the divine using whatever physical and mental disciplines might have been handed down by the Teacher of Righteousness to help attain the inner union. We could also surmise that the low, narrow benches found in the main large room of the excavations, which have been claimed unconvincingly to be writing tables or dining chairs – they are too low and too cramped for such purposes – might have been the very benches where the priests settled to perform their nocturnal acts of communion. Certainly the members of the sect had no time for sacrifices and the other rituals to be found in mainstream Judaism as practiced in the temple in Jerusalem. As Vermes surmises: "Prayer and holy life were the substitutes for the sacrifices and free-will offerings performed by the priests in Jerusalem".

The question arises, could the anonymous Teacher of Righteousness have been a revealer of inner truth, an initiator into the inner light, like Jesus? Throughout this book, and particularly in looking at other traditions, it has been suggested that Jesus might not have been the only 'Christ', but that at other times similar people seem to have had a similar role, saying very similar things, making very similar claims, and apparently enabling people to have a similar experience. We have noted particularly that within the mystical writings of many religions there are repeated references to the ability of a special teacher to raise the dead, heal the wounded, enable the lame to walk and give sight to the blind, indicating that whatever process was being enacted, it was not confined to one particular individual.

It has also been suggested that the experience Jesus was able to give to *his* followers continued to be available from his disciples, and his disciples' disciples, for several generations into the future, until, weakened and diluted, it no longer held the same power and faded from view. Could it be that between the appearances of great, dynamic and charismatic teachers like Jesus, 'the way' they reveal of the path of 'inner experience' does not die out but simmers in a quiet manner, either with lesser leaders, or just depending on memories of the previous great master, until circumstances combine with the appearance of a new teacher to fan the glowing ember into a new burst of flame? In this scenario, the Teacher of Righteousness might have been a master of the same ilk as Jesus. Once he had gone, only a weakened, diluted version of his initiation might have been available, taught by a priestly class similar to the Gnostic teachers of the second and third centuries. Not having the charismatic confidence of Jesus to walk straight into the lions' den, to strike out fearlessly on his own to bring his truth to the world, they needed the structure of a commune with rules to operate in. It would have been a formula that could last for several generations, but in every case there was the possibility that, as with Buddhism in India, the old would return, and 'religion' would creep back in to replace inner experience.

* * *

Ever since the discovery of the Dead Sea Scrolls, it has been thought plausible that Jesus and John the Baptist, but especially the latter, had been Essenes. The scrolls have a prediction of the arrival of a new teacher, as does John. They, like him, had an eschatological approach in their teachings – the technical term for saying the time of destiny is here, God will come soon to save his people.

Interestingly, there is some evidence – a series of bath-like constructions – that the Essenes practiced a form of baptism by immersion, which John could have, if he had left the sect to proceed alone, been replicating in the River Jordan. It is a theory rejected by Geza Vermes, on the grounds that a sect member "who conformed to the basic rules of the community would not have been allowed to proclaim his message indiscriminately to Jewish society at large, as John did, and would have been restricted to passing on his teachings to the select few of the chosen".

He allows however, that if John had *left* the sect, these rules would not apply, and here is the caveat. It could be that both Jesus and John had been members of the Essene sect at Qumran and were increasingly frustrated not, as is commonly supposed, at the Roman occupation of their country, for Jesus makes clear he has no problem with the current occupation of his land by a foreign power, but at the total collapse they saw in the understanding of, and love for, God, and left the community, either in unison or separately, to begin their new endeavor.

John need not have fallen out with his superiors at Qumran. Perhaps given his fervor he was granted a special dispensation to conduct his own baptisms down by the river. Although there is no real evidence that he had belonged to the Qumran sect, it is an inordinate coincidence that the spot where he is believed to have performed his baptisms in the River Jordan was no more than three miles from the settlement, though if the sect did practice baptism, one might have thought they would do it in the local river rather than build their own water containers. Professor Shanks, in his *Mystery and Meaning of the Dead Sea Scrolls*, has also pointed out that John's food and dress were the same as the Qumran residents. A further coincidence is that the location of Jesus' temptation in the wilderness has been identified as less than ten miles away from the Qumran site. In this reading, we also have an explanation for what Jesus was doing during his 'missing' years; it would certainly explain the mystery of why Jesus was at the opposite end of the country to his family home when he came across and received the baptism of John.

There are countless objections to this line of reasoning. Why, for example, is no such connection mentioned in any of the gospels? Why is there no evidence in the scrolls of this new awakening shaking Judea by someone who was recently one of their own? Neither of these objections is insuperable. The presence of the Essenes might have been so well-known in contemporary Judea that it had no need to be mentioned, and, in any event, by the time the gospels were being written, the Qumran community had already been destroyed. On the other hand, the scrolls were not a commentary on life in nearby Jerusalem, but the sacred documents of an inward-looking sect.

An accepted theory in the world of Biblical scholarship is that, even without any direct connection with Jesus, the Essenes had much in common with the early Christians, and after the crucifixion many became followers of 'the way'. It has also been suggested that as the two communities were based in the same part of Jerusalem, near the 'Essene Gate', the location of the last supper could have been an Essene meeting house, borrowed for the occasion. This would explain the mysterious account of Jesus telling his disciples to meet and follow a man carrying a jar of water, "and wherever he enters say to the master of the house, 'The Teacher says: Where is my guest room where I may eat the Passover with my disciples?' " He would then show them a 'large upper room furnished and ready'. If this were an Essene meeting house – possibly also used for subsequent meetings of the disciples, and maybe also the location for the visitation by the Holy Spirit – it indicates that Jesus, whether he had previously been an Essene or not, enjoyed good relations with them which existed apart from his normal circle.

Ultimately, of course, does it really matter? What *is* of interest is the fact that the information contained in the Dead Sea Scrolls reveals that something very similar to, and in its own way just as nobly expressed as the Christian message, was already in existence long before Jesus began his mission.

The scholars soldier on, painstakingly piecing the fragments of manuscripts together, examining the pottery, the inkwells, the baths, and the tools found at the site. Yet, although the work clearly has to be done, and to the highest standard, what is of real importance is not these minutiae but something far more intangible: the spirit that occupied these rooms and buildings, the presence and closeness of an ethereal divine, and the need these long dead sect members felt to dedicate their very existence to it. And although it would answer many questions, it is not absolutely necessary to know where Jesus came from, or how he came to begin his incandescent period of revelatory teaching. As with Shakespeare, the body of work is there. That, not how it began, is the important thing.

Chapter Twenty-Three
Final Thoughts

There is a theme that is found in the scriptures of all the major religions relating to a master figure: the notion that he can take his followers, if they have sufficient faith in his ability, on a journey from a place of illusion, or unreality, or impermanence – the words vary – to a place of safety, the home of the divine. This journey involves crossing a hostile or lifeless terrain, a desert maybe, or an expanse of water, to a land where they can live in peace and harmony, where they can flourish and achieve the fulfillment that has been promised. To scholars familiar with this kind of metaphorical language, a miracle such as Jesus walking on water and calling for his disciples to follow him is instantly recognizable as a variation on this common theme. What is important in the story is not that Jesus could walk on water but that Peter, in his noble attempt to join his master, fails, and begins to sink, until Jesus reminds him in a well-known phrase what the prerequisite condition of salvation is: "O ye of little faith, why did you doubt?"

Both the parables and the miracle stories in the New Testament are linked in this same purpose. The example given above may well have started out as a parable from Jesus' lips, and was transformed over many retellings into an account of an actual incident featuring one of the most loyal apostles. The miracle stories, like the parables, are still waiting for a new interpretation which will reveal their hidden meaning. They are keys relating to the purpose of Jesus' work, not the embarrassment they appear to be to some modern day Christians and scholars.

The writings of the ancient and medieval worlds are full, bursting at the seams, with miracle stories. We do not accept them now. We take from the eighth century *History of the English People*, by the Venerable Bede, the basic facts of the story we would not otherwise know. We accept that he had certain prejudices, and take that into account. But we do not give any credence to the many miraculous cures he cites which were achieved by praying to such and such a saintly king, or by kissing a splinter of wood that might or might not have come from the crucifixion cross itself. This was the world Bede lived in, where the earth was flat, demons lived in the forest, and heaven was behind the sky. We do not hold it against him that he was a product of his time and probably believed such things himself.

But *we* do not believe them. Nor the countless miracles and strange goings on of the gods of the ancient world, any more than modern Hindus believe that their gods could change form, command the elements, or perform amazing feats, such as Hanuman the monkey-god flying through the air holding a mountain in the palm of a hand, as he had not had time to select the actual mountain herb he had been commanded to bring by his master, Rama. In any religion, miracles are used to convey hidden meanings, just as fairy stories and fables in a different way carry hidden morals and truths.

Buddha, we are told, did not believe in miracles. When he was asked by a visiting king to produce one to prove who he was, he laughed: "I eat when I'm hungry and I sleep when I'm tired. That's my miracle". He appears to have been a master who shared with Jesus not only a profound understanding of these matters, but also a name for his work, the way, which is the same as that of Jesus. His quote, "The way is not in the sky. The way is in the heart", is uncannily similar to Jesus' assertion that if heaven is in the sky, birds will get there first.

Like Buddha, it is quite likely that Jesus of Nazareth did not believe in miracles. Yet his followers, in many respects, still do. It is as if what he was, what he did and what he taught were not enough. Something else had to be added. Belief in miracles is, in short, derogatory to Jesus. It is no different in essence from rejecting the theory of evolution in favor of the creation story of *Genesis*. If Jesus walked on water, then Adam and Eve did indeed walk in the Garden of Eden. The twist is, of course that Jesus was telling people there really is a Garden of Eden, where men and women can live with the divine, and which can be attained by undertaking an internal journey.

We have to take the literal understanding of miracles out of the equation from the very beginning, and this is not an easy task. They cannot be made to disappear with just one miraculous wave of a wand. The premises have to be deconstructed, and a more plausible scenario put in their place. The miracles – and in particular the resurrection miracle – have to be understood as the allegories they are.

We have suggested throughout this book that Jesus was able to draw people into a direct experience of God by showing them 'the mystery of the Kingdom of Heaven' and by his very presence providing the essential ingredient which makes the journey possible: faith in himself as the great healer, the guide. This process appears to encompass a revelation, or a means of entry through a previously closed inner door into an internal world of serenity, of light, of 'direct' *gnosis* or 'knowing'. From many examples drawn from a wide variety of scriptures we have seen that uncannily similar analogies have existed elsewhere at various times. We see that the light could be no more than 'a small flame in a niche' or a blazing 'light of lights' that seems to fill the whole body – a reference which resembles Jesus' aphorism, "Your whole body will be filled with light". And with the light, presumably, came a feeling, a sensation, of the presence of a divine being, which is usually described as 'love', and which appeared to be personified by the master. Initiates had a sense that they had not only seen light but were now in the vicinity of God, had entered, no less, even though it might be just the vestibule, the Kingdom of Heaven itself. In a much-quoted passage from Paul it was said that people thought the followers of Jesus were drunk: possibly, instead, they were in a state of immense joy at what had happened in their lives.

* * *

It would seem that no world-changing individual master has appeared on earth since that period of time when the great religions of today had their beginnings, unless we are content to add the 15th century teacher, Guru Nanak, whose followers became the Sikhs. Each religion has had its variations and offshoots, and in India in particular occasional 'sants' have emerged from time to time until relatively recently, but have not achieved wider recognition than their own immediate circle.

In the second half of the twentieth century, a great surge in interest amongst the younger generation in alternative paths to 'God-realization' led to various 'gurus' coming to the west, but for the most part they taught a combination of mantra meditation and the usual array of religious practices, nevertheless providing some degree of internal satisfaction amongst their followers. They have become a small, but significant, fringe activity in the field of western spirituality, alongside a return to pagan religions, and for many these pathways suffice. In funeral ceremonies, beautifully moving services are conducted by humanistic mediators without reference to God or an after-life. Some are attracted by the practical and almost militant atheism of persuasive and deep-thinking people like Richard Dawkins and the late Christopher Hitchens. But for others, there remains a vague disquiet; they sense a creative power, a loving God, but find little in the way of means of reconnecting with him.

It is certainly true that trying to practice a 'good' life of tolerance, kindness, and being of service to others – following 'the golden rule' – does not require religious partisanship. The character in Camus' great novel, *The Plague,* who helps save others, eventually at the expense of his own life, is, to the bewilderment of his Catholic friends, an atheist. The teachers who heroically give their lives to shield their charges in dreadful school massacres are acting not from religious conviction but from the deepest human instinct: sacrificing themselves to protect the children in their care. Jesus may have articulated that such self-sacrifice is the greatest love a man or woman can know, and by extension, such people, if there is an afterlife, will be embraced in the arms of an *abba* whose nature is unimaginable love, but it is not dependent on loyalty to, or belief in, him.

Religion does not necessarily make someone a good person, but it can provide a platform for those who feel a profound need to engage in whatever way they can with what they perceive to be the source of their own being. By way of example, we can take the American authority on Gnosticism, Elaine Pagels. While being challenged in her traditional faith by her realization that the Christian religion today may be far removed from what Jesus actually taught, she describes how, at a time of personal tragedy, she entered a church in New York and was deeply touched and moved by the simple expressions of praise and thanks to the almighty she found taking place there, in the singing of hymns and the comforting ceremonials. One of our other experts, A.N. Wilson, has also returned to the fold of Christianity after the death of a parent.

Many people feel a heartfelt need to acknowledge an unseen divine power, to worship 'him' and give 'him' thanks. The actual religion or form of spirituality is not really so important. Its value can be that it provides a framework for simple human acts of worship and prayer to take place, an acknowledgement that although we know so little about it, there is a creative power, a loving God, who, in the words of Wordsworth, moves through all things. Whether the prism through which one experiences those feelings is Buddhist, Christian, Jewish, Muslim or Hindu does not matter very much, for all their founders were merely pointing, in their own way and in their own language, at the same God.

A considerable proportion of Christians believe that their savior will actually reappear one day, but what would be achieved if he did? If they feel they already have his gift of salvation, what else would be required of him, other than that he could then bestow it on others who do not have it? He had a hard enough task putting his message across the last time he was here; why should he be any more successful on a return visit, and why should his followers want him to take such a risk? The fact is that another appearance of a master of the stature of Jesus may not be necessary. We might already have all we need from his teachings, and from those of other 'masters', to live in peace and harmony, recognizing that all religions are merely variations in acknowledging and relating to the same divine being. But one key ingredient would remain unattainable: the ability to have the inner experience the master could apparently facilitate.

* * *

Once we have decided that Jesus and his teachings actually stand some distance away from their later representation, we are faced with the question, why did it happen? Whether we accept him as unique or as one of a number of other similar people appearing at various times and in different situations – and this judgment very much depends on whether we have a 'Christian' or a general view – we confront the same dilemma. The gradual build up of a tradition about the master or original teacher – we must avoid the term founder – becomes in all cases relentlessly complicated, with the development of a complex web of supporting theology and the branching out of various belief systems that in future years often come into conflict.

There is one essential feature that can be detected whether we are considering Christianity alone or any of the world's major religions. It is, simply expressed, that at the point where the seed of the original teachings becomes the tree of subsequent religion, something real is transformed into something unreal, something genuine into a replica. Nobody subsequently can do what the original man could do, which all came from his essential qualification: he appeared to be, and to his own disciples indubitably was, one with God, or a messenger of God, or, removing such strident language, a pathway to the source of life. Without this original catalyst, the later religion cannot take root. The irony is that in this transference, the essential ingredient is invariably destined to become lost.

Let us examine this development from real to ersatz a little further. The key clue comes in the word 'representation' or 'symbol'. It is this terminology that the religion following a master's period of teachings has to fall back on and develop in the years and centuries after his death, without considering, at the start of the process, whether it is really necessary. It is assumed immediately, without any perceived line of one ending and the other beginning, that this is the case, that this is what the teacher, and by implication God, would have wanted.

So we will find the head of one Christian denomi- nation, let us say the Anglican community, offering a gift to the head of another Christian denomination, say the Catholics, as a 'symbol' of peace, or as a 'symbol of Christ's love'. Likewise, one can no longer be granted entry into the *reality* of God's world, so as a substitute one is granted entry into his 'church' as if it were the same thing, and as if the substitute process were blessed and ordained by the master, or by 'God' himself.

From then on, the symbolism becomes rife, subsum- ing the entire paraphernalia of the particular religion. A good example is found in one of the prime rituals of a branch of Buddhism, which, although not a major offshoot within the entire world of Buddhism, is the most famous one in the west because of the outstanding personality of its leader, the Dalai Lama. The religion he heads treats him, as do the Catholics the Pope, as a living representative of the divine. When he appears at a gathering of the faithful there is a feeling of devout prayerfulness and joy, and this finds expression in a series of time-honored rituals. Each of the faithful is given a white scarf, or neckband. In the days before his holiness's arrival the senior monks painstakingly create a complicated and beautiful mandala – a circular pattern, originally the inner light itself – of different colored sand, some four feet or so in diameter. In the very center is a little representation of Buddha himself. When completed, the mandala takes on the sacred properties of the deity, treated as not just symbolic but the real thing, handled most delicately, protected by four walls of glass, while the faithful are then allowed to file past it, waving their scarves deferentially at it as they pass, the scarf being thereby imbued with the blessings of the divine, which are then passed on to those who wear it. Only the most senior monks are granted the privilege of staying close to the mandala, protecting it and at the same time receiving the enormous blessing a prolonged period in such a proximity to the deity bestows.

When the Dalai Lama arrives, he alone has the power, the authority, to destroy this mandala by wiping his arm across it, disturbing and erasing the intricate patterns of sand. The ceremony is completed when every grain of the mandala is scooped up and placed in a 'sacred' urn, to be poured into a nearby river by the reverend leader at an auspicious time.

Without intending any disrespect, we might ask, has anything been achieved by this many days long spiritual process? Did the faithful really have divine grace come into their lives, or was it merely that they believed divine grace had come into their lives? Certainly if their scarves were actually touched by his holiness, the power of what they received was added to exponentially. And we are familiar with other endearing features of that great eastern religion, possibly founded, and definitely inspired, by someone even Christians regard as the only other human being to bear comparison with the Nazarene himself, for example, the spinning of 'prayer wheels', or the writing of prayers or quotations from scriptures onto colored ribbons which are then left to flutter in the wind, spreading blessings or good feelings to the four corners of the world.

Because we are so familiar with them, we would be wasting good time and mental energy to begin to list or describe the array of comparable rituals and practices to be found in the Christian churches, which might seem as quaint, exotic and of dubious value to others as those Buddhist practices do to many westerners. But we know well what they are, and can see that, in common with their Buddhist equivalents, they have one essential feature: they are not the real thing; they are symbols of the original teachings. 'Symbol', in fact, has become one of the pivotal words in major Christian ceremonial, and the fact that its use is so unquestioningly accepted is the greatest testimonial that real experience has been supplanted by representation. The baptism in the spirit, the experience of the divine, which each religion's particular teacher is claimed to have been able to bestow while he was alive, has also been replaced by a symbolic act.

This is not to deny that religions, of whatever kind, do have their own profound value, and there might well be a place for them in a future world. For many millions, they provide a channel to a feeling that the world, that life itself, is not inherently meaningless but meaningful, underpinned by a caring and kind creator.

There is no harm in words of that original teacher, if they are recorded, being read out to a 'congregation', nor of songs sung in the deity's or the master's honor. Chanting or mantra repetition might also have its place: the 'plainsong' of Christian worship dating from medieval times is ethereally beautiful, and comparable beauty can no doubt be found in the devotional practices of other religions. The fact that Jesus, with the guttural and, to western ears, somewhat harsh sounds of his own language, Aramaic, would probably find those Gregorian chants as unattractive as western people might find the calling to prayers of the Imam from his minaret, is beside the point. The feeling of well-being in the heart that can arise from these practices is indeed not false but real. Even little ceremonials to help bring the love and meaning of the master's message to mind can perform a similar role. And of increasing value in the modern world where essential human qualities sometimes appear to be being undermined, is the voice the churches provide on behalf of the poor, the oppressed and the victims of war, hunger and injustice. What is confusing, and possibly of *negative* worth, is when the symbolic is taken to be real, when an intermediate class comes between the 'lay' people and the divinity, and when certain rules in life are imposed, to go against which would mean a transgression against

God is being committed that only the church has the power to forgive.

* * *

Where do these new revelations about Jesus leave the average 'Christian' in the western world today? They will certainly be supportive for those who like the general message of Christ but sense that the church is removed from it. People in the main have great love, or at least admiration and respect, for Jesus. It could be said that people, not the church, own Jesus. His words and teachings resonate deeply within their hearts. They do not want to abandon him as an iconic figure who did indeed appear to represent the divinity. And many might now feel relief that they do not have to believe in his miracles, nor in his resurrection, in order to have a heartfelt inner relationship with him.

The 'new Christians' who might appear from this re-assessment of Jesus might want to continue remembrance of him in a different style of gathering. The role of a priest as an intermediary will be no longer required. Such people might term themselves 'natural' Christians, as opposed to the 'supernatural' Christians who have held sway for so many centuries. 'New Christianity' might decide to revisit the contents of the Bible, which will no longer require the prefix 'holy', for no book merits that title, marking as dubious or inauthentic those New Testament passages and quotations which most scholars agree are 'later additions', and including those Gnostic and apocryphal gospels that our experts agree are genuine and worthy of inclusion. Rituals and ceremony might be discarded or much reduced. It could be open to discussion whether the cross should remain as the overarching symbol of the new Christianity. In favor would be its symbolism as a remembrance of how Jesus was indeed killed, not by Jews or Romans but by an uncomprehending and intolerant human race, as might possibly, were he to 'reappear' today, be repeated. But a symbol which depicts not the significance of his teachings but the manner of his demise might not be appropriate. The crucifixion is not by any means the most important part of his story. In a new look at this master from Nazareth who deplored the use of symbols to represent what to him was a tangible reality, it might be decided that no symbol of any kind would be required.

Many times we have commented about how little is known about Jesus and his short time in the spotlight of human attention. But at least we have here a real, recognizable man. We simply do not know enough about Gautama the Buddha to be able to make similar claims on his behalf. He lived too long ago, there are no contemporaneous writings, just a few anecdotes that portray him as a cheerful purveyor of inner experience. If anything, the great religion that has developed in his name serves as a huge barrier, hiding the real teacher at its heart.

We have a sense that maybe Guru Nanak, whose followers after his death and under his successors formed themselves into the Sikh religion, gradually accumulating the usual array of symbols their teacher had firmly rejected, was a master, spending his life traveling through modern Pakistan and Iran, teaching that the Muslim and Hindu faiths both had the same 'God' who lived and could be known within the human heart. But the vast difference in culture makes it hard for people from a western background to recognize him as a sympathetic and profoundly human figure. Krishna may be a legend, but he does have a warm and vibrant persona which is attractive today and is represented in an endearing manner by his present devotees and their incessant singing and chanting of his name.

Possibly the fourteenth century Indian mystic, Kabir, was a master. This chirpy argumentative man was an impoverished weaver, sitting on the roadside plying his trade with a small handloom while berating passers-by with powerful, incisive and challenging poetic outpourings about the God within and his resplendent, infinite, unutterable 'word'. Although he was illiterate, many hundreds of his pithy poems have come down to us as strong and beautiful reminders of life's purpose. One of his famous sayings is: "The fish is thirsty in the water, and it makes me laugh". You could well imagine Jesus, Buddha and Guru Nanak too, would have laughed along with him. It is typical that the movement established to remember him and promote his teachings follows, according to the Penguin *Who's Who of Religions*, "Hinduized rituals and practices (which) run counter to much that Kabir stood for".

Not only do we feel an empathy with Jesus the man, but we instinctively sense that our world is the same as *his* world. The four gospels and some of the Gnostic records are uniquely colloquial and direct. They open a window into a scene of ordinary life and ordinary people, with names and feelings, conversations and arguments, pride and humility, betrayal and loyalty to which we can relate and which would otherwise be completely lost to us. This is what makes Jesus and his cohorts, the cast of characters in this profoundly human yet brief drama, so real to people today. He lived in surroundings basically similar to their own. From these accounts, they recognize the society he inhabited, the dramas of life, the cruelties, the warmth, the love, the hopes, the doubts and the faith of people very similar to themselves. And in Jesus they have someone immensely relatable, someone to whom they would like to be loyal, if only the deep layers of mystical clutter and religious posturing covering the story were removed from the picture.

Not much has changed in two thousand years. Most people do not want injustice, cruelty, warfare, abuse; they desire dignity, respect and kindness. Only a sociopath would say he or she does not agree with Jesus' 'golden rule' as a basis for life. It is not a coincidence that on a million Christmas cards, the little town of Bethlehem is depicted in profound peace and covered with deep snow, even though it lies in the searing heat of the Middle East, was probably, under Roman occupation, as troubled then as it is now, and in any event was almost certainly *not* the birthplace of Jesus. It is an aspirational setting that appeals to people's deepest instincts of what they would like for themselves and their world. Peace and goodwill to all men and women is a potent message, but it is not, as we have seen, the essential teaching of Jesus himself. That was something altogether far more profound, a message not for mankind in general but for each individual; the opportunity human life offers to know and experience the inner divine, and by doing so, to fulfill life's fundamental purpose.

People *like* Jesus, but their good sense holds many back from engaging too closely with the institutions which claim to represent him. They do not find him there, but feel 'he', or the 'father' he spoke so much about, does indeed, in some unfathomable way, inhabit the very core of the human heart. It may well be that misunderstandings and misinterpretations, like the snow blanketing Bethlehem, have covered the ground. But now, a different truth is coming to light, and I suspect that, if Jesus were, by some miracle, to be looking down on the world from that distant cloud on the horizon, he would be pleased that, be it two thousand years too late, a beginning is being made on resurrecting not his body, but the real essence of his teachings.

Bibliography

Alderman, Naomi *The Liar's Gospel* (Penguin 2012)

Alexander, Eben *Proof of Heaven* (Piatkus 2012)

Ali, Abdullah Yusuf (Trans) *The Holy Qur'an* (Wordsworth 2000)

Allegro, John M. *The Sacred Mushroom and the Cross* (Abacus 1973)

Armstrong, Karen *A History of God: the 4,000-Year Quest of Judaism, Christianity and Islam* (Ballantine 1993)

Armstrong, Karen *Buddha* (Orion 2000)

Armstrong, Karen *Islam: A Short History* (The Modern Library 2002)

Armstrong, Karen *The Bible: The Biography* (Atlantic 2007)

Aslan, Reza *Zealot: The Life and Times of Jesus of Nazareth* (Random House 2013)

Bauckham, Richard *Jesus: a very short introduction* (Oxford 2011)

Beilby, James K. & Eddy, Paul R. (Ed) *The Historical Jesus* (SPCK 2010)

Bynner, Witter (Trans) *The Way of Life, According to Lao Tzu* (Capricorn 1962)

Campbell, Joseph *The Masks of God: Primitive Mythology* (Penguin 1959)

Casey, Maurice *Jesus of Nazareth: An Independent Historian's Account of His Life and Teaching* (T & T Clark International 2010)

Cook, Michael *Muhammad: a very short introduction* (Oxford 2011)

Cresswell, Peter *the Invention of Jesus* (Watkins Publishing 2013)

Dorje, G. (Trans) & Coleman, G. (Ed) *The Tibetan Book of the Dead* (Penguin 2005)

Goulder, Michael *A Tale of Two Missions* (SCM Press 1994)

Guillaumont, A; Puech, H. Ch; Quispel, G; Till, W; Al-Masih, Yassah Abd (Trans) *The Gospel according to Thomas* (Brill 1976)

Hess, Linda & Singh, Sukhdev (Trans) *The Bijak of Kabir* (Banarsidass 1983)

Hinnells, John R. (Ed) *Who's Who of Religions* (Penguin 1996)

Holy Bible Authorized Version (Oxford)

Holy Bible English Standard Version (Collins 2002)

Huxley, Aldous *The Perennial Philosophy* (Perennial Classics 2004)

Johnson, Luke Timothy *The New Testament: a very short introduction* (Oxford 2010)

Johnson, Paul *Jesus: a biography from a believer* (Viking 2010)

Juergensmeyer, Mark *Radhasoami Reality: The Logic of a Modern Faith* (Princeton University Press 1991)

Kasser, Rodolphe; Meyer, Marvin; Wurst, Gregor (Ed) *The Gospel of Judas* (National Geographic Society 2006)

Le Donne, Anthony *Historical Jesus: What can we know and how can we know it?* (Eerdmans 2011)

Leloup, Jean-Yves, Rowe, J. (Trans) *The Gospel of Mary Magdalene* (Inner Traditions 2002)

Lovejoy, David *Heresy: The life of the monk Pelagius* (Echo Publications 2012)

MacCulloch, Diarmaid *A History of Christianity: The First Three Thousand Years* (Penguin 2010)

Mascaró, Juan (Trans) *The Bhagavad Gita* (Penguin Classics 1962)

Mascaró, Juan (Trans) *The Upanishads* (Penguin Classics1965)

Mead, G.R.S. *Fragments of a Faith Forgotten – the Gnostics; a contribution to the study of the origins of Christianity* (University 1960)

Miles, Jack *Christ: A Crisis in the Life of God* (Arrow 2002)

Miles, Jack *God: A Biography* (Vintage 1996)

Murphy-O'Connor, Jerome *Paul: His Story* (Oxford 2005)

O'Grady, Selina *And Man Created God: Kings, Cults and Conquests at the time of Jesus* (Atlantic Books 2012)

Pagels, Elaine *Beyond Belief: The Secret Gospel of Thomas* (Vintage 2004)

Pagels, Elaine *The Gnostic Gospels* (Random House 1979)

Pagels, Elaine *The Gnostic Paul: Gnostic Exegesis of the Pauline Letters* (Trinity Press International 1992)

Palmer, Martin *The Jesus Sutras: Rediscovering the lost religion of Taoist Christianity* (Piatkus 2001)

Pendergrast, Mark *For God, Country and Coca-Cola* (Weidenfeld & Nicolson 1993)

Pullman, Philip *The Good Man Jesus and the Scoundrel Christ* (Canongate 2010)

Rampuri *Baba: Autobiography of a Blue-Eyed Yogi* (Bell Tower 2009)

Rao, Sushil (Trans) *Trap the Trapper: Poems of Bhagat Kabir* (Hrdaipress 1999)

Sanders E.P. *The Historical Figure of Jesus* (Penguin 1993)

Sanders E.P. *Jesus and Judaism* (SCM Press 1985)

Scholem, Gershom G. (Ed) *Zohar The Book of Splendor: Basic Readings from the Kabbalah* (Schocken 1963)

Shanks, Hershel *The Mystery and Meaning of the Dead Sea Scrolls* (Random House 1998)

Simon, Bernard *The Essence of the Gnostics* (Arcturus 2004)

Singh, T; Singh, B.J; Singh, K; Singh, B.H; and Singh, K (Trans) *The Sacred Writings of the Sikhs* (Allen & Unwin 1960)

Smith, Morton *The Secret Gospel: The Discovery and Interpretation of the Secret Gospel According to Mark* (Gollancz 1974)

Smith, Paul (Version) *Kabir: Seven Hundred Sayings* (New Humanity Books 1988)

Stanton, Graham *The Gospels and Jesus* (Oxford 2002)

Streeter, B.H. *The Four Gospels: A Study of Origins* (McMillan 1930)

Szekely, Edmond B. (Ed) Szekely, Edmond B., Weaver P. (Trans) *The Gospel of Peace of Jesus Christ by the disciple John* (Daniel 1937)

Tagore, Rabindranath (Trans) *Songs of Kabir* (Samuel Weiser 1974)

Thiede, Carsten Peter *The Dead Sea Scrolls and the Jewish Origins of Christianity* (Oxford 2000)

Thurman, Robert (Trans) *The Tibetan Book of the Dead* (Bantam Books 1994)

Tuckett, Christopher *The Gospel of Mary* (OUP 2007)

Vermes, Geza *Christian Beginnings: From Nazareth to Nicaea AD 30-325* (Allen Lane 2012)

Vermes, Geza *The Authentic Gospel of Jesus* (Penguin 2004)

Vermes, Geza *The Story of the Scrolls: The miraculous discovery and true significance of the Dead Sea Scrolls* (Penguin 2010)

Vermes, Geza *The Nativity: History and Legend* (Penguin 2006)

Vermes, Geza *The Complete Dead Sea Scrolls in English* (Penguin 2011)

Vermes, Geza *The Resurrection* (Penguin 2008)

Vermes, Geza *Jesus: Nativity – Passion - Resurrection* (Penguin 2010)

Wallis, Roy *Elementary Forms of the New Religious Life* (RKP 1984)

Wilhelm, Richard (Trans) *The Secret of the Golden Flower* (Kurt Wolff 1970)

Wilson A.N. *Jesus* (Flamingo 1993)

Wilson A.N. *Paul: the Mind of the Apostle* (Pimlico 1998)

Zeolla, Gary F. (Trans) *Analytical-Literal Translation of the New Testament of the Holy Bible* (Author House 2005)

About the Author

Glenville Whittaker was born in 1943 in Manchester, England. Raised first in the northern industrial town of Rochdale and then in the Victorian coastal resort of Southport, he studied history as an open scholar at Oxford University, and became interested at an early age in the various aspects of spiritual life and the search for inner experience. Much of his life has been spent working and developing understandings in these areas. Now semi-retired, he lives and works in Brighton on the south coast of England.

59843060R00217

Made in the USA
Charleston, SC
16 August 2016